Standing Out on the SAT and ACT
Perfect Scorers' Uniquely Effective Stra
Admissions Success

Shiv Gaglani and

Blake Cecil

with Christian Fong

Foreword by Joann P. DiGennaro

k12.osmosis.org

Osmosis Publishing
676 N. 33rd Street
Unit A
Philadelphia, PA 19104
k12.osmosis.org
hi@osmosis.org

Cover Design by PixelStudio
Edited by Allison Hagan
ISBN: 978-0-9960636-3-0
First Edition, Spring 2014

PRAISE FOR *STANDING OUT*

"I wholeheartedly agree with the philosophy behind *Standing Out*. Too many test prep guides today focus on tricks to beat the test rather than building skills in reading and math that will serve students well in college and beyond. By focusing on genuine skill development, this book ensures that you achieve top scores while developing patterns of thought that will lead you to greater heights."
-- Ryan Haynes, Ph.D. in neuroscience, co-founder of Osmosis, Marshall Scholar, and M.D. candidate at Johns Hopkins University

"The authors have captured the essence of learning that it is a journey of discovery rather than a path to the top. Through a unique combination of information, problem solving strategies, and examples, pointing out the vocabulary learned along the way, *Standing Out* persuades that skills are more important than scores and you can achieve both by carefully applying the wisdom shared by Shiv and Blake."
-- Barbara Kurshan, Ed.D., Executive Director of Academic Innovation, University of Pennsylvania Graduate School of Education

"*Standing Out* takes a refreshing and unusually effective approach to doing well on the SAT and ACT, getting into college, and most importantly developing as a person. Throughout the book Gaglani and Cecil clearly lay out dozens of core strategies that helped them achieve perfect scores on both the SAT and ACT. I encourage students, parents, and teachers to read this book, which extends well beyond test prep."

-- Jason Shah, founder of iNeedAPencil

"It is refreshing to read a book that de-emphasizes test scores as an end in themselves, but rather as an opportunity for self-improvement. That being said, it provides all the necessary strategies – and more – to excel in both."

-- Malorie Snider, Rhodes Scholar and perfect scorer on SAT

"*Standing Out* reshaped the way I viewed the SAT and turned it from just a test into an opportunity to better myself. The strategies allowed me to approach the test confidently and improve my score by 140 points, enough to reach my goal and get into the range of Ivy League schools. The most valuable part of *Standing Out* was that it taught me skills and strategies on how to learn in a general sense so that I have gained immensely more out of my college experience and it will continue to benefit me for the rest of my life."

-- Diana Sheedy, Harvard Class of 2017

"One of the most important lessons I took from *Standing Out* is to not look at the SAT as a 'stepping stone'; I will now always view the SAT and other standardized tests as opportunities for learning and gaining foundational skills, instead of just requirements to be met for the next level of education. This strategy has in turn transferred over to my schoolwork, in which I focus more on the attainment of knowledge than on achieving certain required grades. The strategies in *Standing Out* are truly applicable for all standardized tests and tests in general! For example, one of the math strategies for multiple-choice questions mentioned in the book is eliminating the answer choices. This technique really cut down simple algebra mistakes I was making and helped me get a higher score on the math section of the SAT."

-- Varun Bansal, Rice Class of 2017

"As students constantly look for new insights and a leg up on the SAT and ACT, Shiv Gaglani and Blake Cecil have written a finely tuned strategic and practical approach to tests that may otherwise drive parents and kids around the bend. Having been incredibly accomplished in their educational paths, they herald back to what also made them successful test takers and they share that knowledge with their audience through carefully constructed modules of information. Positioned for the student who really wants to excel, not just slide by, this book is a valuable tool."

-- Laurie Racine, co-founder and Managing Director of Startl Education

"I highly recommend *Standing Out* for any student who wants to achieve his or her maximum potential. I especially enjoyed the insights about confidence and testing mentality. A lot of students study and prepare diligently, but in order to stand out and achieve results, students need to trust in their preparation and take tests with confidence. *Standing Out* helps you not only prepare for tests, but also execute on test day."

-- DJ Chung, author, *Build Like an Ant: How My Mom Helped Me Become Valedictorian*

"During my career I've been fortunate to play many roles, ranging from education technology entrepreneur to politician, and have realized that skills such as public-speaking and writing have been common denominators in my success. I would not have been able to communicate effectively and understand innovations without a foundation of rigorously improving and testing my skills through education. Shiv and Blake hit the nail on the head with *Standing Out*: focus on developing your skills and being the best you can be. The rewards will follow."

-- Steve Welch, co-founder of DreamIt Ventures and KinderTown

"The authors provide both highly practical advice and idealistic justification on how and why to increase your standardized test scores. They base their strategies not only on personal experience scoring perfect on the SAT and ACT, but also on years of teaching other students how to do the same. Besides taking practice tests, you should understand how you can most efficiently approach the problems and how the test-makers formulated them. Shiv and Blake provide this kind of invaluable insight."

-- Gen and Kelly Tanabe, co-authors of *The Ultimate Guide to America's Best Colleges*

"The strategies detailed in *Standing Out* not only gave me the tools to improve my critical reading score, but also gave me confidence in my problem solving abilities."

-- Sean W. Carroll, Cornell Class of 2017

"*Standing Out* presents a fascinating and uncommon program that offers much, much more than test prep! It goes beyond communicating and drilling test strategies, deemphasizing test scores as an end in themselves and instead emphasizing the importance of developing mathematical intuition, critical reading, and vocabulary as important life skills. The book also features many related lessons, including the value of establishing good habits for lifelong learning, how investing small amounts of time regularly improving yourself can reap dividends for a lifetime, and the importance of being able to teach something as a means to fully understanding it."

-- Radha Bansal, Parent

"*Standing Out* is an accurate, honest discussion of many commonly perceived myths on test-taking strategy and a valuable resource on the route to standardized examination greatness. The escalator step philosophy is a compelling framework that I employ on a regular basis but wish I had known in high school."

-- Michael Batista, Co-founder, The Smartphone Physical, and Doctoral Candidate in Biomedical Engineering, Johns Hopkins University

"With all the heated debate over standardized testing, it is easy to lose sight of the fact that these tests are designed to measure what you *should* know to get the most out of life. And so, rather than blindly prepare for the test, focus on preparing yourself properly for life as you also try to do well on the tests."

-- Andrew Ackerman, Managing Director of DreamIt Ventures and Former Product Manager at Kaplan Test Preparation

On "Silverturtle's Guide to SAT and Admissions Success"

"Blake's work has always been exceptionally logical, precise, and thorough. He cuts right to the core of what you need to know and how to approach each section of the exam. More importantly, he's honest and direct, speaking from one student to another. He won't waste your time on flashy tricks that don't actually work, instead focusing on real strategies that are tried and true -- ones that he himself used successfully, and ones that worked for me and so many of my friends and thousands of others after we read his online guide. If you really want to score high on the SAT, then his advice is for you. I highly recommend it."

-- Grace Zhang, Yale Class of 2015

"Blake has done an amazing job in his guide by seeing through the information that is not necessary and instead focusing on the essential skills and strategies required to do your best on the SAT. I thought the entire guide was enormously helpful, but the grammar section specifically was clearly a winner in our house. My daughter used this section and tested herself after mastering the information in the book. She was able to recognize any grammar error the SAT threw at her and she increased her Writing score by 100 points! I used this guide to tutor two other students on Writing. After working with them only two times they both increased their scores as well; one by 70 and the other by 80 points! They also both indicated that their AP Language teachers noticed a difference in their timed writing exercises and essays for class. Blake's guide simplifies grammar rules and breaks them down into very recognizable and easily understood concepts. He zeros in on the most common errors encountered on the SAT and arms students with the knowledge needed to easily spot the correct grammatical usage. I highly recommend the whole guide for the best preparation possible."

-- Elizabeth Bergmann, Parent

FOREWORD

Over the past thirty years I have had the singular opportunity to work with thousands of the most intelligent and talented students around the world. These individuals have certainly stood out not only during their high school, collegiate, and graduate years, but most importantly throughout their professional lives. Among them are successful entrepreneurs, such as the founders of Pinterest and General Assembly, professors including Fields medalists (the Nobel Prize equivalent for mathematics), and renowned physicians, lawyers, engineers, and other professionals.

One can trace their success back to their high school days, during which they were standout students: perfect or near-perfect scorers on SAT, ACT, and AP exams; gold medalists at international Olympiads for science and math; and science competition winners. While impressive, these accomplishments ultimately were of less importance than the underlying motivations that drove them to succeed, and the skills they acquired on their respective paths. This, in essence, is the philosophy espoused in *Standing Out*.

It is a pleasure to write the Foreword for this unique book, which was first conceptualized by its authors Shiv Gaglani and Blake Cecil in 2011. Shiv was a 2005 alumnus of the Research Science Institute, a flagship program of the Center for Excellence in Education, and has since remained committed to the success of his younger peers - first by writing *Success with Science* (www.successwithscience.org) and then by founding Osmosis (www.osmosis.org), a novel educational platform used by thousands of students around the world. Equally accomplished, Blake had already helped tens of thousands of students get into college with his invaluable contributions on College Confidential, and participated in a variety of academic competitions. This was before he had even stepped foot at Brown, where he attends college. Both authors have sharpened their teaching skills through extensive personal tutoring.

Shiv and Blake each received perfect scores on *both* the SAT and ACT, an exceedingly rare accomplishment that makes them stand out even among the most distinguished high school students. However, as they write in *Standing Out*, it was not the scores themselves that mattered but rather the skills they acquired in the process of preparing for the tests: a more versatile lexicon, the ability to think critically, and a deep understanding of grammar - all of which helped them write this book in the first place!

Unlike other books on the subject, *Standing Out* eschews gimmicky test-taking shortcuts, which often fall short on all but the most basic questions. Instead Shiv and Blake focus on empowering students with the drive to aim higher – and, of course, the strategic tools, knowledge, and resources to achieve that success. Although the prevailing contemporary attitude among students is that standardized tests are nothing but a waste of time, *Standing Out* will convince readers that there is a deep educational potential in these collegiate entrance exams, opening their eyes to the rich learning possibilities all around them.

I know that this book will appeal not only to the highly motivated students that the Center for Excellence in Education generally attracts, but also to students who have tremendous potential yet need the right encouragement to unleash it. It is an invaluable resource for these students as well as their parents, teachers, and guidance counselors who may also learn more about what it takes to truly stand out.

- Joann P. DiGennaro
President and Co-Founder, Center for Excellence in Education

DEDICATION

To our parents who encouraged us to succeed, and to all the students out there whom we know can do the same.

ACKNOWLEDGMENTS

We would like to thank our friends and family who helped us not only proofread this book, but also to develop the uniquely effective strategies in the first place. In particular we would like to thank our editor, Allison Hagan, for her outstanding job proofreading and formatting this manuscript. In addition we are grateful to Osmosis Publishing (www.osmosis.org) for their support of this book. We also thank the online community for their years of contribution and testing to help find the very best methods for making SAT and ACT success accessible to anyone.

Shiv would like to thank the students and parents in his Brevard Success Program who motivated him to put his ideas onto paper. These students include Ryan Allison, Varun Bansal, Sean Carroll, Emily Catizone, Isabela Rovira, Diana Sheedy, and Sanju Vardhan. He would also like to thank his classmates and teachers at West Shore Jr/Sr High School who, in particular, helped him succeed on the tests including Annie Nery (math) and Michelle Wells (English), as well as the Osmosis team, in particular Ryan Haynes, for supporting this endeavor. Most importantly he would like to thank Malorie, his parents, and his sister, Anushka, for their unwavering support.

Blake would like to thank his parents for surrounding him in an environment that allowed him to improve but without any pressures, as well as his vivacious dog Jakebob and sister, in addition to the inspiration from the faithfully empathetic friends he has met.

TABLE OF CONTENTS

INTRODUCTION
STANDING OUT

Being outstanding is rare. For every Nelson Mandela and Abraham Lincoln, there are thousands of politicians whose influence or fame never reaches beyond their respective constituencies or dominions. For every Albert Einstein and James Clerk Maxwell, there are thousands of physicists whose work will scarcely touch society; their colleagues will read it, and that's the end of it.

Each high school valedictorian stands beside hundreds of his or her less-accomplished peers; each admit to an Ivy League college takes the spot from a dozen fellow applicants; and for every high school senior with a perfect SAT or ACT score, there are thousands who scored lower.

This rarity raises two important questions. First and fundamentally, what is the big deal about standing out?

Position and Pursuit

In our view, standing out does not matter much in itself. The pursuit to distinguish oneself is sometimes just a ploy to keep one's overinflated ego bubble from popping – to rationalize the presumption of individual exceptionalism. This is not a particularly respectable motivation. And in any case, it's a misguided idea that may delude more than motivate. Inevitably, that bubble will pop at some point, despite your best self-aggrandizing efforts. An exogenous[1] paradigm for worth is unstable. Such a mentality is ripe for disappointment when things go amiss, as they do in our world of vicissitudes[2].

Maybe you'll notice that in the first two paragraphs of this introduction, two different standards for valuation underlie the juxtapositions between those who "stand out" and those who do not. In the first paragraph, we use power, prestige, and impact on society as our criteria; in the second, personal accomplishment is the implicit criterion for success. So just what is our philosophy?

Our advocacy is modest. We believe that there can be no sensible doubt that power and prestige are superficial – these are enticing characteristics that some people

---

[1] SAT Word Alert: A strong vocabulary helps on the Critical Reading section of the SAT and in communication in general. We have therefore sprinkled some advanced words throughout this book, which we define here. If you do not know a word (whether footnoted or not), spend some time learning its usage; it may come in handy. Here, *exogenous* (adjective) means "originating from outside, derived externally"

[2] SAT Word Alert: *Vicissitude* (noun) means "a change or variation occurring in the course of something"

seek to others' (and often even their own) detriment. We believe that personal accomplishment and good impact on society are reconcilable. The route to positively changing society begins with bettering oneself. Fill your path with rich opportunities for healthy meaning, and in turn find personal satisfaction in the good you have done.

We wrote that, for some people, attempts to stand out are shallow: Egoists want to do better so their position in society – judged by some concoction of wealth, power, and prestige – is higher than others'. One will use some unsavory methods if this is the goal. *Win by cheating? If it works. Profit by lies? Also fine. Power by tyranny? Still counts.* This comparative mentality for achievement is bad for society. It yields what economists call "positional externalities"; for you to get ahead, others must fall. You are playing a zero-sum game. That's no fun.

On the other hand, however, the drive to stand out can be a wonderful stimulus for *valuable greatness* in its capacity to encourage unabashed individuality, creative nonconformity, and – most relevantly to the topics of this book – the full realization of your potential so that you can feel good and make a positive difference.

Measure your position on a personal path, from which you can admire and aid in others' successes. Pursue greatness for yourself so that others are better off; you can be happy along the way. You don't have to wait for power and prestige: The pursuit for good can begin now.

The prosperity of a productive society relies on its members to achieve. Because no society's members are inherently more able to achieve than those of any other, it is people's *willingness* and *opportunity* to stand out that determine societal flourishing and its members' well-being.

Ultimately, the willingness is up to you. Know, though, that there are strong reasons to will yourself toward your potential. Beyond the cold yet true fact that your exertion improves society and your material wealth lie two surprising – we daresay *profound* – promises: that the journey toward personal greatness leads to deep satisfaction *independent of "success"* and that determination for great things guarantees great things, even if they are not the same great things you were expecting. Ambitious goals work in furtively[3] fortuitous[4] ways.

So if you want to be a politician, aim to be the next Obama (or Reagan, if you prefer). If you're a scientist, work to join the historical ranks of Charles Darwin and Francis Crick. Or maybe you want to be the next Hans Zimmer or Lady Gaga; please do, because more music is always good! More immediately, try to be first in

---

[3] SAT Word Alert: *Furtively* (adverb) means "done in a secret or sly manner"

[4] SAT Word Alert: *Fortuitous* (adjective) means "accidental and fortunate"

your high school class, prepare to achieve perfect scores on the SAT and ACT, and ready yourself to be a competitive applicant for the nation's most selective colleges.

In doing so, you are not risking failure. The crucial point is not, for example, to get 2400 on the SAT but scoff at the – gasp – "imperfect" score of 2200; instead, success lies merely in the dedicated *pursuit* thereof. Measure accomplishment not by how near you are to the end you pursue – and certainly not by the position your neighbor occupies on his or her personal path – but by how hard you worked to improve over yesterday on your personal path. Reflect in order to hone your future efforts, not to ruminate[5] on the past and indulge the useless concept of failure.

Outside the narrow realms of grades and test scores, true perfection is often a meaningless concept. Those who seek perfection and will not be satisfied until they find it will endure a ceaseless sense of inadequacy. Those who pursue it and will be satisfied by the journey's victories, excited by the prospect of progress, and emboldened[6] by its failures will find a path brimming with enjoyable opportunities.

This brings us to the second question: *How do I stand out and forge forward on my personal path?*

Path for Improvement

If, as we have agreed, truly outstanding accomplishments are rare, then they must surely be difficult to achieve. *Maybe*, you'll wonder disheartened, *it's just so difficult that I ought not even try.* This resigning sentiment has resonated in the minds of many; for evidence, look at those in our society for whom just *trying* is embarrassingly stigmatized. Mediocrity is safe. Fortunately, however, it's a sentiment that is rooted in a simple fear of failure, and this is a fear that you should overcome, because genuinely striving toward greatness is success in all the ways that matter.

Yet the question of precisely *how* one goes about standing out remains unaddressed. Knowing our limits, but confident in the power of specific skills to hold generalizable worth, we believe that this book's coverage of how to succeed on the SAT and ACT and in college admissions will be helpful to you in expected and unexpected ways.

Regarding the SAT and ACT, let us get some unhelpful – and thankfully false – ideas out of the way: You are **not** too dumb, too otherwise untalented, or too poor to do well on the SAT or ACT. So what separates the SAT and ACT success stories from the rest of the pack? What, in other words, makes some students stand out on the SAT and ACT?

---

[5] SAT Word Alert: *Ruminate* (verb) means to "turn over in the mind" or "ponder"

[6] SAT Word Alert: *Embolden* (verb) means "to make bold" or "encourage"

There is no one trick, no singular and shocking discovery, that answers this question. Not all perfect or otherwise outstanding scorers earned their scores through a common method, and yes, many of them did so thanks in part to exceptional natural ability. But effort goes a long way in compensating for any disadvantage in the rather unclear "talent" or "intelligence" department; in fact, any perception that you have a deficiency in ability has a greater chance of stifling your potential than does any such deficiency itself. Believe that you can do it, because there is a good chance (and now even better) that you're right.

But for most students, the relevance of effort is an obvious given: To a point, the more work you put into improving, the likelier you are to improve. More practice is better than less. We'll certainly agree to that claim. We will make one critical qualification, however: *How you prepare is more important than how much you prepare.*

Work hard but, more importantly, smart. Millions of collective hours (and dollars) have been wasted by well-meaning and dedicated students preparing for the SAT and ACT simply because they lacked the knowledge and physical resources to prepare in an efficient, effectual[7] way. They misguidedly spent much money and many hours sitting through preparatory classes from the similarly uneducated or misinformed; taking the wrong practice tests; using those practice tests, moreover, in the wrong way; and simply employing *bad strategy* while taking the tests.

Developed and refined through our personal test preparation experience and our educational experiences with others who followed us in the process with great success, the first part of this book offers the best strategies for helping students prepare for and take the SAT and ACT. (In fact, by reading this section, you have secretly been making progress in one of the most basic but important elements for success on the tests: being well-motivated to succeed. In the next chapter, we will attempt to amplify this drive to flourish.)

College admissions – another domain plagued by misconceptions – serve as our secondary focus for this book. In the second part of this book, we attempt to distill the admissions process, to convey its complications simply and clearly but without sacrificing needed nuance. Just as millions of students have wasted time and underachieved by preparing poorly for the SAT and ACT, many students have approached the college admissions process in ways that are too costly, misguidedly (sometimes perversely) artificial, and ultimately ineffective. In both cases, there are smarter, easier, and simpler ways; we share these effective strategies with you.

Here we strive ambitiously. We have worked to communicate and proliferate strategies for testing and admissions success that make today's and tomorrow's students better thinkers. Fair access to these strategies can mollify[8] the presently

---

[7] SAT Word Alert: *Effectual* is synonymous with *effective*

4

undeniable but unnecessary existence of economic and racial disadvantages of opportunity responsible for inequity in education. For both college admissions and standardized tests, our pursuit is to advance preparation efficiency, limit disadvantages born of wealth and other social disparity, and impart an eager and healthy motivation for doing your best – so that, in the eyes of the respective travelers, successful personal paths are less rare. We hope you find this helpful.

---

[8] SAT Word Alert: *Mollify* (verb) means to "mitigate or reduce"

CHAPTER 1
WHY YOU SHOULD CARE

There are no shortcuts to any place worth going.

Beverly Sills (1929-2007)
American Opera Singer, Grammy and Emmy Winner

The Stepping Stone Myth

Like most high school students, you have probably heard something like this before:

"You should go to college."
> Why?
>> "Because getting a college degree is the way to get a great job. It's a stepping stone."

"You should aim for a great job."
> Why?
>> "Because having a great job is a stepping stone to making lots of money."

"You should make lots of money."
> Why?
>> "Because making lots of money is a stepping stone to buying an expensive Ferrari."

"You should buy a Ferrari."
> Why?
>> "Because driving a Ferrari or other expensive car is a stepping stone to happiness."

"But first … you should score high on the SAT and ACT, maintain a great GPA, and do a lot of extracurriculars."
> **Why?**
>> **"Because doing those things is a stepping stone to getting into college and, thus, everything else above!"**

This line of reasoning is apocryphal[9] – but not because it claims that doing well on the standardized tests and in your classes and being student government president will help you get into college; that part is true. The problem is in thinking that the tests, classes, and extracurriculars are *just* stepping stones that you have to cross on your way to eventual happiness. That is a surefire way to be underprepared for college and life. If this is how you look at things – no love lost if so, because it is a common perspective that many subscribe to – let us correct course before your proverbial ship (you) crashes into the proverbial iceberg (reality).

The fact that you are reading this book makes it clear that you care about your future (or at least that your parents care about your future). In either case, *someone* cares about your future, for which you should be glad. The Stepping Stone Myth is an unfortunate byproduct of this care and the fact that college admissions have become more competitive. When Shiv applied to Harvard, there were about 22,000 applicants for 2,000 offered spots, for about a 9 percent admissions rate. At the time of this writing, there were about 35,000 applicants for a similar number of spots – nearly a 6 percent admissions rate! The desire to get into a good college – and the fact that doing so has become more difficult – has produced an arms race among high school students. But instead of stocking up on WMDs (Weapons of Mass Destruction), students are stocking up on the "ETGs": extracurriculars, test scores, and grade point averages.

Amassing[10] any one of the ETGs alone takes a significant commitment, so together they can appear overwhelming. The Stepping Stone Myth is a coping mechanism that makes us think we can cut corners in an effort to "game the system." Examples include cramming for a foreign language test the night before and then forgetting everything immediately after; padding a resume by creatively rounding up your community service hours (*driving* to the soup kitchen counts, right?); and practicing how to guess on or otherwise game the SAT rather than learning how to do math, understand what you read, and use English. If our goal is merely to step to the next stone along our path – present enjoyment and future readiness neglected – we are thinking in narrow and short terms.

Those machinations[11] may help you get into college and may even help you do decently well there. However, the realization that the Stepping Stone Myth actually hurts you rather than helps you will ultimately hit you so hard that you will feel as if the stones themselves fell on top of you. Shiv remembers this happening to him during his second week at Harvard, where it seemed that almost everyone was a polyglot.[12] During high school he viewed the foreign language requirement as a stepping stone to jump over and thus became very good at memorizing long lists of

---

[9] SAT Word Alert: *Apocryphal* (adjective) means "of doubtful authenticity"

[10] SAT Word Alert: *Amass* (verb) means "to collect"

[11] SAT Word Alert: *Machination* (noun) means "scheme or plot, usually for bad intentions"

[12] SAT Word Alert: *Polyglot* (noun) means "one who can speak or write several languages." In fact, during Shiv's senior year at Harvard, his group of five roommates collectively spoke eight languages: Arabic, Chinese, English, French, Hebrew, Italian, Korean, and Spanish.

Spanish vocabulary words ten minutes before a test and then regurgitating them, in the process forgetting what each word meant as soon as he had written it down. Though Shiv "earned" A's in each of those Spanish classes, he was only slightly more fluent than the Chihuahua from the Taco Bell commercials ("Yo quiero Taco Bell"). At Harvard he realized his folly and decided to retake Spanish and even spend a summer in Chile, though his current level of fluency would have been much higher if he had viewed foreign language not as a stepping stone but rather as a useful skill.

A far better perspective is to view each of the ETGs as individual steps on an infinitely high escalator. As opposed to stepping stones, which are independent, disconnected, and based on the idea that ultimate meaning lies just beyond the remaining stones, the steps of an escalator move together and build upon each other. Developing a new skill – whether it is fluency in a foreign language, mastery of a golf swing, or an understanding of fractions and percentages – is tantamount[13] to moving up a step on the escalator. The skill, like the step, will always be behind you, pushing you further up.

Now think about the classes, extracurriculars, and tests that you view as stepping stones and consider why they may be more meaningful than you give them credit for.

The SAT and ACT aim simply to gauge the knowledge and reasoning skills in reading, writing, and math that you have hopefully developed throughout high school. Most of the questions do not technically require any preparation beyond what you would get in regular high school English and math classes. However, what is covered in these classes often varies by school, and even by teacher. Therefore, the SAT and ACT college admissions tests are meant to ensure that all college-bound students are ready for college-level work, after which they should be prepared for the post-college job market.[14]

Let us be clear: The tests should not be viewed as passive measures of what you have learned, but rather as roadmaps for what you need to improve upon before college. For example, Shiv knows that if he had not taken the time to memorize vocabulary words and read more to do well on the tests, he would not have developed the skills that allowed him to do well in his college courses, get admitted to top professional schools, and receive great job offers. Many required readings in college and for jobs are riddled with SAT-level words (like those found in this book). That is why, instead of being "okay" with not knowing the last few, relatively difficult sentence completion questions or trying to game the system by

---

[13] SAT Word Alert: *Tantamount* (adjective) means "equivalent in value, significance, or effect"

[14] Yikes, the word "college" appeared four times in the last sentence: Note that you should spot redundancy as problematic in the grammar sections of the tests *unless* the authors are emphasizing a specific point, like we just did.

guessing, it is better to simply learn the words. A strong vocabulary will stay with you like an escalator step.

Now eliminate the Stepping Stone Myth from your mind and replace it with the reality of the escalator! Each step is not a means toward a vague ideal but an opportunity to derive meaning through personal achievement: new and improved knowledge and skills. This revised attitude will serve you well while preparing for the SAT and ACT and, more importantly, while moving forward into college and beyond.

As many wise men and women have said, "Live not for the destination but for the journey."

Why You Should Care

At a time when most students see a dichotomy[15] between education and anything worth doing – like uncovering the hilarious cultural riches of the Internet, forming meaningful memories with their peers, and plotting their escape to college – a test apparently devoid of humor or life comes along to stand in the way of getting into college.

It is a long test. And, by most honest accounts, it is a challenging and intimidating test, popularly known, among its target population, by such pejorative[16] labels as "standardized assessment," "admissions entrance exam," and even (though on shakier ground) "intelligence test."

It is understandable, then, that the SAT or the ACT is often a dreaded facet of college admissions (and, in turn, the high school experience) of motivated, college-bound students.

One can see the test as a frustrating and uncooperative hurdle, placed in his or her way by mysterious authority figures, which must be stepped over to get to the next stage of life. In fact, most do.

Those who view it in this way will approach the test with a dismissive defeatism: *I'll take a couple practice tests like everyone told me to; maybe I'll even go to a couple prep classes at my school. Then I'll get through the test once – they better not make me retake it! – and get accepted by a college.* They will do worse than they are capable of because they are unmotivated. For almost all students, this lack of motivation means less knowledge, fewer skills, and less confidence, not to mention less ability to earn scholarships and college acceptances.

---

[15] SAT Word Alert: *Dichotomy* (noun) means "division into two contradictory groups"

[16] SAT Word Alert: *Pejorative* (adjective) means "having an unpleasant connotation"

Alternatively, some will approach it with the rabid motivation of necessity and gamesmanship: *I have to get into a prestigious, selective university, for which I need a high score! I must take dozens of practice tests and spend lots of money so that I can learn how to game this unfair, unnecessary, stupid test. What does the SAT or the ACT think it is, and why does it get to determine my future?* They will do worse than they are able to because they are misguided in their motivation and will waste a lot of time and money in the process.

Fortunately, there is a much better approach to the SAT and the ACT. It is the way we espouse[17] in this book, and it begins with a change in your viewpoint, as we brought up earlier in this chapter:

See the difficulty of the test as an opportunity to accomplish something previously beyond your grasp and perhaps even greater than you thought you had the potential to grasp. This feat is in itself meaningful.

See the test not as the product of a group of judgmental enemies who are sitting in a room maniacally concocting[18] tricks but as the work of a well-meaning though imperfect team of educators who want merely to craft a series of questions designed to gauge your readiness for college.

Do not see the occasional frustrations that will invariably[19] arise when you are preparing for the test (no journey worth your time is without hurdles!) as signs that you have run into the boundaries of your intellectual capacity or arrived at the plateau of your potential for progress. These frustrations should instead be a source of motivation. They serve as the objects for your aim to overcome – and then as the escalator steps propelling you to progress further.

Be wary, however, of letting yourself adopt a perverse[20] and exaggerated motivation – a mentality that the SAT and ACT ought to dominate your college admissions priorities or usurp[21] time you would have spent doing other important things. On the first point, extracurriculars and grades matter as well (remember the ETGs). And on the second point, college admissions are not the end-all of high school life; there is room too for cultivating a happy social life.

You should care about the SAT or the ACT because the process is rewarding and the skills gained in the process – both the specific problem-solving techniques that you will master and the more general strategies that you will develop for tackling challenges – are useful forever after, across all domains and at all levels. One

---

[17] SAT Word Alert: *Espouse* (verb) means "to support or advocate"

[18] SAT Word Alert: *Concoct* (verb) means "to create or devise"

[19] SAT Word Alert: *Invariable* (adjective) means "not changing; constant"

[20] SAT Word Alert: *Perverse* (adjective) means "not right or good; corrupt"

[21] SAT Word Alert: *Usurp* (verb) means "to take away wrongfully"

escalator step up is one more escalator step supporting your experience of new heights.

More immediately and practically, you should care about succeeding on the SAT or the ACT because there are also external and very real incentives for doing well on the tests, such as a boost in college admissions and scholarship chances, as you will see.

As abnormal and atypical as it may feel at first, compel yourself to get excited at the chance to do what it takes to succeed on the tests! You will look back proudly, and all of the unpleasant associations with the tests that you may have now will be gone and will, in fact, heighten your sense of accomplishment.

On the way to doing well on the SAT or ACT, you will learn valuable skills. After doing well on the SAT or ACT, you will be exposed to valuable opportunities. These include college admissions, which we touch upon briefly below and heavily later on in the book. They include recognitions, like the Presidential Scholars program through which Shiv received an expense-paid trip to China, and scholarship money, such as the National Merit Scholarship that Blake and Shiv have used to help pay for college. (This latter reason should be motivation enough because, as we will mention in Chapter 3, each test question you get right may be worth up to $100!). And they include other opportunities, such as lucrative[22] tutoring posts, stemming from your increased credibility and desirable reputation.

Though there are plenty of self-interested motives for raising your scores, there is at least one other important reason to live up to your potential on these tests: your responsibility to your community. Many students sit bored in their classes, realizing neither the costs that go into their education nor its societal value. Since the tab for our school is picked up by our parents and other taxpayers, there is a misalignment between how we value our classes and what they are actually worth monetarily (the latter often far outweighs the former). We owe it to our parents, our teachers, and our country to make their investments in us worthwhile. Indeed, in this globally competitive environment, we should hold ourselves responsible for developing the skills to become the educated workforce upon whose shoulders our society will continue to prosper.

As John F. Kennedy so famously said in his inaugural address, "Ask not what your country can do for you; ask what you can do for your country." The advancement of society depends not only on those at the forefront of technological and scientific innovation but also on the population at large to educate and apply themselves. We think that standardized tests are able to provide a compelling, effectively guided stimulus for this education.

---

[22] SAT Word Alert: *Lucrative* (adjective) means "producing wealth"

Okay, maybe it's worth it to try to do well on the tests, you may now grant. *But can I even do it? How do I do it?* Yes, you can. As for how, caring *in the right way* – in other words, adopting the appropriate mentality and motivation – is a productive and great first step. In the following chapters, we will build upon that step to provide you with the tools to escalate your score.

You should (and can) do well on the SAT and ACT. If you are dubious[23] of the above words of encouragement that trying your very best will bring you success, cast those doubts aside! When you do, you will realize the fruits of applying yourself. They taste like achievement: incorporeal,[24] but sweet.

College Admissions

The college admissions process is often abstruse[25] and marked by nuances[26]. The role of test scores in admissions is no exception; this is particularly true of the admissions practices of the nation's highly selective colleges and universities. (Thankfully, many schools, including most public universities, have more clear-cut procedures within their admissions offices.)

These very competitive schools have adopted what they like to refer to as "holistic"[27] admissions policies. In effect, this means that their admissions officers – the people who review your application and decide whether to admit you, deny you, or hold you in some sort of decidedly undesirable limbo (waitlists) – mine through the large amount of information that they have on you as an applicant and try to establish an overall sense of your "fit" for their school.

One crucial element of this fit is your academic credentials, which the admissions officers rely upon to develop confidence in your ability to succeed at the college without unreasonable amounts of effort or overextension on your part. This is both to your benefit – you do not want to find yourself in a situation in which *just passing* your classes is a lofty goal requiring interminable[28] study sessions – and to the benefit of the university, which has an interest in maintaining high graduation rates, keeping professors happy with the quality of the students, and recording impressive statistics on its admissions profile.

In addition, the admissions officers are keenly concerned with accepting applicants who will form a cohesive, collaborative, and extracurricularly vibrant student body. They want some students who occupy the traditional niches of the school, and they

---

[23] SAT Word Alert: *Dubious* (adjective) means "doubtful"

[24] SAT Word Alert: *Incorporeal* (adjective) means "not physical or tangible"

[25] SAT Word Alert: *Abstruse* (adjective) means "hard to understand"

[26] SAT Word Alert: *Nuance* (noun) means "a subtle difference or variation"

[27] SAT Word Alert: *Holistic* (adjective) means "related to the idea that an entity is more than the sum of its parts"

[28] SAT Word Alert: *Interminable* (adjective) means "having no end"

want some students who do not. In so doing, they aim to cover a panoply[29] of interests and personalities in their student body.

To that end, beyond the initial academic stages of applicant review, admissions to highly selective colleges are often more an art than a science, replete[30] with subjectivity, propensity[31] to err, and uncertainty. Though the SAT no longer features analogies, we still believe they are important and will use one to clarify the above point:

Consider your college application a painting, and you are the artist. There are a myriad[32] of elements that need to come together seamlessly for a painting to be considered a masterpiece: the hues and lights of the colors, direction and force of the brushstrokes, composition of the paints, and texture of the canvas, among others. Curators and critics spend hours poring over and analyzing these details, deciding whether the painting is a good fit for their museum or worthy of acclaim – subjectively, of course, because, as anyone who has been to a museum of modern art knows, beauty is often in the eye of the beholder.

Like a painting, your college application is composed of a number of elements: your test scores, GPA, extracurricular activities, background, recommendations, essays, and others. And it, too, will be reviewed by well-intentioned though subjective "curators and critics" – admissions officers – who will decide whether the painter behind the application – you – should be accepted into their school. Some of these curators will not even consider the painting if it is clear that a fundamental element that they seek for their art collection – say, brushstrokes – is absent (imagine if Leonardo da Vinci had tried finger painting the *Mona Lisa*). Similarly, admissions officers may scarcely even consider your application if the fundamental ingredient of high SAT and ACT scores is missing.

It is therefore among our goals to help you improve the chances that your college applications will be accepted by providing you with the right ingredients and tools – test scores and skills – and instructions for how to put them together artistically. Fortunately, we developed this artistic sense in time to have collectively been accepted to a number of those "highly selective colleges," including Brown, Columbia, Duke, Harvard, MIT, Princeton, Stanford, the University of Chicago, and Yale. Wielding the insights we have gained from these application experiences, we have devoted an extensive portion of this book – Chapter 10, "The Art of College Admissions" – to preparing for and succeeding in college admissions. Consider us your personal Bob Ross in helping you make your application painting a college admissions masterpiece.

---

[29] SAT Word Alert: *Panoply* (noun) means "a wide-ranging and impressive array or display"
[30] SAT Word Alert: *Replete* (adjective) means "full or abundant"
[31] SAT Word Alert: *Propensity* (noun) means "a tendency"
[32] SAT Word Alert: *Myriad* (noun) means "a great number"

CHAPTER 2
GETTING TO KNOW THE TESTS

In the previous chapter, we established why you should think of the SAT and ACT as your (challenging but worthwhile) friends rather than as obstacles. The next logical step is to stalk them on Facebook, right? Unfortunately, the SAT and ACT do not have profiles with amusing or incriminating[33] pictures, but their creators do provide a lot of valuable information that you can capitalize on to do better. Information can be turned into knowledge, and knowledge can be turned into power. Many students do not understand the SAT and ACT on a fundamental level, which contributes to their fear of the tests and, in turn, poorer performances on them.

In this chapter, we aim to provide everything that you will need to know about the tests themselves; hopefully, you find our coverage perspicuous[34]. This information will provide the knowledge to undergird[35] your learning the strategies for doing the best that you can on the tests – which is likely to be quite good, perhaps even better than you expect.

Both the SAT and ACT are standardized tests designed primarily as college admissions exams. *Standardized* means that the tests' structures, the types of questions that are asked, the administrations of the exams, and the scoring are constant across the country (and internationally) and from one test date to the next. With the exception of IB and AP exams, this is likely in stark contrast to tests that you take in your high school classes, which vary significantly across the country depending on the teacher, even for the same class.

The consistency of the SAT and ACT enables colleges to compare scores from tests that were not exactly the same or taken on the same day: A score of 2040 on the SAT from May 2013, for example, should in theory represent about the same level of proficiency as a 2040 achieved in October 2014. And for the most part, the makers of both the SAT and ACT do a pretty good job of standardizing the exams, as statistically revealed by reliability metrics. This means that official practice tests will predict with good accuracy how you will do on a formal administration, which we will discuss more in the next chapter.

This standardization also means that you can know what is coming. Let's leverage this predictability to your advantage.

---

[33] SAT Word Alert: *Incriminate* (verb) means "to imply guilt or wrong-doing"

[34] SAT Word Alert: *Perspicuous* (adjective) means "clearly presented"

[35] SAT Word Alert: *Undergird* (verb) means "to provide with a sound basis"

The SAT

The SAT has historically been the most taken college admissions test, although the ACT has been gaining popularity. Development, administration, and scoring of the SAT are completed by the College Board and the Educational Testing Service (ETS).

The SAT has been around for a long time – over one hundred years – and has undergone many changes, including its name. "Scholastic Aptitude Test" was eventually thrown out because it suggested too strong an association with IQ tests; next came the "Scholastic Assessment Test"; and today the formal title is the SAT Reasoning Test. ("SAT" now stands for nothing, which is safe, we suppose.)

Until 2005, the test had two sections: Verbal and Mathematics. The test you will be taking, dubbed the "New SAT," has three sections: Critical Reading, Mathematics, and Writing. (In 2016, an even newer version of the SAT will replace the current test.)

Here is a breakdown of the current SAT:

Critical Reading

The Critical Reading section of the SAT has three subsections on each administration of the test, totaling 70 minutes. Two are 25 minutes in length; one is 20 minutes. Spread out over these subsections will be 67 questions, for each of which you are given five choices.

There are two main types of questions on the Critical Reading section: passage-based questions and sentence completion questions. You will face 48 passage-based reading questions, which test your ability to read text effectively and with a keen analytical eye. There will be a mix of short passages, long passages, and dual passages, which you will have to compare and contrast. Sentence completion questions round out the final 19. These questions test your vocabulary and your ability to apply that vocabulary, using an understanding of how the words fit into the sentence.

Mathematics

As with the Critical Reading section, the SAT's Math section is allotted 70 minutes and divided into three subsections (two 25 minutes long, and one 20 minutes long). It tests a variety of algebraic and geometric concepts and has 54 questions in total: 44 multiple-choice questions and 10 free-response questions. You will likewise have five choices for each multiple-choice question. On each free-response question, you will be given a grid on which to bubble in your numerical answer.

Writing

The Writing section is a bit shorter, clocking in at a total of 60 minutes. This section is also divided into three subsections, though the distribution is different: There are two 25-minute subsections and a 10-minute one.

The first subsection of the SAT is always a 25-minute Writing section: the essay. You will be asked to respond with a draft in support of your opinion on the given prompt. The second Writing subsection on the test will be comprised[36] of a mix of Improving Sentences questions, which test your ability to identify the phrasing that most clearly, grammatically, and laconically[37] conveys a point; Identifying Errors questions, which test your ability to recognize grammatical errors; and Improving Paragraphs questions, which focus on clear phrasing of sentences and on organization of a paragraph.

The final section of the SAT is always a 10-minute, 14-question subsection including only Improving Sentences questions. Considered a nice respite[38] after hours of testing, this mini-section proves that the test creators have mercy.

The SAT has ten subsections on each administration, and thus far we have accounted for only nine of them. The tenth, experimental subsection is 25 minutes long and can be in any of the three subjects. It is "experimental" because the test creators use it to vet[39] newly developed questions, and thus it will not affect your score. You may be wondering why anyone would expend the time and mental energy to answer the questions on the experimental section. If you have seen the *Matrix* trilogy, you may remember the scene where Agent Smith clones himself and Neo cannot tell which one is the real antagonist. The test creators adopted a similar strategy and made the experimental section indistinguishable from the other nine sections. Thus, when you are taking the test, you should try your best on each of the ten subsections.

So the grand time tally is 3 hours and 45 minutes, in addition to the breaks. Yikes, that seems long! With practice and the dedication needed to focus, you will be able to limit the negative effects of mental fatigue; with effort, you can surmount what may now seem like insuperable[40] length.

Scoring

Each correct response on the SAT is worth 1 point. A non-response to a multiple-choice question yields zero points. An incorrect response to a multiple-choice question results in a deduction of .25 points. This penalty for wrong answers is

---

[36] SAT Word Alert: *Comprise* (verb) means "to consist of, be made up of"

[37] SAT Word Alert: *Laconically* (adverb) means "concisely, or expressed in few words"

[38] SAT Word Alert: *Respite* (noun) means "an interval of relief"

[39] SAT Word Alert: *Vet* (verb) means "to examine"

[40] SAT Word Alert: *Insuperable* (adjective) means "unable to be overcome"

designed to account for random guessing and diminish the influence of luck in one's score. We will discuss the strategic implications of this in the next chapter.

In order to calculate your raw score on a given section of the SAT, take the number of correct responses to all multiple-choice and free-response questions and subtract one quarter of the number of incorrect responses to multiple-choice questions. (While the opportunity cost of not answering a question is still one point, this implicit cost need not be taken into account explicitly when you are calculating your raw score.) Finally, round your score to the nearest integer, remembering that a score that ends in .5 rounds up in your favor.

In keeping with its standardized nature, the SAT is curved so that the slight differences in difficulty from one test to another do not influence the score. At the end of this chapter, you will find approximate raw-score-to-scaled-score conversion charts for the SAT.

The essay subsection of the Writing portion of the SAT is scored by two graders, each of whom awards a score between 1 and 6. (The lowest score is reserved for responses that are utterly digressive[41].) The highest achievable score is 12, yielded by two perfect scores of 6.

The essay graders for the SAT do not do a particularly good job of scoring essays in a consistent way. As much as the College Board attempts to establish objective, generally applicable standards for the scoring of the essays, the process is ultimately subjective and decidedly human. That, for example, scores of 11 occur approximately three times as often as scores of 12 – meaning the two graders disagreed on whether the essay deserved a 5 or 6 – reflects this unfortunate reality. In fact, almost 5 percent of essays are sent to a third grader, meaning that the original graders disagreed by 2 or more points out of 6. Not impressive.

Worry not, however: All hope need not be consumed by the partial randomness, thanks to the way in which the Writing section is scored. Scoring the Writing section involves two steps. To find out your essay-independent scaled score, you convert your raw score on the multiple-choice questions (for which there is a maximum score of 49) to a scaled score out of 80. Refer to Table 2 at the end of this chapter for an example conversion set.

To calculate your overall scaled score, convert your multiple-choice raw score (the one out of 49, not 80) into your score on the Writing section (out of 800) by using your essay score (out of 12). This will all make sense when you look at the tables – specifically, Table 3 at the end of this chapter is the relevant guide here.

---

[41] SAT Word Alert: *Digressive* (adjective) means "tending to wander away from the main purpose or topic"

As you will see, achieving an excellent Writing score is achievable even if you do not get a perfect or near-perfect essay score. Clearly, however, an excellent score on the essay is helpful in compensating for less-than-ideal performance on the multiple-choice questions.

In total, there are 10 subsections derived from three sections, each worth 800 points –2400 points in all.

Logistics

All administrations of the SAT are on Saturday, but late testing on Sunday is offered under certain circumstances. The SAT is offered in October, November, December, January, March, May, and June and, at the time of writing, costs $51 for registration. Fee waivers are available. The test begins at 8:00 a.m.; arrive at least 30 minutes earlier than this in order to reduce stress on testing day.

Bring all of the following:

Your SAT Admission Ticket, which can be printed out on the College Board's website. Do this well ahead of time so that you are not left panicking at the last second to get it printed. The test proctor will not be as hospitable[42] as that kind English teacher in middle school who let you print out your forgotten assignment when you arrived at school.

A photo ID, such as your driver's license or school ID.

Your skills. Never leave home without them – especially on this day, for which you have hopefully prepared diligently.

Water and snacks for the breaks. Nothing too significant, of course – just to tide you over until you finish the test.

A watch whose alarm you know how to disable so that you can quietly keep track of time on each subsection. Practice with your watch ahead of time to ensure that you understand how to use it.

Pencils, lots of them. The College Board recommends two, but – within reason – the more you bring, the safer you are (as long as you don't keep them in your pocket). They also need to be No. 2 so that the scoring machines can best read your answer sheet.

A calculator. A scientific or graphing calculator that is approved by the College Board will do. If you are comfortable with a graphing calculator, that should be the preference, because some questions on the Math section are more easily solvable through graphing. Consult the College Board's website for a list of acceptable calculators, but most commonly used ones are fine, including the advanced TI-89 graphing calculator. Also bring some extra batteries of the appropriate type in case of the dreaded mid-test power failure. However, after you read and follow the advice in the Math chapter of this book, your calculator will be more of a paperweight than a necessity.

---

[42] SAT Word Alert: *Hospitable* (adjective) means "friendly and welcoming"

The ACT

Introduced in 1959, the ACT is the primary competitor of the SAT and is produced, administered, and scored by ACT, Inc. It is most popular in the Midwestern and Southern US but has been gaining currency[43] in other regions. Nationally, it has approximately matched the popularity of the SAT.

Like the SAT, the ACT used to be an initialism[44] – in this case, for "American College Test" – but presently has no such meaning. Six states – Tennessee, Wyoming, Kentucky, Illinois, Michigan, and Colorado – require that high-school students take the ACT in order to graduate.

Depending on how you label the parts of the test, the ACT has one or two more sections than the SAT. The ACT's four primary sections are English, Mathematics, Reading, and Science. There is also a fifth, optional section: Writing.

None of the sections on the ACT are broken into subsections as on the SAT – just four or five consecutive sections.

English

The ACT's English section is 45 minutes long and has 75 questions. You will be given five passages with corresponding multiple-choice questions that test your ability to apply grammatical and organizational skills to those passages.

Mathematics

The Mathematics section is 60 minutes long, and all of its questions are multiple-choice. Like the SAT's Math section, it covers a range of algebraic and geometric topics. Topics from a basic pre-calculus curriculum, such as trigonometry, are also included.

Reading

Comprised of 40 questions spread over four passages, the Reading section is relatively brief at 35 minutes in length. The purpose of this section is to test your reading comprehension and analysis skills.

Science

The Science section is also relatively short at 35 minutes and 40 questions. It is divided into seven "information sets," which can be represented graphically or in

---

[43] SAT Word Alert: *Currency* (noun) means "general acceptance or prevalence"

[44] SAT Word Alert: *Initialism* (noun) means "acronym"

prose. The questions will require you to interpret data, analyze experiments, and determine relationships, among other common scientific skills.

Writing

The final section of the test is the Writing section. In contrast to the SAT's Writing section, which has a combination of multiple-choice questions and the essay, the Writing section of the ACT is solely an essay. You will be given 30 minutes (five more than the SAT allots for its essay) to respond to a prompt. Grading is the same as for the SAT's essay: two graders each provide a score from 1 to 6, for a total score of between 2 and 12.

The Writing section is optional, but, for most students, taking it is strongly advisable. The only situation in which opting out of the Writing section is a sensible idea occurs when you are certain that the colleges you will apply to do not consider it.

Not including breaks, the ACT lasts 2 hours and 55 minutes without the Writing section, or 3 hours and 25 minutes with it. Thus the ACT is slightly shorter than the SAT.

Scoring

Scoring of the ACT is similar to that of the SAT with one salient[45] distinction: Wrong answers to multiple-choice questions on the ACT do not result in point deductions. Therefore, your raw scores are equal simply to the number of questions that you answer correctly.

Sample ACT conversion sets for raw scores to scaled scores appear at the end of this chapter.

Each of the four sections on the ACT is scored out of 36. Whereas on the SAT the sections' scores are summed to arrive at a total, sections on the ACT are averaged and then rounded to arrive at a composite score.

For example, scores of 36 on English, 34 on Mathematics, 30 on Reading, and 33 on Science will yield an average of 33.25 and a composite score of 33. The Writing score is not factored into the composite score.

Logistics

Test-day practicalities for the ACT are similar to those for the SAT. Each testing administration occurs on Saturday and begins at 8:00 a.m., though, again, arriving earlier is wise, especially for those with pesky dilatory[46] tendencies. The months when the ACT is offered differ from those for the SAT: For the ACT, they are September, October, December, February, April, and June.

---

[45] SAT Word Alert: *Salient* (adjective) means "prominent or conspicuous"

[46] SAT Word Alert: *Dilatory* (adjective) means "tardy" or "tending to delay"

You should bring your printed admissions ticket, your photo ID (such as a driver's license or school ID), multiple No. 2 pencils, a watch with an alarm that you know how to disable, and a calculator. The list of approved calculators can be found at the official website for the ACT; it is similar to those allowed for the SAT except that the TI-89 calculator is prohibited on the ACT.

Score Submission and Consideration

Score Choice

The SAT's Score Choice option allows you to select specific SAT testing dates' scores to send to colleges rather than submitting all of them. So if you took the test on, for example, three testing dates (say, June, October, and December), you could choose to send all three or pick one or two to selectively show to colleges. The unsent score or scores would go unseen by college admissions officers. Note, though, that if you wish to send the score for any section of an SAT testing date, you must send the other two sections' scores from that date, as well.

Score Choice does allow you to send only the SAT Subject Test scores that you want to, even if the tests were taken on the same day. (Chapter 9 has more information on Subject Tests.)

There is an important qualification to make here: Some schools – Yale, for instance – request that you not use Score Choice and instead send all scores to them. All evidence points to mechanisms for the enforcement of these anti-Score Choice policies being nonexistent; such schools rely on applicants' honesty.

Score submission for ACT scores naturally follows a process similar to that afforded by the SAT's official Score Choice policy, since a student may submit whichever testing day's scores he or she wishes.

Superscoring

Unlike Score Choice, superscoring is performed not by the applicant but by colleges' admissions departments. Superscoring involves considering only the highest score on each section of one of the exams, even if this means looking at multiple test dates. For example, if on the SAT a student scores 670 in Critical Reading, 720 in Math, and 790 in Writing – for a total of 2180 – on one test date and then 700 in Critical Reading, 700 in Math, and 610 in Writing – totaling 2010 – on another test date, the superscore is 700+720+790 = 2210.

Most colleges superscore the SAT, and some also superscore the ACT. A small minority of colleges even superscore *across* the SAT and ACT, taking the best subject performances on each test and equating them to arrive at a maximized combined score. See a representative SAT-ACT score concordance in Table 5 at the end of this chapter.

Chapter 10 discusses in detail the role that test scores play in college admissions.

Score Conversion Charts

Table 1. These charts provide raw-score-to-scaled-score conversion for the SAT. The raw score is, as described earlier, a function of the number of questions answered correctly and the number answered incorrectly. Conversion varies from one test administration to another, but these offer a representative approximation. (This information is based on curves from the New SAT reported from 2005 through 2012, averaged and compiled by Erik Jacobsen and posted on www.erikthered.com/tutor/.)

Critical Reading Raw Score	Critical Reading Scaled Score		Mathematics Raw Score	Mathematics Scaled Score
67	800		54	800
66	800		53	780
65	800		52	760
64	780		51	740
63	760		50	720
62	740		49	710
61	730		48	700
60	720		47	690
59	700		46	6870
58	690		45	670
57	680		44	660
56	670		43	650
55	660		42	640
54	650		41	640
53	640		40	630
52	630		39	620

51	630	38	610
50	620	37	600
49	610	36	590
48	600	35	580
47	600	34	570
46	590	33	560
45	580	32	560
44	580	31	550
43	570	30	500
42	560	29	490
41	560	28	490
40	550	27	480
39	550	26	470
38	540	25	470
37	530	24	460
36	530	23	460
35	520	22	450
34	520	21	450
33	520	20	440
32	510	19	430
31	500	18	430
30	500	17	420
29	490	16	420

28	490	15	410
27	480	14	400
26	470	13	400
25	470	12	390

Table 2. This conversion approximates what your SAT Writing Multiple-choice Score would be, given your raw score on the non-essay portion of the Writing section. This scaled score does not directly affect the total composite score out of 2400. (This information is also based on curves from the New SAT reported from 2005 through 2012, averaged and compiled by Erik Jacobsen and posted on www.erikthered.com/tutor/.)

Writing MC Raw Score	Writing MC Scaled Score		Writing MC Raw Score	Writing MC Scaled Score
49	80		35	57
48	78		34	56
47	75		33	55
46	73		32	54
45	71		31	53
44	69		30	52
43	68		29	51
42	66		28	50
41	65		27	50
40	63		26	49
39	62		25	48
38	61		24	47
37	60		23	46

36	58	22	45

Table 3. This conversion offers a way to approximate the scaled score (out of 800) you would receive on the SAT Writing section, given your multiple-choice raw score (out of 49) and your essay score (out of 12).

Essay Score

MC	12	11	10	9	8	7	6	5
49	800	800	800	800	790	760	750	730
48	800	800	790	770	750	730	710	690
47	800	780	760	750	720	700	690	670
46	780	760	750	730	700	680	670	650
45	760	750	730	710	690	670	650	630
44	740	730	710	700	670	650	630	620
43	730	720	700	680	660	640	620	610
42	720	700	690	670	650	630	610	590
41	710	690	680	660	630	610	600	580
40	700	680	660	650	620	600	590	570
39	680	670	650	640	610	590	570	550
38	670	660	640	630	600	580	560	540
37	660	650	630	620	590	570	550	530
36	650	640	620	610	580	560	540	520
35	650	630	610	600	570	550	540	510
34	640	620	610	590	560	540	530	500
33	630	610	600	580	560	530	520	490
32	620	610	590	570	550	530	510	490
31	610	600	580	560	540	520	500	480

30	600	590	570	560	530	510	490	470
29	600	580	560	550	520	500	490	460
28	590	570	560	540	520	490	480	450
27	580	570	550	530	510	490	470	450
26	570	560	540	530	500	480	460	440
25	570	550	540	520	490	470	460	430
24	560	550	530	510	490	470	450	430
23	550	540	520	500	480	460	440	420
22	540	530	510	500	470	450	430	410
21	540	520	510	490	470	440	430	410
20	530	520	500	480	460	440	420	400
19	520	510	490	480	450	430	410	390

Table 4. These four conversions apply to the ACT. As for the SAT, these are subject to variation. Note also that on the ACT, the raw score is not lowered by a wrong answer to a multiple-choice question, as it is on the SAT.

English Raw Score	English Scaled Score		Mathematics Raw Score	Mathematics Scaled Score
75	36		60	36
74	35		59	35
73	34		58	34
72	34		57	33
71	33		56	32
70	32		55	32
69	31		54	31

68	30		53	31
67	30		52	30
66	29		51	29
65	29		50	29
64	28		49	28
63	28		48	28
62	28		47	28
61	27		46	28
60	27		45	27
59	27		44	27
58	26		43	27
57	26		42	26
56	25		41	26
55	25		40	25
54	24		39	25
53	24		38	24
52	24		37	24
51	23		36	23
50	23		35	23
49	22		34	22
48	21		33	22
47	20		32	21
46	20		31	21

45	20		30	20

Reading Raw Score	Reading Scaled Score		Science Raw Score	Science Scaled Score
40	36		40	36
39	36		39	35
38	35		38	34
37	34		37	32
36	33		36	31
35	32		35	29
34	31		34	28
33	30		33	28
32	29		32	27
31	28		31	27
30	28		30	26
29	27		29	25
28	27		28	24
27	26		27	23
26	25		26	23
25	24		25	22
24	23		24	21
23	22		23	20
22	21		22	19
21	21		21	18

Table 5. In order to evaluate all applicants in an equal way despite receiving scores from different standardized tests, admissions officers will convert the scores using an SAT-ACT concordance[15] table. Each school has its own table, but the tables will all be quite similar to that suggested by the ACT. Here is what the ACT has estimated the relationship to be (information from www.act.org/aap/concordance/estimate.html):

ACT Composite Score, out of 36	Corresponding SAT Composite Score, out of 2400
36	2390
35	2330
34	2250
33	2180
32	2120
31	2060
30	2000
29	1940
28	1880
27	1820
26	1770
25	1710
24	1650
23	1590
22	1530
21	1470
20	1410
19	1350
18	1290

And here are some percentiles to give you an idea of where these scores fall, relative to the performance of the rest of the test-taking population; the percentiles reflect the results of the college-bound members of the recent high school graduating classes (calculated based on specific score tallies provided by the College Board for graduating seniors in the class of 2011):

SAT Score	Percentile
2400	99.98
2300	99.56
2200	98.43
2100	96.36
2000	93.00
1900	88.05
1800	81.20
1700	72.45
1600	61.88
1500	49.92
1400	37.62
1300	25.96

Earning a score at a percentile of 85 would mean that you did better than 85 percent of the test-takers, and a score whose percentile is 40 would be lower than those of 60 percent of the test-takers.

In the next two chapters, we will detail our patent-pending (not really) PERFECT[47] Approach, which can only be described as "the P90X of Test Prep." Just as that program advocates[48] regular workouts and healthy eating for getting a ripped body

---

[47] Perhaps the all-caps format is misleading. "PERFECT" is not a meaningful acronym (unless you count "Positively Extraordinary, Ridiculously Fail-proof, Exact, and Correct Technique," which you shouldn't because it's lame) but rather an approach that we want to emphasize. Many of our peers and students have benefited tremendously from it – not just on standardized tests, but in their daily lives.

[48] SAT Word Alert: *Advocate* (verb) means "support or promote"

and six-pack abs, the PERFECT Approach offers proven strategies for getting a ripped brain and six-pack test scores. It, too, requires commitment and motivation but is well worth the effort. If you are still building up your drive, we suggest going back and (re)reading the chapter on *Why You Should Care*.

We have organized our method into two chapters. Chapter 3 concerns how to prepare for the SAT and ACT, and Chapter 4 focuses on strategies to use when taking the tests. Each half of the PERFECT Approach has been divided into four fundamental pieces of advice. Without further ado…

CHAPTER 3
THE PERFECT APPROACH: TEST PREPARATION STRATEGY

1. **Hold Yourself Accountable: Aim for a Perfect Score**

2. **Take Official Practice Tests**

3. **Master Every Question**

4. **Take Both Tests**

Hold Yourself Accountable: Aim for a Perfect Score

Imagine that you are window shopping at the mall and see something you really want to buy that's marked at $20. Having misplaced your credit card (uh-oh, time to cancel your card and prepare for a contrived[49] mathematical dilemma), you only have a ten-dollar bill and some spare change in your pocket. Luckily for you, it is 40 percent off! Even better, you have a store card that gives you a 15 percent discount on top of that! Before you zip off to the checkout counter, you need to know *beforehand* if you have enough money to buy it, especially because you do not want to embarrass yourself in front of that cute cashier. Sound familiar? (No? Well, keep reading anyways.)

Unfortunately, real-life problems like this one do not come in multiple-choice format. An SAT test writer doesn't pop up from behind a clothing rack and say, "Hey Johnny, after the discounts, will it cost (a) $9.00, (b) $10.20, (c) $11.50, (d) $12.00, or (e) $14.60?"[50] The point is that, in real life, you have to figure out the answer for yourself. (In Chapter 4, we describe why it is also valuable on the SAT and ACT to "Solve for the Answer Itself," even when you are given choices.)

Granted, you probably have a cell phone with a calculator that you can whip out any time you get a whiff of something that smells like math. But what will your date think while you fumble with it to work out a 20 percent tip on a $40 dinner[51]? And besides, even if you have the calculator do the "hard work" – a myth about mental math that deserves to be wiped off the face of the planet – you still need to know what numbers should be added or subtracted, multiplied or divided. Don't

---

[49] SAT Word Alert: *Contrive* (verb) means "create intentionally and obviously"

[50] The answer, by the way, is (b), so assuming that your spare change is more than 20 cents, you're golden – unless you needed to save some of that money to take the subway back, in which case you're hopefully buying some comfortable shoes.

[51] $8, for a total of about $48 dollars. At minimum wage, that's almost seven hours of flipping burgers. Whoever your date is better be a keeper!

worry, though! We have devoted a chunk of our chapter on the math sections to helping you kick that calculator habit.

Most important, however, is that as the pace of daily life has sped up, we (paradoxically) have become lethargic[52] and have lost our sense of accountability. Computers have emancipated[53] us from the "tedious"[54] tasks of applying math (calculator), learning vocabulary (dictionary), spelling and using grammar (autocorrect), sending letters (e-mail), and remembering our to-do lists (smartphones) – in essence, they have freed us from thinking.

Our mistakes are almost always reversible: For egsample, these statement have bad seplling and grammur, which we can spot immediately on our word processor by the red and green squiggly underlines and correct with a quick right-click if they have not been autocorrected already. It is a mistake to develop an attitude that all mistakes are reversible, because if tests and real life have one thing in common, it is that some mistakes are not. The best way to train yourself for both, then, is to hold yourself accountable.

Relying on your calculator for the math sections, for example, is a decently reliable way of quickly solving most easy questions. But here's the important answer to the frustrated objections posed by students when they are perennially[55] compelled to limit their use of their calculators: defaulting to the calculator hampers creative problem solving. To maximize your potential for a truly outstanding performance on the math sections – to stand out – you must learn to figure problems out first with your brain, then leave only the largest figures to the calculator. (Using mental math for calculations, in addition to contributing to smarter approaches to hard problems, is also quicker for all but the most challenging calculations.)

You may ask yourself, *What if I do not expect to get a perfect score? Can I settle for easier methods that will merely help me pass?* We answer with an emphatic "No!"

Only those who will risk going too far can possibly find out how far one can go.
T.S. Eliot (1888-1965)
Nobel Laureate, Literature

We initially considered opening up this chapter with the well-known quote, "Shoot for the moon. Even if you miss, you'll land among the stars." However, we changed our mind once Shiv remembered that one of his college roommates majored in astronomy and astrophysics and would shoot *him* if he featured that flagrantly[56] unscientific statement.

---

[52] SAT Word Alert: *Lethargic* (adjective) means "lazy, indifferent, or apathetic"

[53] SAT Word Alert: *Emancipate* (verb) means "to free"

[54] SAT Word Alert: *Tedious* (adjective) means "dull or boring"

[55] SAT Word Alert: *Perennial* (adjective) means "lasting" or "enduring"

The essential point of both quotes is that by aiming high you can achieve things that you never thought possible. People often set their goals too low for a number of reasons. Some do not have confidence in themselves and underestimate their abilities. Others do not want to be disappointed if they cannot reach the goal. A few may lack motivation or are, frankly, indolent[57].

A common reason people set their scoring goals too low on the SAT and ACT is that they are aiming for the "minimum" score that will get them into college or earn them a scholarship. For example, Shiv has taught many students who want to qualify for the Florida Bright Futures Scholarship (close to full tuition at public universities in Florida). At the time of this writing, the minimum required SAT and ACT scores were 1290 (Critical Reading plus Math) and 29, respectively. For most students seeking the scholarship, those scores transform into the goals that they aim for on practice tests. Unfortunately, perhaps due to the pressure or formality of test day, students often score slightly lower than they did on the practice tests, and as a result barely miss the cut-off requirement for the scholarship. The lesson: If you aim high to begin with, you will be much more likely to achieve, if not exceed, the score you want.

Another reason to aim for a perfect score while preparing for the SAT or ACT is **accountability**. If you do not aim for perfect, you may become apathetic[58] when it comes to doing and correcting practice problems. You may fall into a pit of carelessness and come up with false justifications, like, *Oh, it's all right if I miss those last few questions – I don't need to get them right to get the score I'm aiming for.* Rationalize mediocrity, and you will become mediocre.

This sloppy attitude often leads to under-preparation and underperformance. People who do well on these tests (and, more generally, in any endeavor they strive for) hold themselves accountable for every single problem. That way, they will be prepared for anything the test-makers can possibly throw at them. Remember that *every point counts*! This sense of accountability – both during games *and during practice* – is also what separates the best athletes from the average ones.

For some, money can be the most compelling reason to take our advice and hold themselves accountable during practice. Consider again the Florida Bright Futures Scholarship. At the time of writing, the scholarship was worth $101 per credit hour; since a four-year bachelor's degree is 128 credit hours, the total scholarship is worth about $12,928. In order to score the minimum 1290 on the SAT to earn the scholarship, you would only need to get about 100 questions correct. ***That means each question you get right is worth about $129.28.*** What would you rather do: flip burgers for 20 grueling hours or get a single question right on the test? Now, if

---

[56] SAT Word Alert: *Flagrant* (adjective) means "offensive or egregious (extremely bad)"

[57] SAT Word Alert: *Indolent* (adjective) means "lazy"

[58] SAT Word Alert: *Apathetic* (adjective) means "lacking concern or emotion"

that is not reason enough to view every question as crucial and aim for a perfect score, then we do not know what is.

Remember, then, that a fundamental strategy of the PERFECT Approach is –

Hold yourself accountable for each question: aim for a perfect score!

Take Official Practice Tests

A student who is just beginning to learn about his or her preparation options for the SAT and ACT finds many: official guides, preparatory sessions by his or her high school, companies' test prep classes, unofficial guides, and online advice.

In response to these choices, some students reason that the official guides do not fit into the "beating the test" mentality espoused by the unofficial guides – *How can the College Board's and ACT's official materials give me a special leg up on the other test-takers? I need the secret tricks that the unofficial guides have uncovered.*

For similar reasons, students turn to test prep classes offered in their areas or online. Some well-known ones are administered by The Princeton Review and Kaplan, both of which also produce popular written guides. These courses are also attractive by virtue of how expensive they can be – hundreds to thousands of dollars for the most popular programs and many thousands for the courses that are billed as more "elite" – because these high costs imply quality and efficiency. Do they follow through?

No. Students' most common method is buying a few unofficial guides with advice and practice tests and enrolling in a local test prep course offered by one of the big names. Most of these students are wasting significant time and money.

The tutors for the test prep programs and the writers of the unofficial guides often revert to generic, gimmicky strategies that sound a lot better than they work because they are easy to market. Occasionally, you will find a tutor (most likely one working independently or for a specialty company) who really knows his or her stuff and employs this deep understanding of the tests to offer productive and specifically catered advice. Such sage[59] tutors are the exception, however.

So what is the right choice? Buy all of the official practice tests you can get your hands on and an unofficial guide heavy on advice that works and light on questions that pretend to replace the real thing. Only when your official materials run out should you turn to unofficial practice exams. This combination not only is cheaper than what most students elect for but also prepares you better[60]. For some students, especially those who need help *learning* math concepts, pairing those resources

---

[59] SAT Word Alert: *Sage* (adjective) means "wise and experienced"

[60] This is what they call a win-win situation.

with reference books (such as Gruber's) works well – just don't rely on those source books to refine your test-taking skills.

The writers of unofficial tests struggle to match the type, style, and difficulty of the real tests. As a result, those writers' questions are frequently poorly illustrative[61] of what you will face on the official administration, and your unofficial practice test scores are deceptive. Practice tests written by the makers of the SAT and ACT are, therefore, indispensible as sources for preparing for the exams.

For the ACT, unfortunately, there are fewer official tests to practice with, so it is particularly important that you take advantage of those that exist. Get *The Real ACT Prep Guide*, which includes three official tests. Also purchase the ACT Online Prep course at act.org; this gives you access to two tests, which you can print out, as well as full explanations by the people who wrote the questions. Once they have exhausted these resources, students are usually most satisfied by The Princeton Review's practice tests.

Thankfully, there is more official material available for the SAT. Get *The Official SAT Study Guide,* a compilation of advice and ten tests published by the College Board and accompanied on its website with official explanations. Also consider getting *The Official SAT Online Course* for many additional full-length tests. At its online store, the College Board sells many previously administered PSATs, which are helpful in preparing for both the SAT and PSAT.

It is important to note, however, that you should not buy these official guides with the expectation that you will find especially meaningful advice: The utility[62] of the strategies is minimal, even to those who have no prior knowledge of good test-taking strategies.

Instead, the power of the official practice tests comes in their ability to provide you with accurate representations of what you will face on exam day. When properly used by the motivated student – which your reading of this book strongly suggests that you are – as opportunities to acclimate[63] to the test's format and questioning style, understand all of the questions that will be faced, and experiment with the application of the strategies learned in the accompanying unofficial guide, the official practice tests will "up your score" prodigiously[64].

For the SAT, you may also want to purchase a supplementary vocabulary book; this is discussed further in Chapter Six, "Boosting Your Reading Scores."

---

[61] SAT Word Alert: *Illustrative* (adjective) means "serving as an example or demonstration"

[62] SAT Word Alert: *Utility* (noun) means "practical usefulness"

[63] SAT Word Alert: *Acclimate* (verb) means "to become accustomed to"

[64] SAT Word Alert: *Prodigious* (adjective) means "extraordinary in amount or extent"

Official practice tests should be your go-to resource for improving your scores. Everything else is merely supplemental.

So how should you get the most out of those practice tests?

As we have said, the official guides' test-taking strategies are too obviously commonsensical or generic to be of much help. So you would do fine to skip immediately to the practice tests in these guides once you have read this book as a strategic foundation.

Practice tests provide a good opportunity to experiment with various paces for each section, since you must find what speed works for you by providing the best balance between getting to as many questions as possible while not rushing you so much that you cannot focus on any of them.

Yet that should not be your initial use of the practice tests: Before moving on to finding your sweet-spot paces, you need to learn how to answer the questions on the SAT and ACT. Merely reading through strategies and worked-out practice questions is insufficient; you must also form and internalize your own process for approaching each type of question – *What method that I've seen before works fastest on this math question?* – and your subjective sense for distinguishing between subtly varying answer choices – *Was the author's attitude ambivalent or skeptical[65]?*

These skills are complex but nonetheless fully attainable through repeated exposure to questions written by the people who are responsible for writing the questions on the test's official administration.

The usual method for taking practice tests represents an enormously inefficient way of developing those question-answering skills: taking the sections timed, skipping questions that you do not have time for, grading the test, recording your score, and then moving on to the next test.

Rather, in the initial phase of taking practice tests – in which you try to form your question-answering skills – you need to worry not about your scores or time limits but about *understanding* the questions themselves. To this end, you should spend as long as you need to on your first practice tests, giving no worry to the sections' time limits. Once you are finished, check the answers (but not the explanations) against your selections; then begin the process of trying to independently figure out exactly

---

[65] It is tempting to conflate (SAT Word Mini-Alert: *Conflate* (verb) means "to merge or fuse two or more separate entities or ideas") such similar terms, but there is a meaningful difference here: While both *ambivalent* and *skeptical* imply that the author is undecided about the topic at hand, the latter adjective goes one step further and indicates active doubt about some claim. If you ask me to mentally multiply 6,879.38 and 8,912.28 and present me with two near and plausible choices, I will be *ambivalent* about which is correct. But if you present me with two choices that are implausibly low—say, 27,802 and 31,795—I will be highly *skeptical* that either is correct. (That's justified skepticism in that case, I should add—or maybe multiply.)

why you missed each question that you missed and how you could have arrived at the correct answer.

After you have completed this process as best you can (perhaps you cannot understand a question despite your best attempts, and that's okay), turn to the answer explanations, making sure to read them in such a way that you understand not only this specific question but also how the explanation would generally apply to similar questions. You can also do this even for questions that you answered correctly but struggled with, in case you were not thinking about the question in the way that the test writers were or in the most efficient way.

You want your successes to be reproducible and your mistakes increasingly rare. **Do not move onto the next test until you have understood how to best approach every question on the previous test.** In doing so, you may get more out of one test than those who are less meticulous can get out of many.

Eventually, you should begin to take the tests within the allotted time in order to better simulate the stress and pacing conditions of the real test administration, when you will not be able to spend all the time you need. At first, you will probably find yourself crunched for time and unable to think as carefully as you had been about each question; this is normal and, with practice, can be assuaged[66] to such a negligible extent that you will ultimately be able to condense your thorough question-answering skills within the time limit without losing accuracy.

In the pursuit of that goal, you should work out any questions that you were unable to get to in the allowed time, even when you have decided to take the tests in a timed fashion. You will thereby be able to strengthen your question-answering skills without compromising your exposure to the timed conditions. All the while, you should of course ensure that you understand every question before moving on to the next test.

Along the way to achieving your goal of succeeding on the SAT or ACT, you will likely face a mix of pleasant surprises or accomplishments – such as improving significantly after just a couple tests or feeling proud after you fully comprehend a question whose solution had previously eluded[67] you – and troublesome disappointments, such as reaching a temporary score plateau or making the same mistake recurrently[68]. Revel[69] in the pleasant and transcend[70] the troublesome.

---

[66] SAT Word Alert: *Assuage* (verb) means "to mitigate or lessen"

[67] SAT Word Alert: *Elude* (verb) means "to escape or evade"

[68] SAT Word Alert: *Recurrently* (adverb) means "happening again and again"

[69] SAT Word Alert: *Revel* (verb) means "to take pleasure"

[70] SAT Word Alert: *Transcend* (verb) means "to overcome"

Take Both Tests

Unfortunately, there is an extant[71] belief that some colleges (especially those in the Northeast, such as colleges in the Ivy League) prefer the SAT over the ACT. This notion is now a misconception: The SAT and ACT are considered on equal ground at nearly every university in the United States.

Every college has its own table for equating scores from the SAT and ACT so that fair comparison is possible. The ACT organization has a recommended concordance table on its website, which indicates that a composite score of 36 (out of 36) on the ACT translates to 2390 (out of 2400) on the SAT, 33 to 2180, 30 to 2000, 27 to 1820, and 24 to 1650. We shared a more complete chart along those lines in Table 5 of the last chapter.

Many people believe that the ACT is easier than the SAT or even that the ACT is the fairer test. They claim that the SAT is corrupted by tricks or that the SAT is just a veiled intelligence test, whereas the ACT tests what actually matters for college. It seems, however, that this sentiment is mostly the product of rumors or general frustration with the test.

In any case, the SAT and ACT are rather similar: Both assess your reading, writing, English, and math skills. The ACT throws science in the mix as well, though the fundamental assessment in even that section is closely related to reading comprehension. Another notable difference in content is that success on the SAT's Critical Reading section more explicitly relies on having an advanced vocabulary than does the ACT's Reading section (which is why we call the vocabulary reviews in this book "SAT Word Alerts"). We will discuss these differences and more in the section-specific chapters, but the important take-away is that there are few, subtle distinctions between two otherwise-alike tests. (Differences in format were explained in the last chapter.) In fact, with the upcoming 2016 SAT changes, the tests will be more similar than ever.

Because of that similarity, it is reasonable to expect that most students would perform at a comparable level on both tests. This is usually the case, but the scores of a student who takes both exams may still differ to a meaningful degree – and in cases in which the differences between the tests happen to make one test particularly well-suited to a student's strengths, the difference can be quite large.

We have not found that students are accurate in their prediction of which test they will do better on. For this reason we recommend that you **try both the SAT and ACT in order to discover which test you prefer**. A modest degree of open-mindedness and patience is needed here: Do not give up on the SAT in favor of the ACT (or vice-versa) after just one practice test; give at least one more practice test a

---

[71] SAT Word Alert: *Extant* (adjective) means "existing"

try to see whether there is promise for greater improvement on that test. You certainly do not need to continue practicing with both tests, though, if it remains clear that your strengths lie in one over the other. That being said, the skills you acquire in preparing for both exams will continue being useful in the longer term. For example, exposing yourself to the ACT's Science section is a good idea, since it is our collective societal responsibility to be able to understand and make informed decisions on scientific debates.

When you have prepared for both tests and find that your performance levels are similar, it is a good idea to try your hand at official administrations of each. But in most cases, students will develop a preference during the preparation process.

CHAPTER 4
THE PERFECT APPROACH: TEST-TAKING STRATEGY

1. **Solve for the Answer Itself**

2. **Be Ruthless**

3. **Be Confident**

4. **Answer Every Question**

Solve for the Answer Itself

Duh, right? Actually, this part of the PERFECT Approach is not as obvious at it seems.

One thing school has definitely taught us is to be robots. Each of us is now an expert at bubbling in the correct answer while, of course, making sure to stay within the oval and using ONLY a No. 2 pencil[72]. Call us jaded, but we do not think being able to fill out a Scantron form is a vital skill for daily life. On the contrary, we actually think that it has been detrimental[73] to our problem-solving abilities!

Life is full of choices: Jeans or shorts? Skim or whole milk? Read this book or watch TV? Sometimes there are even multiple choices: Jeans, shorts, or capris? Skim, whole, or chocolate milk? Read this book, watch TV, or sleep? You get the point. However, most of these decisions are based on personal preference, not objective truths. Once in a while, we do have choices with clear "right" and "wrong" answers, like whether or not to cheat on a test (*umm*…don't), though most of the time, we have to come up with the right answer without being given any choices. Therefore, unlike on standardized tests, most important questions and problems in daily life require us to first identify our own choices. Then, as on standardized tests, we need to use reasoning skills, such as math or critical analysis, to come up with the correct answer.

Just a few examples of important questions and problems you will need to answer within the next few years include:

- Deciding which college to attend based upon your interests as well as your required loans

- Buying a car based upon the initial price as well as gas mileage

---

[72]Consider this gem from xkcd: xkcd.com/499/

[73] SAT Word Alert: *Detrimental* (adjective) means "tending to cause harm"

- Choosing credit cards and bank accounts based upon rewards and fees

- Opening a mortgage when buying a home, based upon interest rates and terms

Fortunately, *all* of the problems you encounter on the SAT and ACT are even easier than those in real life, because there is always a single right choice.

It is therefore good to be able to come up with your own choices and then to decide between them. Hence, the first strategy of the PERFECT Approach is –

At first, do not even look at the multiple choices; instead, solve the question directly for the answer itself!

Most of the exercises in this book do not have multiple choices, so that you will be able to learn how to solve them cold, without guessing or using a process of elimination. If you practice solving every problem as if it were free response, you will be much more confident in your answer if it matches one of the choices. It may seem paradoxical, but if you practice solving problems without using the choices, the test will actually take *less* time to complete than it would have if you had relied on the choices. Trust us. In fact, we require our students to conceal the multiple choices when they are taking practice tests – it works for them, and it will work for you!

This strategy applies to all sections: Math, Critical Reading, Writing/English, and Science. As you implement the high-impact strategies and guidelines in this book and your math, vocabulary, grammar, and reading comprehension skills improve, you will frequently and pleasantly surprise yourself by anticipating the correct answer. Consider this sentence completion question:

Because his desire to marry a divorcee named Wallis Simpson outweighed his desire to be king, Edward VIII became the first British monarch to voluntarily _____ his throne.

a) Clean

b) Devour

c) Abdicate

d) Reprimand

e) Assemble

As you read the sentence above, chances are your mind automatically began to predict the correct word or synonym: *give up, renounce, forfeit, resign, relinquish,* and *abdicate* (the last choice is typical when discussing royalty). If you cover up the multiple choices, you will become skilled at recalling words in your mental dictionary and thesaurus, and both your writing and speaking abilities will improve. As we discussed in "The Stepping Stone Myth," this is the true purpose of learning vocabulary and one that will also help you ace the SAT and ACT. The same goes for math, grammar, and comprehension.

Another benefit of covering up the multiple choices is that the question will become less distracting. This is especially the case with long, boring, or confounding[74] problems, for which it is all too easy for your eyes to drift between the question stem and the multiple choices. For (admittedly exaggerated, but nonetheless telling) example:

> If Bob is 4 years older than Susan, Susan is 2 years younger than Zach, and Zach is five years younger than Jennifer, what is the difference in age between Bob and Jennifer?
>
> a) ***LOOK OVER HERE***
>
> b) !!!NO, LOOK OVER HERE!!
>
> c) FORGET ABOUT THE QUESTION; PAY ATTENTION TO ME
>
> d) 3 years
>
> e) ❑❑❑❑❑❑❑

If you get in the habit of physically covering up the choices and focusing instead on the question itself (go ahead and try it for the one above), you will become a seek-and-destroy missile, relentlessly hunting out the right answer without getting distracted or misled by the four other decoys. This will make you doubly effective at solving the question correctly and quickly.

For all the positives that come from this strategy, we would be remiss[75] if we did not mention two small caveats[76]. First, if all else fails, we admit that guessing strategies can help you get some extra points on the test. Hence, we have included a section on guessing strategies, such as process of elimination. Second, there are some questions on the SAT and ACT that will actually require you to look at the multiple choices *before* you can solve the problem. For example, consider the question:

> *For any negative integer, x, which of the following is the largest?*
> *a) x*

---

[74] SAT Word Alert: *Confound* (verb) means "to confuse or baffle"

[75] SAT Word Alert: *Remiss* (adjective) means "negligent or failing to take care of"

[76] SAT Word Alert: *Caveat* (noun) means "an explanation to prevent misinterpretation"

b) x^2
c) x^3
d) x^4
e) x^5

It would be impossible to solve[77] the problem above without looking at the choices! Though this happens more often on reading sections than on math sections, the majority of problems in both sections can be solved without looking at the multiple choices.

So remember: *When you see a question, solve it directly for the right answer!*

Be Ruthless

A student, Sarah, thinks that she has correctly identified the answer to a question among the available choices, only to find out that this choice is "wrong." She wonders aloud, "All right, I guess I understand why that choice is correct. But couldn't mine be right, too?"

There is a reason that the SAT and ACT instruct you to select the *best* choice rather than the *correct* answer. This knowledge probably will not assist you very much on the math sections of the tests, but for questions that rely on any amount of subjective reasoning – such as the majority of the English and reading sections of both tests – the distinction is crucial. Your job is not to find the singular, objective truth among the choices; one of the choices is simply better than the others, and you must figure out which that is.

This realization explains why the frustrated student missed the question: Her answer may have been acceptable, but there was apparently a better choice that she overlooked. However, there is a deeper, significantly more powerful lesson to be learned here.

When the SAT and ACT deem the difference between a "good" answer and a "better" answer to be tantamount to that between a wrong answer and a correct answer, one suspects that they are treading in dangerous territory. In our litigious[78] society, the College Board and ACT organization would face an onslaught of frustrated test-takers whose responses could be defended against the testing agencies' claims. Indeed, some have tried, to little avail.

---

[77] Answer: (d). There are two important realizations to solve this problem. First, x is an integer (…, -2, -1, 0, 1, 2, …). If x is negative and you raise it to an odd power (x^1, x^3, x^5), the result is still a negative number, so (a), (c), and (e) are wrong. Second, since x cannot be a decimal between 0 and 1 or 0 and -1 (e.g. 0.5 or -.25), x^2 and x^4 must both be higher in value than x itself. x^4 will be the larger number. Try it out with a few integers and prove it to yourself.

[78] SAT Word Alert: *Litigious* (adjective) means "having a tendency to settle disputes through the law"

Thankfully for us and them, there is a paradigm in which the seemingly subjective differentiation between a good answer and a better answer can be treated in a refreshingly objective manner, and it is both the reason that the testing companies are safe from this sort of controversy and, it turns out, one of the most helpful strategies for doing better on the tests. **A necessarily correct answer trumps a possibly correct one**, every time.

Sarah's answer wasn't wrong in a universal sense; it *could* have been right, after all. Let's imagine that this was Sarah's passage-based reading question:

> After the events described, Jake from passage 1 meets Bob from passage 2. It is reasonable to believe that
>
> (A) Jake has a friendly conversation with Bob.
>
> (B) Jake yells at Bob.
>
> (C) Jake asks Bob for a favor.
>
> (D) Jake forgives Bob.
>
> (E) Jake tells Bob a joke.

Let's say that all the passages mention about Jake or Bob is that Jake has an angry temperament and that Bob tried to steal Jake's prized lemur but was caught in the act. Remembering the incident, Sarah figures that it would be logical for Jake to forgive Bob, so she picks (D). This makes some sense; it certainly could happen, since that is one of the things that may naturally follow from witnessing wrongdoing.

The only other choice that seems to have anything to do with what could happen after an attempted theft is choice (B). In this sense, both (B) and (D) are potentially correct. But because this is a simplified example, it is probably clear to you that the one detail we know about Jake – that he is a generally angry person – implies that he would not forgive Bob but would instead convey his anger over the planned prized-lemur-napping.

This illustrates an effective general principle. If an answer choice is the best among the options on an SAT or ACT question, you know that it will have two characteristics: *You will have reason (i.e., support in the text) to believe that it is correct, and you will have no reason to believe that it is wrong.*

In the example, there is no affirmative reason to believe that choices (A), (C), and (E) are correct. There is reason to believe that choices (B) and (D) are correct (Bob has done something to Jake that could be forgiven or not), but Jake's angry predisposition is reason to believe that choice (D) is wrong. By this method, only choice (B) remains.

A faster way to apply this strategy on the reading sections of the SAT and ACT is to first rule out irrelevant answers, of which there is almost always at least one, usually more. This eliminates choices (like the previous (A), (C), and (E)) that you have no reason to believe are correct. Next, go through the remaining options and attempt to **justify why each choice could be wrong**. If some indication exists in the text (as we will stress in the chapter on the reading sections, all of your evidence must be stated or clearly implied in the passages) that a choice may be wrong, don't pick it. Be ruthless about it: Correct responses will never be contradicted by the text.

Hard reading questions can usually be distilled[79] down to two choices. In almost every case, one of the choices is either possibly correct but unsupported by the text or potentially supported by the text but contradicted by another part of the passage. The correct answer will be thoroughly supported by what can be read or inferred from the passage.

This thinking can be applied to the English questions on both tests. If a choice for revision of a word, phrase, or sentence contains or results in a grammatical error, this is absolute reason to believe that it is wrong, so don't pick it. Correct answers will never yield bad grammar. Another reason to believe that a response is wrong is that it detracts from or otherwise alters the original meaning of the sentence.

So if multiple choices remain even after this filtering, what's an affirmative reason to believe that a response to an English question is correct? You have a couple options here: clarity (admittedly subjective though usually apparent) and brevity (it is objectively clear which option is shorter). It is rare for multiple choices on an English question to be both grammatical and consistent with the originally intended meaning; when this occurs, one choice will usually be so clumsily worded or long-winded that it calls out to be eliminated from consideration.

Be Confident

In addition to the logistical necessities of test day that were discussed in Chapter 2, such as bringing your pencils and admission ticket, those tangible items (yes, you newly developed sticklers, your skills are in fact palpable) do not fully cover everything you need to bring with you on test day. One of your most powerful assets for gaining an upper hand on the SAT and ACT is your test-day mentality. You need to come mentally prepared to succeed.

Focus is especially important if you are to realize your potential: One of the most oft-cited reasons for underperforming on the tests is that nerves reared their distracting heads, taking your mind off the task at hand. To some extent, being nervous is completely expected and can indeed be helpful, so that your brain is

---

[79] SAT Word Alert: *Distill* (verb) means "to purify"

firing on all cylinders. However, when we become so nervous that we begin to question our ability to do as well as we had on practice tests, we just may find that the fear becomes self-fulfilling.

It would be simple and pithy[80] enough to say that you should be confident while taking the SAT and ACT; this much is certainly true. But here are some additional thoughts that you can run through your mind to really help that idea resonate:

All you have to do is take on the test. As you sit ready to take the test, remind yourself that you are about to be handed a booklet, at which point your only objective over the next few hours is to use your capabilities to read the passages and questions and then find the answers. Nothing else matters at that time. Dig deep to muster all your austerity[81]. We don't welcome provincialism[82], but some intense narrow-mindedness is quite helpful.

More specifically, stay focused on correctly answering the one question you are working on. Unhelpful distractions arise from stressing out over perceived less-than-satisfactory performance thus far, fear of tough upcoming questions, or worry that missing the question you are on will derail your score. Ignore the big picture of how you will do or are doing on the test and commit yourself to tackling the one question in front of you. Rinse and repeat.

Each question has one correct answer; you need to find it. If a question seems impossible or with multiple correct answers, don't rationalize[83] your struggle as a mistake on the test writers' part: They almost never make errors. Instead, approach each question with the resolute[84] assumption that each question is perfect and that its sole answer is sitting on the page, waiting for you to figure it out.

Each question ought to be seen not as a chance to mess up but as an opportunity to succeed. This mindset tends to be self-affirming.

Visualize your success. An excellent way to reduce test-day stress is to imagine yourself ahead of time doing exactly what you want to do: moving through the test comfortably, finding the answer to each question. But the thoughts of this ideal, perhaps quixotic[85] scenario should be accompanied with visualization of how you will comfortably handle more realistic situations, such as the nerves that are bound to flare when you struggle with a couple questions in a row. The processing that

---

[80] SAT Word Alert: *Pithy* (adjective) means "concise and forcefully expressive"

[81] SAT Word Alert: *Austerity* (noun) means "rigorous self-discipline"

[82] SAT Word Alert: *Provincialism* (noun) means "ignorant narrowness of mind"

[83] SAT Word Alert: *Rationalize* (verb) means "to justify to oneself"

[84] SAT Word Alert: *Resolute* (adjective) means "firmly resolved or determined"

[85] SAT Word Alert: *Quixotic* (adjective) means "unrealistically or romantically idealistic." Related to the classic book from the 1600s, *Don Quixote*, written by Miguel de Cervantes.

your brain does while you are practicing these techniques makes the ideal scenario more likely and the realistic scenario closer to the ideal.

The fear is all in your head; you can actually do well once you've prepared effectively!

Answer Every Question

We will get the simple one out of the way first. The ACT does not deduct points for incorrect responses, so there is no reason to ever leave a question unanswered. Even if you are about to run out of time and cannot read any of the remaining questions, it is to your probabilistic favor to bubble in random guesses: All A's, all B's, a smattering of each letter – it is your choice.

Now the SAT. It would be better for students' scores if they simply never learned that the SAT awards 1 point for each correct response but deducts .25 points for each incorrect response to a multiple-choice question. They misapply the knowledge and employ excessively conservative guessing practices. Most people are not excellent at spontaneously approximating their confidence in a choice; when any significant amount of doubt exists, many students opt to leave the question blank rather than "guess." This is a bad strategy.

A better strategy – one that has become rather popular – is to guess as long as you have eliminated at least one possible answer. This is not a terrible approach, but we would rather advocate that you answer every question, every time.

This advice comes from the fact that, if there are only four choices (as would effectively be the case if you cross one out as incorrect) and you guess, the odds say that you will not only compensate for the wrong-answer penalty but *come out ahead*. One correct response (value of 1 point) minus the deduction for three incorrect responses (.25 times 3, or .75) is a positive .25. So you are in good shape there.

But even if you blindly guess on every question when there are five choices and incur the penalty for four out of every five, you would break even: 1 point minus .25 times 4 comes out to zero. You may think, then, that it does not really matter which approach you take, but the important thing to know is that you do not need to blindly guess. You can always budget to give a question a mere ten or twenty seconds of analysis, after which consideration your "guess" is actually bound to be slightly better than random chance would suggest.

So if you guess blindly all the time, it will be as if you left every question blank – no harm. But if you exert even a little brainpower toward the questions that stump you, guessing – whether or not you can absolutely eliminate any choices – will tend to yield a higher score than omitting. Hopefully, though, you will have the strategies and practice you need to *know* the answer.

CHAPTER 5
ACING THE MATH SECTION

The advancement and perfection of mathematics are intimately connected with the prosperity of the state.

Napoleon Bonaparte (1769-1821)
Emperor of France

Neglect of mathematics works injury to all knowledge, since he who is ignorant of it cannot know the other sciences or the things of the world.

Roger Bacon (1214-1294)
English Philosopher and Doctor Mirablis ("Wonderful Teacher")

One of the best things about math is that it rarely changes. The Pythagorean Theorem you learned about in geometry class is the same one that Pythagoras and his crew figured out around 500 B.C.! (By the way, you should know that the theorem is for finding the side lengths of a right triangle: $a^2 + b^2 = c^2$.) In fact, many of the math concepts tested on the SAT and ACT were developed over 2,000 years ago, mostly by the Greeks, Indians, Arabs, Chinese, and Persians. That means that if the test-makers administered the SAT or ACT math sections back then (test-makers are old, but not *that* old), those ancient people would probably do really well! Now, are you going to lie back and let a bunch of dusty 2,000-plus-year-old geezers school you in...school? We're hoping that your answer was a vehement[86] "No!" so let us proceed.

When it comes to the math sections of the SAT and ACT, there are basically three types of test-takers: those who breeze through, those who do decently well but never mastered the material, and those who often precede the word "math" with *another* four-letter word. Category One generally includes students in higher-level courses, such as AP Calculus, because they mastered the foundations and have been applying them ever since. Category Two is usually comprised of students in mid-to-upper-level high school math classes who can do straightforward math but have not developed mastery or intuition yet, simply because they have not practiced enough problems. Category Three includes students with just as much potential to do well but who for whatever reason – such as initial difficulty that compounded, lack of interest, or poor teachers – have psyched themselves out and so subscribe to the idea that "math is hard[87]."

---

[86] SAT Word Alert: *Vehement* (adjective) means "forceful, strong, impassionate"

[87] An even worse viewpoint is that "math is lame," because as Napoleon and Roger said earlier in this chapter, math is essential not only to the prosperity of the state, but also to your individual potential for success. In addition, being good at math and being popular are not mutually exclusive. Just Google "Danica McKellar."

Regardless of which group you are in, rest assured that you can improve quickly if you diligently follow the strategies we prescribe in this book. In fact, consider it a good thing if math is the section you need to improve on the most because, along with grammar, it is arguably the easiest topic in which to make rapid and significant improvements.

Overview

As we alluded to above, the SAT and ACT cover only concepts that the average 11th grade math student should know. While the College Board somewhat ambiguously[88] describes the SAT as covering arithmetic operations (adding, subtracting, multiplying, dividing), algebra, geometry, and (not as frequently) statistics and probability, the ACT breaks the content of its test down meticulously[89] : pre-algebra (23%), elementary algebra (17%), intermediate algebra (15%), coordinate geometry (15%), plane geometry (23%), and trigonometry (7%). A brief and important digression: You should get in the habit of actively checking numbers and figures, because that will help you do well on the tests, not to mention life at large. That means that you should be adding the percentage values to make sure that they reach 100 (23+17+15+15+23+7), signifying that the ACT did not make a mistake. While this particular example may have (okay, *will* have) little bearing on your life, you can imagine the serious consequences that may come from not actively checking numbers like your credit card statements, college loans, and mortgage payments.

The SAT math section consists of 44 multiple-choice and 10 free response questions, which are contained in one 20-minute subsection and two 25-minute subsections. Based on that, you should be able to figure out about how many seconds you have per question (again, just getting you in the habit of actively working with numbers).[90] The ACT math section features 60 multiple-choice questions in 60 minutes, or about a minute per question.

Upon hearing that information, some students may prefer the SAT because there is more time per question, whereas others may prefer the ACT because it is solely multiple-choice – though as we discussed in our PERFECT Approach, you should try covering up the multiple-choice questions so they all look like free response anyways. Some may prefer the SAT's three interspersed math sections to the ACT's long section, while others may have antipodal[91] feelings. In our experience,

---

[88] SAT Word Alert: *Ambiguous* (adjective) means "uncertain, or capable of being understood in two or more ways"

[89] SAT Word Alert: *Meticulous* (adjective) means "marked by excessive care in the consideration of details"

[90] 70 total minutes / 54 total questions ~ 1.3 minutes per question, or about 78 seconds.

[91] SAT Word Alert: *Antipodal* (adjective) means "entirely opposed." You may remember this because there are actually islands south of New Zealand called "The Antipodes Islands." The British named them this because if one were to drill a hole through the Earth from Britain, she would reach

we found the SAT math to be a little more annoyingly tricky, while the ACT math is fairly straightforward (though it does include more trigonometry than the SAT). In any case, we recommend taking both tests, because your performance may vary based on which layout you feel more comfortable with.

A fortunate result of the significant overlap of math concepts tested on the SAT and ACT is that preparing for one test will help you do better on the other (the same goes for the other sections as well). Hence, without further ado, let us begin our quest for world (or at least SAT and ACT Math) domination.

Outstandingly Effective Math Strategies

The reason why we said the math section will be relatively easy to make gains on is that there are a limited number of question types and concepts that the test-makers can throw at you. With active practice, pretty soon these questions will become simple or even predictable. For example, if they show you a line intersecting two other parallel lines, you will know that they are testing your knowledge of opposite interior angles. If they give you two points on a coordinate plane, they will want you to find the $y = mx + b$ line equation and maybe even notice that a parallel line will have the same slope (m) whereas a perpendicular line will have a negative reciprocal slope ($-1/m$). The focus of this section, therefore, is to help you take advantage of this fact so that you never miss the same concept or question type more than once.

To this end, we equip you with the arsenal of highly effective, proven strategies that we and our students have used to decimate the math sections of the SAT and ACT. Regardless of whether you are starting out as a Category One, Two, or Three math test-taker (see the introduction to this chapter), if you adopt and practice these strategies, you, too, can ace the test. Fortunately, as with most things worth doing, the only required input is motivation. The output: success.

Solve for the Answer Itself

This is such an important strategy that it bears repetition, even though we devoted a whole section to it earlier. Though you should apply this strategy while practicing the other sections, it is most effective for training your brain to solve math questions. Multiple-choice questions give you five choices, four of which are wrong and some of which are intentionally meant to trick you. For example, if you were given two variables, x and y, and were asked to solve for x, you can be all but positive that the multiple choices will give you both the value for x (correct) as well as the value for y (incorrect). By physically covering up the choices (with a piece of paper or index card) and treating every question as a free response, you will be more focused on the problem itself and less prone to making silly mistakes or falling into traps. Once you solve the question, you will also be more confident of

---

the Antipodes.

your answer if it matches one of the choices. Do not worry if it doesn't; that is what the following strategies are for!

Hold Yourself Accountable for Each Question

Insanity is doing the same thing over and over again and expecting different results.
Albert Einstein (1879-1955)
Nobel Laureate, Physics

Aiming for a perfect score by holding yourself accountable for each question – a key element of the PERFECT Approach – ensures that you will reach your maximum potential. This means that you should review not only the practice test questions you missed, but also the questions you guessed on (by marking them while taking the test). Reviewing means actually understanding why you missed or guessed on the question and how you can solve it – and any other question like it – in the future. Based on what Einstein said above, it would be insane of you to keep taking practice tests in the hope of improving without reviewing and learning from your mistakes. Even if you are a Category Three math test-taker, you can still hold yourself accountable for those last few questions which are typically more difficult and, in the process, learn enough to get them right on the actual test. Remember that each question can be worth over $100, so blowing off even one is sort of like being too lazy to bend down and pick up a Benjamin Franklin off the floor!

Think Like a Test-Maker

This is a highly effective strategy that Shiv developed when he was preparing for the tests and, ever since he achieved the perfect scores, has been passing on to his students. It naturally follows from the above strategy of being accountable. Here it is:

For every question that you miss or guess on during practice, write and solve three new questions that test similar concepts.

As we mentioned and as you may have already realized if you have taken a couple practice tests, question types often repeat. You can accelerate the rate at which you learn how to solve these questions by shifting your perspective from test-taker to test-maker. If you can write and solve your own question, which is sometimes as easy as changing the values of a given question and re-solving, then you will have a complete understanding of the concept(s) being tested and will (hopefully) never miss another one like it again. Note that you need not come up with false multiple choices, although you can make note of potential red herring choices (such as the value for *y* instead of *x*) that often lead to silly mistakes and wrong answers.

Review (or Learn) Concepts You Do Not Know

We understand where you are coming from, Category Three math test-takers. Early on, you had a math teacher who was so bad that he could not have taught the Cartesian coordinate system to its inventor, René Descartes. Or you fell a little behind and by the time you understood the stuff that was taught in week one, you were already in week four. That is one of the difficult properties of math: It is cumulative. You can do poorly in US History but recover in time for World History. You may not "get" physics, but you were number one in your biology class. These other subjects are fairly independent at the high school level, but that is not the case with math. If you do not learn Algebra 1 properly, you will have a really tough time in Algebra 2, and the same goes for geometry and trigonometry. Even though you may have been able to put a Band-Aid on it at the time and hobble by with a satisfactory grade, it is now SAT/ACT time, and you realize that the wound is much deeper than it appeared.

There is no way around this basic truth: You have to (re)learn the fundamentals of arithmetic (operations, fractions, percentiles, ratios, etc.), the algebras, and geometry. Fortunately, it will not take you another five years of sitting through Mr. Jones's and Mrs. Smith's math classes to accomplish this. This time, you have at least *seen* the material before and not *all*, or even a majority, of it will be tested (it is important to count the small victories). The College Board's *Official SAT Study Guide* and *The Real ACT Prep Guide* both have good reviews of the concepts that you will need to know to perform decently well on the math sections. It is imperative[92] that you read through and understand these reviews.

If you do not recall every concept in the review, you are lucky we now live in a time when you can learn almost anything if you have access to the Internet. This is a crucial theme that we touch upon in Chapter 11 of the book: the importance of becoming autodidactic[93], or being able to teach yourself. The first step is to recognize what concepts – such as functions or triangles – you are weak on, often through doing practice problems, and commit yourself to learning them (*motivation* is key, again). Next, you must find resources that will help you learn the concepts at *your own pace*, as opposed to being confined by the teacher's in-class agenda and syllabus which in turn are governed by the school board. We highly recommend the popular Khan Academy (www.khanacademy.org), a collection of free, short online tutorials, through which many of our students have learned concepts that they never understood in their courses. For example, one of Shiv's students learned how to graph lines by watching the Khan Academy video "Algebra: graphing lines 1," which at the time of writing had close to 500,000 views! The third step of becoming self-taught is to do more practice exercises, which can be found in the official SAT and ACT guides and, conveniently, right below certain Khan Academy videos.

You can do this review while taking practice tests, though you should emphasize getting up to speed early, because thereafter your practice test scores will be much higher and you will be synthesizing and implementing your newly learned concepts. This practice will also help you learn and memorize formulas that you will forever be able to apply; at a minimum, you should know the ones given in the directions

---

[92] SAT Word Alert: *Imperative* (adjective) means "necessary"
[93] SAT Word Alert: *Autodidact* (noun) means "a self-taught person"

part of the math section (e.g. areas of shapes, 30-60-90 and 45-45-90 triangles, etc.). With the right amount of determination, you will smoothly transition from a Category Three to a Category One math test-taker! *Math* will no longer be associated with a certain four-letter word.

Learn the Hit List

Certain types of questions often show up on the SAT and ACT but may not be formally taught in your courses. Even though they can be initially challenging, these questions become extremely easy to our students because we teach step-by-step how to approach and solve them. Here is an example from our hit list (many more examples will appear in our SAT/ACT app):

> Bob can paint a wall in 4 hours. Mary can paint the same wall in 2 hours. Working together, how long will it take Bob and Mary to paint the wall?

Some people will instinctively try adding Bob's time with Mary's time to get the total time; in this case, 6 hours. A quick logical check will make them realize that that would be impossible since Mary, while working *alone*, can paint the wall in 2 hours (unless Bob and Mary make a *really* bad team; fortunately, hypothetical scenarios like this are not tested).

There are two simple and infallible[94] ways to solve this problem. The first is to reason the problem out by giving a value to how big the wall is. Let's say that it is 100 square feet. Based on that, we know that Bob paints 100 square feet in 4 hours, or 25 square feet/hour, while Mary can paint 50 square feet/hour (which makes sense because Mary is done faster). Together, they can paint (25 + 50) = 75 square feet/hour. Since the wall is only 100 square feet, and the team of Bob and Mary can paint at 75 square feet/hour, they will be done in (100 square feet) ÷ (75 square feet/hour) = 4/3 hours or about 1 hour and 20 minutes – faster than each could do individually, which makes sense.

The second way to solve this problem is related to the first but relies on the following equation:

$$\frac{1}{Bob's\ Time} + \frac{1}{Mary's\ Time} = \frac{1}{Bob\ \&\ Mary's\ Time}$$

If we plug in *4 hours* as Bob's time to paint the wall and *2 hours* as Mary's time to paint it, we can solve for their total time working together by first making a common denominator (4) and then adding the fractions:

$$\frac{1}{4\ hours} + \frac{1}{2\ hours} = \frac{1}{4} + \frac{2}{4} = \frac{3}{4} = \frac{1}{Bob\ \&\ Mary's\ Time}$$

---

[94] SAT Word Alert: *Infallible* (adjective) means "absolutely trustworthy or effective"

If we take the reciprocal of this answer, we get Bob & Mary's total time required to paint the wall:

$$\frac{1}{Bob\ \&\ Mary's\ Time} = \frac{3}{4}$$

$$Bob\ \&\ Mary's\ Time = \frac{4}{3}\ hours = 1\ hour\ 20\ minutes$$

This equation is related to the first way we solved the problem (by saying the wall was 100 square feet) because in that case our common denominator was 100, but in this case it was only 4 since we could see the fractions. The beauty of the equation is that you can apply it to *any* problem that asks you to combine any number of productivity rates. For example, how long will it take to paint the wall if Bob and Mary also work together with Susan, who can paint the wall alone in 3 hours? Let's set the equation up the same way:

$$\frac{1}{Bob's\ Time} + \frac{1}{Mary's\ Time} + \frac{1}{Susan's\ Time} = \frac{1}{Bob,\ Mary,\ \&\ Susan's\ Time}$$

$$\frac{1}{4\ hours} + \frac{1}{2\ hours} + \frac{1}{3\ hours} = \frac{3}{12} + \frac{6}{12} + \frac{4}{12} = \frac{13}{12} = \frac{1}{Bob,\ Mary,\ \&\ Susan's\ Time}$$

$$\frac{1}{Bob,\ Mary,\ \&\ Susan's\ Time} = \frac{13}{12}$$

$$Bob,\ Mary,\ \&\ Susan's\ Time = \frac{12}{13}\ hours$$

This also makes sense because the more people who work together, the faster the job should get done.

Do It without a Calculator

A silent yet pernicious[95] epidemic is permeating[96] our society. Unfortunately, teenagers are most susceptible to the disease, which, once contracted, will be deleterious[97] to its victims throughout their lives. Moreover, studies have shown that smartphone addicts stand a higher risk of acquiring the disease and that a common indication is loss of brain function.

The disease is known as *calcoholism.*

---

[95] SAT Word Alert: *Pernicious* (adjective) means "destructive or harmful"

[96] SAT Word Alert: *Permeate* (verb) means "to spread throughout or saturate"

[97] SAT Word Alert: *Deleterious* (adjective) means "causing harm"

Okay, we admit that the account above may be a little over-the-top (another affliction that is common these days is hyperbole, so give us a break). But the dangers of calcoholism are very real. We cannot tell you how many times our students have pulled out calculators to add or subtract two-digit numbers, like 47 and 15. When this happens, we often take away their calculators (tough love) and, despite some initial protest, eventually persuade them to attempt the math in their heads. Some pause for a few seconds before saying the right answer (add: 62; subtract: 32). Others struggle more. Their voices become higher-pitched and they stammer a little; their faces become slightly flushed, and small beads of sweat start forming on their foreheads; their hands are either clenched tight or open if they are trying to count on their fingers to find the answer; finally, they blurt out an answer that shows that they were on the right track (e.g. 52 instead of 62), which they almost invariably follow up with, "Right?"

Let us be clear here. Anyone capable of reading this book is also capable of doing SAT and ACT math without a calculator. If this is true, why are so many people calcoholics? Here's our theory on the origins of calcoholism:

After elementary school, when we have (hopefully) mastered addition, subtraction, and our times tables, we get drawn in by the convenience of the calculator. We say to ourselves, *Oh, I know how to do that, but let me save time by just using the calculator.* Initially, this is so infrequent and for large enough numbers that no harm is done. Gradually, however, the calculator starts coming out more often, and the numbers become simpler and simpler. Our brains, like our muscles, can atrophy[98] from disuse so that we eventually become completely dependent upon and addicted to our calculators. From that point on, our calculators are our crutches; without them, we lose confidence in our math abilities. That is why when two overly zealous[99] guys from Florida and Illinois ask you to add two numbers without a calculator, you qualify your answer at the end by asking, "Right?"

You may be asking yourself, *Wait, we get to use a calculator on the test. And I have my smartphone calculator wherever I go. So why is it important to do it without a calculator?* Great question! Don't worry: We're not going to answer with another question (What if your battery runs out?) or a contrived scenario (Oh, it's a solar-powered calculator? What if a meteor strike sends a gigantic plume of dust in the air, blotting out the sun?) Nor are we Luddites[100] (Shiv is writing this on his MacBook Pro as he listens to music on his iPod/Bose Sound Dock and has a

---

[98] SAT Word Alert: *Atrophy* (verb) means "to wither away or decay"

[99] SAT Word Alert: *Zealous* (adjective) means "fervent or filled with eagerness in pursuit of something"

[100] SAT Word Alert: *Luddite* (noun) means "one who is opposed to technology or innovation." Interestingly, the Luddites were a social movement of 19th-century British workers who destroyed the technology – factory machines – that was replacing them. Their (perhaps fictional) leader was Ned Ludd.

Facebook page open on his smartphone). Then why are we so committed to helping you get rid of your tenacious[101] calculator habit?

There are two key reasons why you should restore your basic mental math skills: first, so you redevelop confidence in your mathematical abilities, both for the test and for daily life; second, so you actually score higher on the SAT, ACT, and any other test involving math. It is fine to rely on computers for some things (like storing phone numbers), but for the basic logic and math skills that we are talking about, you should put away that calculator and clear the cobwebs from your brain. Plus, there are often really simple and logical ways to solve questions that, if you were to simply default to button mashing on your calculator, you would utterly miss. Now (wo)man up and go through the following quick mental math tools and workouts.

Welcome to Calcoholics Anonymous: Tools and Workouts for your Brain

Patience and perseverance have a magical effect before which difficulties disappear and obstacles vanish.

John Quincy Adams (1767-1848)
Sixth President of the United States

In this section, we will go through some of the fastest and easiest ways to improve your mental math skills. The practice problems in this book can be completed without a calculator. Therefore, from this point on, let us go cold turkey and abstain[102] from using a calculator when working on test prep.

Mental math essentially consists of two types of skills. The first one is the ability to perform basic numerical functions in your head. This includes memorizing your times tables so that you know off the top of your head that, for example, 9 times 7 equals 63. The second skill is the ability to hold numbers in your short-term memory – what psychologists call your *working memory* – while you finish calculating a problem. Sounds complicated, right? Don't worry, because it sounds more difficult than it is; in fact, we rely on our short-term memory daily. Consider this example that illustrates both types of mental math skills: Say you have to calculate the final cost of a $15 item that is 30 percent off. You first need to be able to find and remember 30 percent of $15 (.30 * $15 = $4.50) and *then* you need to subtract $4.50 from $15, which gives you a final answer of $10.50.

Though we have relegated[103] our calculators, you should absolutely feel free to begin redeveloping your mental math skills with the aid of paper and pencil. Eventually you will be able to write down numbers less and less often, until you can

---

[101] SAT Word Alert: *Tenacious* (adjective) means "persistent or stubborn"

[102] SAT Word Alert: *Abstain* (verb) means "to refrain from doing something"

[103] SAT Word Alert: *Relegate* (verb) means "to assign to a specific place, or to banish"

do most of the calculations in your head and then, ultimately, do calculations on *those* calculations (as we did in the discount problem). Let's get started.

Change Numbers to Suit Your Needs

The easiest numbers to work with are usually those that end in -5 or -0, perhaps because we are so used to our monetary system. We have coins that represent 1, 5, 10, 25, and 50 cents. Similarly, we have 1, 5, 10, 20, 50, and 100 dollar bills. Because of our daily interactions with money, most anyone can rattle off the times tables for 5 and 10.

A key to mental math, therefore, is to change numbers to suit your needs. For example, you could add 6 and 7 by writing them down, counting on your fingers, or just remembering that the answer is 13. Or you could add them by changing them around using basic properties, such as association:

$$6 + 7 = 6 + (4 + 3) = (6{+}4) + 3 = 10 + 3 = 13$$

Consider a slightly more difficult example:

$$46 + 27 = 46 + (4 + 23) = (46 + 4) + 23 = 50 + 23 = 73$$

Notice that we kept one number the same (46) and just changed the other number so it would be simpler to add. The same idea applies when subtracting numbers:

$$46 - 27 = 46 - (26 + 1) = (46 - 26) - 1 = 20 - 1 = 19$$

Subtracting numbers can become a little trickier when you are subtracting a larger number from a smaller number and therefore will get a negative number. There are two ways to make this simpler in your mind. First, you can instead subtract the smaller number from the larger number and then merely put a negative sign in front of the result:

$$25 - 84 = -(84 - 25) = -[84 - (24 + 1)] = -[(84 - 24) - 1] = -[60 - 1] = -59$$

Alternatively, you can change the numbers so you get 0 immediately:

$$25 - 84 = 25 - (25 + 59) = (25 - 25) - 59 = 0 - 59 = -59$$

Numbers can also be broken down and changed according to your needs for seemingly difficult multiplication problems. Let's begin with an easier example:

$$35 * 20 = 35 * (2 * 10) = (35 * 2) * 10 = 70 * 10 = 700$$

The key here is to change 20 into 2 * 10, because it is easy to multiply anything by 1, 10, 100, or 1,000 (as well as by .1, .01, .001, etc.) – you just shift the decimal point to the right or left and place the right number of zeros in between. But what happens when you cannot make one of the numbers into something times 10?

Fortunately, you can pretty much change any number out there into something plus a number ending in -5 or -0.

For the above example, you could have also changed 20 into 10 + 10, as follows:

$$35 * 20 = 35 * (10 + 10) = (35 * 10) + (35 * 10) = 350 + 350 = 700$$

A few slightly more complicated examples:

$$8 * 43 = 8 * (40 + 3) = (8 * 40) + (8 * 3) = 320 + 24 + 344$$

$$12 * 15 = 12 * (10 + 5) = (12 * 10) + (12 * 5) = 120 + 60 = 180$$

or

$$15 * 12 = 15 * (10 + 2) = (15 * 10) + (15 * 2) = 150 + 30 = 180$$

In summary, whether you are adding, subtracting, multiplying, or dividing, the goal is always to make the numbers easier to work with. For most people, that means getting at least one number to end in -5 or -0.

We recommend that you continue Calcoholics Anonymous workouts for other topics, such as decimals, fractions, percentiles, and ratios, as the investment will certainly be worth it.

Make it Simple

Math has a proclivity[104] to seem more complicated than it really is. Variables, foreign symbols, abstract geometric descriptions, and big numbers scare many students. Remember when you first started to learn algebra and seeing an x in an equation terrified you? That was some time ago. Don't let these fears recur[105]. You are older, smarter, and better prepared these days; you know that, if anything, variables make questions simpler because you can *substitute any number you like*.

Many questions with multiple variables in them (especially when the generous test writers tell you for what variable range the equation is valid), accompanied by numerical answer choices, have two paths to solution: (A) spend a minute or more algebraically simplifying the equation – or even tougher, writing your own equation based on a verbal description and then simplifying that – into a form that explicates[106] the numerical answer, or (B) simply plug in some numbers to make the equation seem less abstract, and often you'll find one of the answer choices emerge. The latter is less prone to error and quicker.

Some geometry questions on SAT and ACT Math seem hard to visualize in the mind. For whatever nefarious[107] reason, the test writers occasionally omit[108] pictures

---

[104] SAT Word Alert: *Proclivity* (noun) means "a tendency to choose or do something regularly"

[105] SAT Word Alert: *Recur* (verb) means "to occur again, periodically or repeatedly"

[106] SAT Word Alert: *Explicate* (verb) means "analyze or develop in detail"

[107] SAT Word Alert: *Nefarious* (adjective) means "wicked or criminal"

of the described shapes and figures. How can you hold in your mind the abstract form they describe while also trying to figure out whatever property about it they want you to discern? Similarly, what do you do when the test writers *provide* a figure, but it is "not drawn to scale"? The answer to both of these scenarios is simple: fix the "mistake" the test writers made by *drawing the picture yourself.* You do not have to hold the shape in your mind; you've got a mighty pencil!

Another way to make things simpler for yourself is to *avoid the tough questions*. We must clarify our meaning here: We absolutely do not recommend *not* attempting the harder questions (double negatives can be tricky, especially on the test, so be sure you understand this sentence). As we stated earlier, we think that during your practice test preparation, it is imperative that you attempt and ultimately understand every single question, *especially* the more difficult ones. Learning only comes after a bit of struggle.

So what do we mean by "avoid the tough questions"? When you are going through the math section, time is of the essence, and the last thing you want is to spend ten minutes tackling the toughie, have time be called, and then glance at an unanswered question that you could have solved with ease. Every question is worth the same point value; get all your easy points in the bank and on the answer sheet before dedicating time to the more elusive[109] points. Mark on your answer sheet any tough questions that you skip and be careful not to get out of sync on your answer sheet. When you've completed the relatively easy questions, attempt the ones you've marked.

Fortunately, the SAT usually arranges the questions by increasing level of difficulty, so in theory you will only encounter the tough questions at the end of the section. Difficulty is subjective, however, so individualizing your prioritization by *temporarily* skipping difficult questions is more efficient.

One final way to simplify matters: *simplify*. Natural enough, right? We wrote earlier that plugging numbers into variable equations can give you a quick route to a numerical answer. Sometimes, however, the equation's form just doesn't lend itself to plugging in; it is not clear to you what compatible variable values you could input to yield a valid equality. This probably means you have stumbled upon an SAT or ACT question meant to distinguish the good students from the outstanding: *All very complicated-looking equations that seem impenetrable to plugging in can be greatly simplified with a bit of algebraic manipulation.*

No question on the SAT or ACT requires any advanced mathematics (like calculus) or even particularly witty algebraic manipulations. Some basic crossing out, rewriting of terms, and consolidation to common denominators can turn a scary,

---

[108] SAT Word Alert: *Omit* (verb) means "to leave out or exclude"

[109] SAT Word Alert: *Elusive* (adjective) means "difficult to find, catch, or achieve"

large equation into a friendly, small one. Most students who do not try to attack the equation with algebra will be left just staring at it, hoping or praying that a great insight will come to them. Do not be one of those students. Instead, dive in with a few algebraic moves.

Stamp Out Silly Mistakes

So you have kicked your reliance on your calculator, you know your mathematical fundamentals as well as you know your phone number, and you have mastered the application of that knowledge to all the question types that the SAT and ACT may throw at you. But one problem remains: silly mistakes.

You know what kind of errors we are talking about: plugging numbers into your calculator incorrectly, misreading the questions, and mis-bubbling the answers. As with anything, achieving 100 percent extermination of silly mistakes may not be possible. However, there are some powerful ways to make silly mistakes an extremely rare – albeit[110] unsightly – occurrence.

With the SAT's and ACT's curves being as unforgiving as they are – the margin for error for those who want a perfect 800 on a given section and, especially, a 36 is almost always nonexistent – working to reduce the number of silly mistakes that you make is an important part of your late-game strategy in moving from great scores to ones that truly stand out.

Incidentally, two effective methods for increasing accuracy have already been discussed: limiting your calculator use and covering up the answer choices.

When you are panicked, you are liable to press a wrong button if you are using a calculator; similarly, you may make a mental math mistake if you try to calculate without computer help. So why does reducing your reliance on calculators help you avoid silly mistakes? The difference is that, when you are mentally calculating an operation, you are *thinking*: You are constantly (whether you know it or not) searching for ways to simplify the mathematical process. The benefit of this thinking is that when you get a result that should not make logical sense or is, for example, of the wrong magnitude, you will notice. On the other hand, students have a tendency to place incredible amounts of allegiance in their calculator's outputs and hardly give a thought to whether they are reasonable; no mental check exists.

The benefit of covering up the multiple choices is probably obvious: If you come up with an answer that is wrong because it qualifies as one of the aforementioned "silly mistakes," it probably won't be one of the choices, because there are so many possible combinations of miscalculations and misinterpretations of the question. However, covering up the answer choices does not assist much in cases similar to

---

[110] SAT Word Alert: *Albeit* (conjunction) means "although"

that mentioned earlier, in which a student solves for *x* instead of *y* because he or she read the question carelessly.

This leads to the third helpful tool for increasing accuracy – proper pacing. There are no hard and fast rules for what pace is ideal; you must experiment so that you can find the best speed for optimizing your concentration and ability to carefully read the question while still being able to attempt every question.

If you find a pace that leaves you time for checking after you have finished all the questions, you have another option for reducing the frequency of silly mistakes. But you are better off not merely glancing back through every question you have completed in search of a small mistake. This is both ineffective (because you are very likely to get in the habit of seeking to *affirmatively confirm* rather than *skeptically check*) and inefficient (because you are spending time reviewing questions that presented very little opportunity for silly mistakes).

You can, instead, hone in on the questions most likely to be plagued by silly mistakes. As you are going through the section the first time, mark on your answer sheet the questions that you feel you may have made an error on. Aim to mark around 20 percent of the questions. Rather than reviewing these questions to confirm that you did not make a mistake, completely rework these "high-risk" questions if you have time after finishing the section; if you again reach the same answer, chances are good that you did not make one of the silly mistakes. (Place these pencil marks on the answer sheet to the left of the question numbers so that the grading machines are not thrown off.)

One final tip: In order to reduce mis-bubblings, you may find it helpful to say the question number and corresponding letter choice in your mind as you are moving from the question booklet to the answer sheet. So under this scheme, if you are on question #7 and think that the answer is (B), you would mentally recite "7B, 7B" as you make your way to bubble it in on your answer sheet.

After all your hard work, it would be a bit frustrating to fall short of your potential because of a little silly mistake. In your final stages of preparation, make sure you've practiced applying those easy insurance policies!

Some Math Strategies in Action

As we've indicated, you will amass your own individually suited toolset of math techniques – and the practiced sense of when to use each – as you begin practice tests, making sure to read the explanations for each question as you go through the tests. Each question has multiple routes to the solution, but some will be more efficient and less error-prone, depending on the circumstance. Here is a sample of how we would approach some questions.

The product of x, y, and z is 1,936. The product of y and 3 is 33, and x divided by y is 4. What is x?

If you haven't solved a question like this before, it can be intimidating. There are three variables, and we aren't directly told any of them. We are supposed to solve for *x*. Where do we begin?

There are two primary avenues to solution here. For the first method, let's try to employ the advice we recommended you attempt whenever feasible during practice: **Solve for the answer first**, before reading the choices. We believe this is an effective preparatory method for developing a foundation of skill that you can confidently call upon before you turn to some of the time-saving tricks you can use in a pinch, which are valuable but should not be your default and only reaction to a question. Moreover, grid-in questions don't supply you any answer choices.

In order to solve for the answer first, in this question we need to **relate the variables using equations**. Whenever a question verbalizes the relationship among variables, we should write an equation to symbolically represent the relationship in order to set ourselves up for a bit of algebra. You likely practiced this a lot earlier in your math career.

Here we would write

$$x * y * z = 1,936$$

$$y * 3 = 33$$

$$\frac{x}{y} = 4$$

We can solve this system of equations by algebraic simplification now. If you look carefully, it should now be clear that the question was not nearly as involved as it appeared. Because *y* is the only variable in the second equation and *x* and *y* are the only two variables in the third question, you don't even need the first equation! Solve for *y* in the second equation, yielding 11. Plug 11 into the third equation and solve *x* to be 44.

A second popular option for this sort of question would be to **plug in the answer choices**. Let's say they were

(A) 36

(B) 44

(C) 48

(D) 56

(E) 58

The idea would be to pick an answer choice and work backwards; instead of intending to use algebra, you would desire to employ only basic operations. Here we would choose a number, perhaps 44, plug it in as *x*, and see if the relationships specified in the question were true. Here they would be, so 44 is correct.

Here are some notes on plugging answer choices in:

This strategy works best when there are variables in the question but numbers as the answer choices.

It's generally a fast strategy, but the slightly more effortful techniques used to solve questions for the answer first may still be required. In this example, for instance, in order to ensure *x* divided by *y* is 4, we would need to know *y*, so solving the second equation would still be necessary. (It was probably apparent enough to do in your head, though.)

Plug in the median answer choice first. The median is the number in the middle when the choices are arranged in ascending or descending value, typically choice (C). This speeds up the process because you can often get a sense of whether the chosen value was too big or too small, allowing you to immediately eliminate two of four remaining choices.

Of course, we much prefer and highly encourage the first option since "plug-and-chug" is not a sustainable way to improve your mathematical and, more broadly, problem-solving abilities.

> You receive your monthly paycheck in the mail. Your base salary has a 20 percent bonus added to it to arrive at the total salary. Off your total salary, 15 percent in taxes is removed, after which you set aside 15 percent for savings. The money you save is what percent of the base salary amount?

In this example, we see the usefulness of **plugging in a new number**. It's probably unnecessarily time consuming and hard to keep track of a compounding series of fractions, especially because we are dealing with two different base numbers. Instead, let's simply plug in a number and see what percent the result we obtain is of the starting number. 100 should be your go-to selection on percent questions.

A 20 percent bonus added to 100 is 120. 85 percent (1 - .15) of 120 is 102. 15 percent of 102 is 15.3. So the saved money is $15.30, which is simply 15.3 percent of our original 100. And that's the answer.

Here are some notes on picking a number to plug in:

This strategy works best when there are variables or percentages in the question and variables or percentages as the answer choices. Say that you see 2x + 3y as an answer choice. If you aren't able to algebraically simplify an equation derived from the original question to reach an expression like those in the choices, plugging in real numbers for x and y can be a powerful workaround.

Ensure the answer choice fits the variables' parameters as indicated in the question. Some numbers, the question will specify, should be integers, positive, or prime. Plug in a number that is appropriate in the context.

Pick a simple (but not too simple) number. We don't want to have to work with numbers that contain many decimal places or are unnecessarily great in value. Also avoid numbers that may yield results that may not be fairly representative of general relationships, like 0 and 1. Three is often an easy, effective choice. Here's another example:

$$\frac{2x(x^2x^3)^3}{3yx^{15}} - 1 = \frac{(1/3)yx^{17}}{y^2x^{44}}$$

What is 2x divided by 3y?

Here we see the potency of **simplification**. The equation looks daunting in its current form. Luckily, we can use algebra to uncover a clearer expression of the relationship. Questions that require simplification will be salient on the SAT and ACT once you've practiced a bit. Any equation whose relationship appears beyond conceptualization because of the complexity of the terms can surely be pared down to its secrets.

First, simplify exponents within the parentheses in the numerator of the first fraction and the denominator of the second fraction. Recall that multiplication of terms with a common base is accomplished by adding the exponents (2 + 3) and that a term and a power raised to a further power is equal to that term raised to the product of those powers (5 * 3 and 4 * 4). Also, we'll change 1/3 in the numerator to a 3 in the denominator.

$$\frac{2x^{16}}{3yx^{15}} - 1 = \frac{yx^{17}}{3y^2x^{16}}$$

Terms with a common base that are divided by one another equal that term raised to the difference of the powers, subtracting the denominator's power from the numerator's. So x to the 16th power divided by x to the 15th power is simply x, and x to the 17th divided by x to the 16th is x, too. y over the square of y is 1 over y. At this point, we will also add 1 to both sides and subtract the second fraction from both sides.

$$\frac{2x}{3y} - \frac{x}{3y} = 1$$

Now that we have a common base, we can subtract the second fraction from the first. 2x minus x is x. So we have

$$\frac{x}{3y} = 1$$

Consistent with our hope, the fraction is very similar to the (2x)/(3y) specified in the question. All we have to do is multiply both sides by 2 to see that the answer is 2.

> If x is the product of two distinct prime numbers z and y, which of the following could not be y?

This question has two aspects that may fool you, but not if you are **watching out for tricks**. The information about x is merely a red herring; the question asks nothing about x. All that matters is the specification that y is a prime number. Also note that the question asks what y could *not* be. The answer choice is going to be the only one that isn't a prime number.

Make sure that whenever multiple variables are given, you circle the one that the question wants you to find. Don't do all the work in a question, only to give the value for a different variable. You should also immediately circle any key negation words, like *not* and *never*.

> Triangle ABC is equilateral with sides of length 4. Segment BD is perpendicular to AC, and point D lies on segment AC. What is the length of BD?

Geometry questions on the SAT and ACT highlight the importance of **marking up your test book**; don't be afraid to use your pencil to interact with the booklet in any ways that help you. Most geometry questions will include small diagrams that provide some illustration of figures needed to solve each question. In those cases, write every piece of information you know about the picture on it, whether it was directly given in the question or you figured it out yourself.

This question doesn't give us an illustration, so you should draw one rather than exert the mental energy to precariously hold a conceptualization of it in your head. Once you've drawn triangle ABC, label each side length as 4. Draw a segment from B to D. Since BD is perpendicular to AC and ABC is equilateral, you'll see that D bisects AC; so AD and DC have length 2.

The perpendicular relationship between BD and AC yields two right angles, ADB and BDC. Mark these, along with the original 60-degree angles of triangle ABC (characteristic of an equilateral triangle). Angle ABC is now bisected, so we have angles ABD and DBC that are each 30 degrees.

Now your figure should show two right triangles, each of which is the same. The short leg of each is 2, and its angles are 30, 60, and 90 degrees. Now comes the time when you must **know your stuff**, to put it a bit bluntly.

There are a number of pieces of information that are useful on the math sections, such as the route to solve a word problem that we discussed earlier. But there is more basic knowledge you should have going into the test, such as the distance formula used to derive that special case: distance equals rate multiplied by time. You should also be confident in your abilities to simplify exponents and other expressions, using methods like factorization. Familiarize yourself with combinations and permutations and how to use your calculator to help you on those. If you are taking the ACT, you ought to review your trigonometry as well.

Anyways, on this question, your knowledge of triangle properties is key. A special right triangle with angles of 30, 60, and 90 exhibits particular side-length proportionality: the leg opposite the smallest angle is half the hypotenuse, and the other leg (that opposite the 60 degree angle) is the short leg multiplied by the square root of three. In this case, the short leg is 2, so the hypotenuse is 4 and the other leg is 2 times the square root of 3. *BD* is therefore $2\sqrt{3}$.

CHAPTER 6
BOOSTING YOUR READING SCORES

Reading without reflecting is like eating without digesting.

Edmund Burke (1729-1797)
Irish statesman & philosopher

No matter how busy you may think you are, you must find time for reading, or surrender yourself to self-chosen ignorance.

Confucius (551 B.C. - 479 B.C.)
Chinese teacher & philosopher

First, let's quickly review what you will encounter on the reading sections of the SAT and ACT.

The Critical Reading section of the SAT is 70 minutes long, made up of one 20-minute subsection and two 25-minute subsections. It contains 48 passage-based reading questions, with some long passages and some short, and 19 sentence completion questions – 67 questions in total.

Here is the specific breakdown for how each subsection on the SAT's Critical Reading section will look. Any potential additional subsection would be the unscored, experimental section mentioned earlier.

25-minute subsection:
    16 passage-based questions (a short passage pair and a long passage)
    8 sentence completion questions
25-minute subsection:
    19 passage-based questions (two short passages and two longer passages)
    5 sentence completion questions
20-minute subsection:
    13 passage-based questions (one pair of longer passages)
    6 sentence completion questions

The Reading section of the ACT is 35 minutes long. It contains four passages, one each on social studies, natural sciences, prose fiction, and humanities; forty passage-based reading questions, ten about each passage; and no sentence completion questions.

Vocabulary

The basic tool for the manipulation of reality is the manipulation of words. If you can control the meaning of words, you can control the people who must use the words.

Philip K. Dick (1928-1982)
American novelist, whose stories were popularly adapted
into *Total Recall, Blade Runner,* and *Minority Report*, among others

The difference between the right word and the almost right word is the difference between lightning and a lightning bug.

Mark Twain (1835-1910)
American author and humorist

Possessing a deep and broad lexicon[111] is an attribute that will assist you in your academic career as well as your everyday life by allowing fuller comprehension of what you read and hear, more precise communication of what you wish to convey, and better categorical organization of the concepts that you think about.

The most natural and common way that people establish their vocabularies is through ordinary experience: occasionally looking up words in dictionaries but mostly inferring from what is read and heard. Because this method of lexical acquisition is experiential, however, it is of course limited – no one knows all of the words in the English language or even a sizable fraction of them – and varies from person to person.

For these reasons, testing vocabulary on standardized tests is a tricky endeavor: The test writers want to focus on skills rather than knowledge, and they do not want to disadvantage any specific populations.

In order to keep the concentration on skills, whenever vocabulary is tested on the SAT or ACT, it is done in an applied manner; context matters. A question will never simply ask for the general denotation[112] of a word but will instead require that you apply your knowledge of words' definitions to piece together a sentence – as on the sentence completion questions of the SAT – or that you understand which sense of a word is being used in the context of a passage, as occurs occasionally on the passage-based reading questions of the SAT and ACT.

Understandably, the test writers are less successful at keeping the indirect assessment of vocabulary fair to all groups. A teenager who is living in an impoverished[113] Southern community is far less likely to have been exposed to the

---

[111] SAT Word Alert: *Lexicon* (noun) means "a particular language's or person's vocabulary"

[112] *Denotation* refers to the dictionary's explicit set of meanings for a word. [Why is this not an SAT Word Alert?

[113] SAT Word Alert: *Impoverished* (adjective) means "reduced to poverty"

difficult words tested on the SAT than, for example, a teenager who attends an opulent[114] private high school in Cambridge, Massachusetts.

This specific, stark social contrast touches upon the broader, relevant fact that the typical teenager has not encountered all of the words that will be tested on the SAT's sentence completion questions, for which an advanced vocabulary is most important. In fact, many of the words seem unintelligibly[115] esoteric[116] (the surfeit[117] of footnotes means that vocabulary is on the mind!) to most teenagers.

So what can be done? If you do intend to take just the ACT and not the SAT, studying vocabulary in order to better position yourself is certainly not worth your while (at least for the test, but remember "The Stepping Stone Myth"). But if you do plan on taking the SAT and do not come into this test prep process with a vocabulary that allows you to ace the sentence completion questions, some vocabulary review is appropriate.

You do not have to read a dictionary from cover to cover or studiously memorize those three-to-five-thousand-word lists. For all except those who have a very basic grasp on the English language, studying such lengthy lists certainly takes too much time to be of advisable productivity; that time would be better spent working through practice exams.

Finding a book with a high hit ratio – in other words, one that tends to have a relatively high percentage of its words appear on real administrations of the SAT – and of modest length is your best bet. *Direct Hits Core Vocabulary of the SAT: Volume 1* and *Direct Hits Toughest Vocabulary of the SAT: Volume 2* seem to fit the bill by offering several hundred words, many of which were correctly predicted to appear on recent tests.

One efficient strategy for studying vocabulary books is to make an initial scan of all the words to identify those whose definitions you are unfamiliar with. Then write these down on flashcards and study just those. Once you have solidified your knowledge of a word's definition, you can remove it from the deck of flashcards so that no time is wasted re-covering crystallized information.

Of course, there is no way to learn every word that could appear on the SAT (or ACT); the English language has enough words to ensure the possibility that even the most erudite[118] test-taker, perhaps one who spent his or her time mastering thousands of "SAT words," may face the unknown. Remember, though, that these

---

[114] SAT Word Alert: *Opulent* (adjective) means "wealthy or affluent"

[115] SAT Word Alert: *Unintelligible* (adjective) means "unable to be understood"

[116] SAT Word Alert: *Esoteric* (adjective) means "comprehended by only a few"

[117] SAT Word Alert: *Surfeit* (noun) means "an excessive amount"

[118] SAT Word Alert: *Erudite* (adjective) means "scholarly or characterized by great knowledge"

tests are curved and that the other test-takers will likely be in the same boat of uncertainty.

Sentence Completion Questions

Now for the application of vocabulary: sentence completion questions. Again, these appear only on the SAT.

In essence, the sentence completion questions of the SAT test your knowledge of words' definitions and your ability to apply these definitions to sentences using the surrounding sentences' structures. They can be tersely[119] described as *vocabulary in context*.

You will be given sentences with one or two blanks each, which you must fill in using one of the five answer choices. The single-blank questions will look something like this (minus the alliterative animal name):

Because he was a/an ------- diver, Waldo the Wonderful Walrus spent much time preparing for each swim meet.

(A) skilled

(B) audacious

(C) dedicated

(D) amateur

(E) experienced

And here is what a two-blank question will look like:

Always looking for a chance to ------, Eduardo the Enigmatic Emu was a/an ------ scientist.

(A) cheat .. honest

(B) experiment .. adventurous

(C) retire .. experienced

(D) eat .. healthy

(E) clean .. angry

---

[119] SAT Word Alert: *Terse* (adjective) means "sparing in the use of words; laconic"

In order to figure out which words are appropriate for the blanks, you must understand the structure of the sentence and the implications of that structure on meaning.

Since each single-blank question has just one correct answer that must be inferable from the given sentence, you will never be introducing new information. Instead, you must look at the information given in the sentence, determine the relation of that information to the blank, and then select the most logically fitting word.

In the first question, for example, we see two grammatical clauses. *Because he was a/an diver* is the first clause. Does this information alone reveal the answer? No, since divers can be any of the choices: skilled, audacious, dedicated, amateur, or experienced. The more telling clause is the second: *Waldo the Wonderful Walrus spent much time preparing for each meet.*

We should now be thinking that Waldo is a committed or very careful diver. Your next question must be *How does this information relate to the blank of the first clause of the sentence?* To determine that, look at the structure of the sentence. The two clauses are linked semantically by *because,* which means that the first clause explains the second. Therefore, the word that goes in the first blank should be directly consistent with our previous conclusion that Waldo is committed or very careful.

Could he be, as suggested by choice (A), skilled? Or experienced, as suggested by choice (E)? Yes to both, but we would be merely speculating to say anything more than "could": The answer needs to be *directly* supported. A committed or careful diver could be skilled and experienced, but he could also be an amateur; we simply do not have enough information to support these choices. Remember the advice from our PERFECT Approach: We are looking for reasons a choice could be *wrong*, because most answers are in some sense possibly correct. **We want to select the necessarily correct answer** – on sentence completion questions, **the word that fits just right**.

More clearly, the answer is not *audacious* (choice (B)) because an audacious (or bold) diver would be likelier to spend little time preparing for meets – which we know to be false here – or to perform dangerous stunts while diving, which is unsupported by the little information that we are given.

Choice (C), however, does explain why Waldo "spent much time preparing for each meet": He was dedicated to diving, so he tried to improve.

Suppose now that the sentence had instead been

> Although he was a/an ------- diver, Waldo the Wonderful Walrus spent much time preparing for each meet.

In this case, the information that the sentence provides is the same as before. The relationship between the provided information and the blank has now changed, however: Instead of explaining the second, informational clause of the sentence, the first clause now contradicts it, so the meaning in the blank must also contradict the thrust of the second clause.

Ideas contradictory to the inference that Waldo is a committed or very careful diver are that Waldo is a feckless[120] diver or that he is an imprudent[121] diver. Being semantically near to *imprudent*, *audacious* (choice (B)) then fits the blank in this alternate phrasing of the sentence.

The approach to two-blank sentence completion questions is similar, except that you will often be given very little to no helpful information in the sentence itself. You must rely instead on your understanding of the relationship between the two words in the blanks, which you also obtain by looking at the structure of the sentence.

Like the first question, the second question is relatively straightforward in that the structure of the sentence is simple: The first clause[122] is directly related to and in explanation of the second clause. So you simply should go through each choice and ask yourself whether it makes sense.

Choice (A): Would an honest scientist often try to cheat? Definitely not. Choice (B): Would an adventurous scientist often try to experiment? Yes, necessarily by definition. Choice (C): Would an experienced scientist want to retire? He may, but not necessarily; many experienced scientists continue to happily work for additional decades. Would a healthy scientist eat all of the time, as suggested by choice (D)? Well, it depends on the way in which that eating frequency is consonant[123] with the proper diet of an emu, so not necessarily. Would an angry scientist frequently clean? Again, perhaps, but the connection seems tenuous[124].

The only specifically supported answer choice, then, is choice (B): *experiment* in blank one and *adventurous* in blank two.

When you are attempting to determine the relationships among the words, phrases, and clauses in a sentence so that you know how to apply the definitions of the answer choices, you should be on the lookout for some simple trigger words and parallel structures; they will help you to conceptually organize the sentence's syntax.

---

[120] SAT Word Alert: *Feckless* (adjective) means "having no sense of responsibility or lazy"

[121] SAT Word Alert: *Imprudent* (adjective) means "incautious or rash"

[122] Actually, *Always looking for a chance to ------* is technically not a clause but instead a participial phrase. More on this in "Mastering the English and Writing Sections," the next chapter.

[123] SAT Word Alert: *Consonant* (adjective) means "consistent or in agreement"

[124] SAT Word Alert: *Tenuous* (adjective) means "unsubstantiated or weak"

Here are three general structures that suggest that *clause A* is **directly related** to <u>clause B</u>:

Subject, who/which *clause A,* <u>clause B</u>.
Example: Toby the Tubby Tomato, who *frequently helps his fellow fruits in their times of need*, <u>has been hailed as a kind tomato</u>.

Participial phrase serving as clause A, Subject <u>clause B</u>.
Example: *Devouring everything in her path*, Beth the Beautiful Llama <u>cannot control her large appetite</u>.

Subject *clause A;* <u>clause B</u>.   or   Subject *clause A:* <u>clause B</u>.
Example: Gordo the Giddy Gecko had bunches of fun no matter the circumstances; everything was an exciting opportunity for him.

Some trigger words that indicate an **explanatory or causal relationship**: because, therefore, thus, accordingly, so that, as a result of, due to

Example: Because *she was an inexperienced orator*, Sally the Sappy Salamander <u>gave an incoherent speech to the group of nematodes</u>.

Example: Fred the Frozen Flatworm *wanted everyone to know that he was extremely wealthy*; therefore, <u>he constructed a decidedly ostentatious[125] abode</u>.

Some trigger words that indicate negation or a contradictory relationship: though, although, albeit, even though, despite, in spite of, nonetheless, nevertheless, no, not, however, but, yet, instead

Example: Despite *his predilection[126] for occasional self-indulgence*, Sean the Chivalrous Shrimp <u>was generally selflessly concerned with others' welfare</u>.

Example: Normally, Joe, though *nice*, is not <u>social</u>; tonight, however, Joe, instead of *avoiding others*, <u>actively sought their company</u>.

Let us take an analytical look at that last sentence. (You do much of this processing naturally, but taking the time to objectively parse the structure of a sentence helps

---

[125] SAT Word Alert: *Ostentatious* (adjective) means "characterized by pretentious show in an attempt to impress others"
[126] SAT Word Alert: *Predilection* (noun) means "tendency to think favorably of"

you to tackle convoluted[127] ones in a more accurate, comfortable, and confident way.)

The sentence can be thought of on two organizational levels. First, we will sort out the higher level of organization: clause A (*Normally, Joe, though nice, is not social*) and clause B (*tonight, however, Joe, instead of avoiding others, actively sought their company*). Before looking at the lower organizational level, first consider the relationship between clauses A and B: The trigger word for this broad comparison is *however*. So clause A ought to contradict clause B.

The ultimate meaning of clause A is that Joe is unsocial. Does clause B say something contradictory to this? As we would expect based on our trigger word, it does: The ultimate meaning of clause B is that Joe is social. (The specification that his being unsocial is *typical* and that his being social is *isolated* is not relevant to this analysis because the "contradiction" we speak of here needs merely to be superficial and grammatical. If this were not the case, no one could ever write "but" or "however" without tacitly[128] admitting incoherence and hypocrisy!)

Within clause B we have two sub-clauses, which we will dub B1 (*avoiding others*) and B2 (*actively sought their company*). The relationship between these sub-clauses is indicated by the contradictory trigger *instead*: Indeed, seeking others' company is antithetical[129] to avoiding them.

Likewise, clause A is comprised of two sub-clauses: A1 (*nice*) and A2 (*social*). The relationship between A1 and A2 is complicated by the presence of two triggers; both *though* and *not* determine the sub-clauses' relationship. Since each of these triggers is contradictory or negating, they can be thought of as cancelling each other out, leaving A1 and A2 to be directly related.

We admit this careful analysis was probably difficult to follow on a first read. Ultimately, as long as you know the definitions of the relevant words, succeeding on sentence completion questions is a matter of applying commonsensical but careful logic to the situations described in the sentences and utilizing your skills of analytical syntax to determine relationships. With some practice, they can become quite consistently manageable.

Passage-Based Reading Questions

Education is the ability to listen to almost anything without losing your temper.

Robert Frost (1874-1963)
American Poet and Four-Time Pulitzer Prize Recipient

---

[127] SAT Word Alert: *Convoluted* (adjective) means "extremely complex and difficult to follow"

[128] SAT Word Alert: *Tacit* (adjective) means "understood or implied"

[129] SAT Word Alert: *Antithetical* (adjective) means "directly opposed or contrasted"

Not all readers are leaders, but all leaders are readers.

Harry S. Truman (1884-1972)
33rd President of the United States

Ah, the passage-based questions. These questions require not only the ability to *read* English passages but also the *skill* and the *will* to critically analyze and in turn understand what one is reading.

To that end, these are well-written questions: The questions on the SAT's and ACT's reading sections generally strike a smart balance in testing whether you can form accurate, well-considered inferences from writing while also avoiding the trap of moving so far from the explicit meaning of the text that the concept of a single correct answer breaks down.

Quite possibly, the strategic approaches and reasoning mentalities that test-takers employ on the passage-based reading questions are more influential on their scores than are the strategies for any other part of the SAT or ACT. A poorly conceived or ineffectively executed mindset and process on the reading sections can spell the difference between, say, a 500 on the Critical Reading section and an 800.

Indeed, internalizing and practicing a few simple ideas about the sections has the strong potential to yield significant score boosts. Lest this reality impress you with the unreality that the *simplicity* of improving on the passage-based questions implies *ease*, note that the perfection of the techniques takes practice – and lots of it. Luckily, the sort of practice that helps you improve on these sections has incidental but important benefits for your general reading abilities. And being good at reading is always nice.

Approaching the Passages

There is no single, objectively correct way to logistically tackle the passages. You should, therefore, experiment with slightly different techniques while making sure to give each one a fair try before jettisoning[130] it; whatever works for you is the best approach. Similarly, you will need to practice repeatedly with different paces until you are able to get through the section within the allotted time but at minimal expense of accuracy.

Here is an advisable process for approaching the long-passage questions on the SAT – a strategy that will make the short-passage questions a refreshing respite in their relative ease – and the reading questions on the ACT, subtle variations on which have proven to be highly successful for many test-takers when paired with an appropriate mentality, often taking them from sub-600 scores to nearly or precisely 800 on the SAT's section:

---

[130] SAT Word Alert: *Jettison* (verb) means "to cast off or discard"

1. Read the introduction to the passage. The introductory sketches tend to be longer and more specific on the SAT, but reading them on either test is worthwhile. They do not take up much time and can helpfully contextualize the succeeding passages.

   The introduction is sufficiently short that you need not have any anxiety over reading it slowly and carefully, in the interest of knowing where the author is coming from before you get into the thick of it. These passages are *excerpts*, after all; you're often missing 98 percent of what else the author wrote in the original complete work, so the introduction is necessary for establishing your orientation. The introduction is a rich resource for determining the author's general point of view.

2. Skip the passage for the time being and go straight to the questions. Do not study or even read the questions; just scan them for numerical line references, as in

   7. The changing tone from lines 23 to 26 can best be characterized as

   In that case, you would then go to the passage and quickly mark lines 23 through 26 (the left margins of the passage columns will contain line numbers by intervals of five); also include the corresponding question number next to the lines. This step of marking line citations may seem time-consuming initially, but it is one of the most effective ways of dissecting the text as you read, and the time commitment can, with practice, be reduced to mere seconds.

3. Start to read the passage. Intend to read all of it, with some question-answering interventions as will be mentioned in step 4. Skipping over large chunks of the passage is inadvisable, even if those parts are not explicitly referenced in the questions because you will then be poorly equipped to handle the general inference and purpose questions that appear.

4. Just before you arrive at a section that you marked in step 2, go read the corresponding question but not the answers. Then read the relevant, marked lines and any context. Read with emphasized purpose and care; you *know* your time spent reading this part is valuable because it is certainly used in a question.

5. Predict a general answer to the question once you have read the relevant chunk from the passage. Go back to the question and read the answers. If, after reading the question and then the relevant section, you find that you can answer the question, do so; if not, forge ahead and save it for later when you feel that you have read enough to respond. The vast majority of the time, however, you should be able to answer the questions with line references immediately after reading those referenced lines and what came

before them. (But if you cannot, don't feel compelled to dwell. There's more reading to do.)

Once you have continued this process and arrived at the end of the passage, begin answering any yet unanswered questions – hopefully mostly those that pertain to analysis of the passage as a whole, such as questions on the author's overall tone, purpose, or attitude. On the dual-passage sections of the SAT's Critical Reading section, this is also where you would answer questions that require comparison or synthesis of the passages. Since you have read the passage all the way through, you will likely know where in the passage or passages to look for the answers.

Again, the details of this method are not set in stone, but it does work for many people, and those for whom it is not ideal usually settle on a productive approach that is very similar. In particular, for the short passage questions on the SAT, students usually find that this method is unnecessarily rigorous and opt to read the whole passage before checking out the questions. This seems like a fine idea, though in preparation it may be preferable to get as much practice as possible in using the line references of questions to guide and hone the speed at which you read each line.

Patience is needed in the application of this method, as it is designed to provide the best method for ultimately achieving a high score – not to confer the highest score out of the gates. Almost everyone who begins to use this technique will initially find that it pushes them over the time limit. But with enough practice, we have found that, for all students, this issue evaporates. Once you have a good strategic foundation, as is provided here, you can feel confident that practice tests are your way of improving the efficient employment of this methodology.

Answering the Questions

Beyond how to logistically approach the section – studying the introduction, marking the line references, reading the passage interspersed with answering questions, and finally cleaning up the general question loose ends – the other main concern for doing your best on the SAT and ACT reading sections is how to answer the questions.

Figuring out how to answer passage-based questions is probably the hardest part of the SAT and ACT. You have to really think. Your outside explicit knowledge is all but irrelevant; only your skill to interpret reading really matters.

Yet most students know almost every word in the passages, as they are not designed to stretch your vocabulary. If most test-takers can read the words, presumably they can understand the passages, in turn rendering them able to answer all the questions, right? What trips students up? Is it because the questions are so subjective?

Let us extirpate[131] right now the idea that the passage-based questions are subjective. Yes, they are not as mathematically demonstrable in their logical unimpeachability as the questions on the tests' math sections. But they are not a mind game in which you have to differentiate based on opinionated whim between two answers that are equally in harmony with the given passage or passages.

Why is that? Recall from earlier in this chapter that for the SAT's sentence completion questions, the correct word had to be necessarily correct, rather than just *possibly* so. The same principle – summed up in our PERFECT Approach as the need to "be ruthless" – applies here. For the sentence completion questions, our determination was informed by the definitions of the words in the choices and how the sentence fits together.

For passage-based questions, quite naturally, we base our answers on the passages. Instead of imagining, as the title implies, that the *questions* emerge from the passage, recognize that **the answers emerge from the passages**. Of your five choices, one is correct and four are wrong. The one correct answer will be necessarily correct, as indicated by the passage. Every correct answer will be entirely supported by the passage; the others will not. Think of the section as not passage-based questions but passage-based answers.

To decide whether a choice is correct – i.e., that it is passage-based and in fact the relevant choice at hand – run these three questions through your mind as you read each possible answer to a question:

Does the answer make sense? With surprising frequency, some choices on the passage-based questions have nothing to do with the facts of the passage. That is, no matter what the question could be, these statements are just demonstrably *false* as far as the passage is concerned. Say that a question asks why the author chose, for example, to join the army, and one answer choice is that he was moved by his father's sacrifices in the military for his country. If you recall that the author never stated that his father served in the military and was in fact a butcher, do not spend time second-guessing your straightforward interpretation; the passage clearly contradicts the choice, so it doesn't make sense and is thus wrong.

On other occasions, the answer may be factually consistent with the passage, even interpretatively well-supported, but wrong because it does not make sense in light of the question. Imagine again that the question asks what the author's motivation was for joining the army. Let us say one of the answers this time is that his father was a butcher. This is true. It makes sense internally. But given the question, it is illogical: Why would having a father who cuts meat inspire service to one's country? Such a choice would be supported by the passage but not relevant. Do not choose it.

---

[131] SAT Word Alert: *Extirpate* (verb) means "to destroy or remove entirely"

Is the answer choice supported by the passage? If it is the correct answer, it will be. Some guidebooks on passage-based questions are careful to point out that "supported by the passage" doesn't necessarily mean that the answer is communicated by the passage explicitly. It may be *inferable*, they say. This is accurate: Some level of reasonable interpretation still grounded in the passage is sometimes needed. However, we find that "inference" in the more commonly interpreted sense of reasonably supported, possibly correct speculation is never needed on the SAT or ACT.

Imagine that the passage corresponding to the hypothetical question about the author who joined the military were in part this:

> I joined the military because I had become a nationalist. My internal nationalistic fervor was kindled and cultivated early in my life. On the way to school, signs solicited me to join the efforts for peace through non-peace. They struck me as ironic. I walked to school many times, though, and saw the signs many times too. Eventually they were resonant logic in my eyes: Without sacrifice and loss, peace is unattainable.

This passage is a bit opaque[132]. With some thought, it is certainly not unclear, though. The following question is not explicitly answered by a technical reading of the grammar of the passage; but, as (hopefully) reasonable people, we can figure out the answer without resorting to any bold sort of inference:

"How had the author become a nationalist?"

The passage never technically says. It states explicitly why he joined the military ("because I had become a nationalist") but not how this nationalism came about, other than when it did: early in life. But we can clearly (though not explicitly) read that the signs he saw that solicited him to join and the explanations they gave amounted to his nationalistic inculcation[133].

One could make a strong case based only on the passage for the correctness of the claim that the author became a nationalist and thus joined the military because of his exposure to the signs on his way to school. Such an answer would be thoroughly supported by the passage. But there is one more question to ask yourself before committing to a choice.

Could the answer be wrong? This final question is a powerful tool for the elimination of answer choices, because correct answers must not only have support in the text but also not be contradicted by anything in the text. **A strong case *can* be made *for* the correctness of the answer, and a strong case *cannot* be made *against* its correctness.**

---

[132] SAT Word Alert: *Opaque* (adjective) means hard to understand or not clear"

[133] SAT Word Alert: *Inculcate* (verb) means "to cause or influence someone to accept an idea"

You may think these criteria are one in the same, but sometimes there are two answer choices, each of which satisfies at least one criterion. To use our simple example passage, imagine that a question asked "What was the author's attitude toward the signs when he joined the military?" Say too that you have narrowed the choices down to "skepticism" (a word that makes frequent appearances on passage-based attitude and tone questions) and "agreement."

The passage first says that the signs seemed "ironic," reasonably interpreted to be because "peace through non-peace" is in some ways a contradiction between means and goal. That part of the passage supports "skepticism" as the choice. But two sentences later, we hear that the author's attitude later changed into belief: the logic of the signs' message resonated in him. He came to agree with it, in other words. This newer attitude supports "agreement" as the answer.

The reason that either of these would be wrong is that the time when the attitude was held does not match that in the question. A consideration of why each choice may be wrong reveals that the interpretation of the signs as ironic was merely temporary, passing before he joined the military. There is no reason to believe, based on the passage, that he did not agree with the signs when he joined. "Agreement" is the correct answer: There is textual support that it is correct and, under a careful reading, no textual support that it is incorrect.

On the problem-solving skills and general mentality for approaching the passage-based questions of the SAT and ACT, we have some final points to make. Here are these golden nuggets of helpful advice (hopefully!):

Correct answers will be supported by the text. We are saying it again. Do not forget it. Every single correct answer choice will have proof, whether explicit or implicit, that can be found in or very reasonably inferred from the passage; the other choices will not.

So if you narrow the options down but find yourself stuck between two answer choices whose distinction is nuanced and that both seem correct, remember that one is correct and that one is incorrect, wherein the difference can be found by a careful and objective analysis of the passage. One of the answers may be potentially or nearly correct, but the other one will be directly, necessarily, and completely supported – find reasons that the former choice could be incorrect; do not rationalize why it could be right. Devil's advocacy works on the SAT and ACT.

Predict the answer before you read the choices. Our PERFECT Approach advice to "solve for the answer itself" is relevant here. When the reading sections trip up a student, it is usually because he or she gets tricked by confusing answer choices, losing sight of the passage and question. A smart strategy to minimize the occurrence of this unfortunate potentiality is to not get biased by the answer choices: Predict the answer based on just the question and the passage.

You likely will not be able to find a word-for-word copy of your guess among the choices, but usually, you will find one that is close enough to vindicate[134] your prediction without needing to bother much with – or get biased by – any of the other choices. Your answer was a pure product of the passage and channeled through the question, the ideal for what we call the "passage-based answer" section of the SAT and ACT.

Naturally, there are times when you should give a serious comparative look to a couple of the answer choices if they are both rather near to your prediction. At this point, you can call upon the toolbox of clarifying questions we shared earlier: Is each choice a relevant response to the question? Is each choice precisely supported by what the corresponding text communicates? Finally, is this precise support also *complete* support – is there any passage-based evidence that the answer is wrong?

Answer prediction is also a good tool for helping to answer the rare in-context passage vocabulary question, of the form "In lines x through y, the word z most nearly means…." Do not try to find the answer choice that matches your preconceived notion of the word's definition. (Oftentimes, the test-makers choose a common word z that has alternative definitions; for example, *vet* could refer to "a health professional who cares for animals" or to "the act of checking." Thus it is better to withhold your conclusion until you look at the passage.) Head to the passage and open-mindedly read the word's context to determine its particular use there. Predict the answer on that basis. Find the choice closest to that prediction.

For questions of tone, first sort out negative versus positive, then move to nuance.
For passage-based questions that ask about an author's attitude toward a topic or his or her tone, the answer choices can almost always be sorted into categories of "positive" and "negative." Determining which of these applies usually allows you to rule out two or three of the choices, making your job easier.

The difference between a scientific journal article and a newspaper opinion piece illustrates well how to identify tone. Scientific articles are basically toneless; they can be described as "neutral" or "objective." Opinion pieces, on the other hand, characteristically brim vividly with tone; the author may be derisive[135] toward a public figure, excited about a book he or she is reviewing, or angry about a policy.

There are numerous trigger words that signal to us as readers whether an author has a non-neutral tone and then what that tone is. (From this tone, we can reasonably infer the attitude of the author.) They tend, conveniently, to be words that jump out at us as we read. They are usually adjectives, particularly subjective adjectives. Would a scientist writing in a formal journal ever describe something as "disgusting," "upsetting," "beautiful," "ugly," "shocking," or "enjoyable"? Rarely,

---

[134] SAT Word Alert: *Vindicate* (verb) means "show or prove to be right, reasonable, or justified"
[135] SAT Word Alert: *Derisive* (adjective) means "exhibiting contempt or mocking"

if ever. In other contexts, this sort of word would be commonplace and amount in totality to the author's tone.

Descriptiveness obviously transcends simple binary "positivity" and "negativity." Such a distinction is nonetheless a helpful starting point, one that can come after a mere moment of reflection after reading a passage. To differentiate with greater nuance, you must look to the tonal trigger words mentioned above. They are subjective and relate to the author's personal interpretation. When he or she describes something as "beautiful" or as any other similar adjective, the author makes an internal claim that others would be able to disagree with because their points of view vary, even if they agree on the facts and perhaps even carry a similar ultimate message. Tone is not just about what is said but also about *how*; pay attention to the adjectives that convey the latter and you will recognize the tone.

Physically engage with the passages and questions. We have two primary means of engagement in mind here. The first is to mark up your test booklet. We already mentioned the helpfulness of indicating line references before you begin to read a passage, but there is another valuable practice to try: Circle important words and phrases.

There is plenty worth circling in both the passages and the questions. If a question inquires along the lines of "All of the following except…," you should instantly circle "except." When a question or answer ever has a word that negates or indicates frequency, like "not" or "never" or "always" or "sometimes," circle that word. It is also worth pointing out here that extreme answers on the SAT and ACT – i.e., those that use words like "never" or "always" – tend to be wrong. The correct answer, as in other parts of life, is usually more nuanced.

In the passages, you can circle the tonal trigger mentioned just previously; any seemingly important adjective or other expression of the author's opinion may be worth a circle. Transitions are also words to grant some attention to. When an author shifts message or tone with any contrasting word (such as "but" or "however"), take notice and mark it. Noting emphatic indicators – like italics, dashes to offset extra thoughts, and transitions that connect ideas (for example, "therefore" and "indeed") – is also a helpful way to clarify meaning.

The second way to physically engage with the passage and questions is to use your finger. It may feel a bit silly at first, but tracking along the page with your finger as you read helps you to control your pace, stay focused on the task at hand, and avoid skipping over any important words.

Read quickly and with a purpose. While practicing, you should work to refine your pace to a point at which you read fast enough to finish the passage but not so fast that your eyes are ahead of your brain. Comprehension is imperative; read actively but not in a panic. This will ensure the appropriate balance of time management so that you do not attain an understanding of the passage but lack time to apply it to the questions.

Practice, practice, practice. Practice helps enormously on the reading sections of the SAT and ACT. Knowing the best strategies in the world does you little good if you walk into the test center without any experience in applying them. Strongly favor the use of official practice tests over unofficial ones: Unofficial tests usually are not counterproductive (though some particularly bad ones can be), but nothing beats tests from the people who write the real thing.

When you are practicing, understand the answers and how to get them. This advice, which we shared in our PERFECT Approach, warrants reiteration. The ability to confidently, consistently, and correctly distinguish among the aforementioned choices that seem quite similar can only come through repeated practice, ideally with questions written by the people who work for the College Board or ACT. Do not move past a practice test until you are comfortable with the reasoning for each correct answer, and do not read that reasoning until you have spent time on your own trying to understand why a choice is correct and the others are wrong.

Love the passage.

> *It is well to read everything of something, and something of everything.*
> Henry P. Brougham (1778-1868)
> Lord Chancellor of Great Britain

If you are uninterested in what you are reading, you will not be able to retain its content or understand its message as well as you would otherwise. Let us rephrase: If you cannot *fool yourself* into thinking that you like what you are reading, you will not do as well. The topics are not ordinarily particularly interesting, and this brings many students to read the text lazily and slowly. If you can convince yourself that you are keenly aroused by the topic and hang onto every word as if it were divine revelation, you will read much more quickly without compromising comprehension. This will not be accomplished easily at first, but soon it will become natural.

We also strongly encourage you to read broadly and to thoroughly expose yourself to a wide range of writing styles and ideas. Read everything from the *Economist* to *Sports Illustrated* to *Better Homes and Gardens*; not only will you improve your speed and comprehension, you may also learn a thing or two and set yourself up as a great conversationalist.

Skill in reading will surely assist you in college and beyond.

CHAPTER 7
MASTERING THE ENGLISH AND WRITING SECTIONS

Grammar is the logic of speech, even as logic is the grammar of reason.
Richard C. Trench (1807-1886)
Anglican Archbishop and Poet

As shared in Chapter 2, "Getting to Know the Tests," these are the key things to remember about the format of the ACT and SAT's English and Writing sections:

The Writing section of the SAT is 70 minutes long, composed of three subsections – two 25 minutes long and one 10 minutes long. There are 25 Improving Sentences questions, 18 Identifying Errors questions, 6 Improving Paragraphs questions, and one essay, which occupies one of the 25-minute subsections – 49 questions overall, in addition to the essay.

The English section of the ACT is 45 minutes long. 75 questions are said to be divided between those testing rhetorical skills and issues of usage and mechanics.

The optional Writing section of the ACT is 30 minutes for one essay.

For simplicity of reference, hereafter we will refer to the multiple-choice portions of the English and Writing sections of the SAT and ACT as "the English sections" and to the essays as, clearly enough, "the essay sections." In keeping with that –

English

Humans have the special capacity to conceive unusually complex thoughts. The standardized tests' reading sections assess your ability to interpret and analyze the written forms of these thoughts and the intentions behind them. The math sections are based upon logical conceptualizations – often numerical – of those thoughts, and the science section presents ideas that have been formed through observation and the application of mathematics.

Communication is our way of sharing thoughts. Among the forms of communication, language allows for the most precise conveyance of abstract ideas. In order for a language to be generally understandable by its speakers and writers, it must be standardized through grammar.

The English sections of the SAT and ACT test your ability to distinguish clear practices of communication from unclear practices of communication. *Clear* here may mean something different from what you initially interpret, however. Consider this sentence:

Three of my Brothers' is more hungrier then me is.

Actually, we might be better off calling this a feeble attempt at a sentence: It is bulged with seven grammatical blunders, whose corrections yield

> Three of my brothers are hungrier than I am.

But you probably already knew that, because you understood what the original sentence was *trying* to say; the communication itself was clear in this case, despite not conforming to the formal grammar of English. (The original sentence would be decidedly incorrect on both the SAT and ACT!)

However, these instances when meaning can be conveyed using improper grammar are the exception, not the rule. Nor is clarity the only relevant consideration for communication. For example, there are times when improper diction distorts meaning, when incorrect verb conjugation leads to misinterpretation, and when misused punctuation obscures or changes the meaning that one is trying to convey.

And even if your (willful or otherwise) ungrammatical habits lead only rarely to miscommunication, that one of your listeners or readers will be slowed down in interpreting what you convey, distracted by the errors, or therefore hold a negative impression of your ability to communicate is all but inevitable.

The writers of the SAT and ACT, at least, seem to think so. The English sections of the tests are a bit unfair, though: Depending on how grammatically those around you speak and write – which is correlated with, among other factors, race and family/community affluence – you will have a better or worse mental "ear" for what is right.

And this has important implications for students' performances on the test, since most people's approach to the questions is to simply ask *Does this sound right?* They tend not to engage any analytical skills or pull from their (usually underdeveloped) knowledge of English grammar.

If you fall in the privileged group of students whose peers and family observe the rules of grammar to a better-than-average extent, using the ear method can serve you fairly well, as long as your goal is to earn a score that at least slightly bests the national average because you can answer the moderately challenging questions yet not those that are designed to fool those using the ear method.

But if you want a great score regardless of your previous exposure, you will need to familiarize yourself with grammar. Most guides to the SAT and ACT English sections significantly simplify the relevant grammar to make the material friendlier, more approachable. These guides often succeed in improving students' scores to some point – a point well below mastery – but don't provide a solid, objective foundation for a confident approach to the Writing section and are certainly not comprehensive.

Because grammatical parlance relies on terminology that most people don't use when thinking about language, grammar is intimidating to many. Don't let yourself be one of these people!

We don't believe that in trying to teach test-takers to distinguish between good and bad grammar, we have to avoid teaching grammar itself. Consistent with its goal to standardize language communication, grammar is a fixed set of mostly objective rules that can be mastered and that – as it relates to the SAT and ACT – is tested in a predictable way, in which certain skills are assessed recurrently. And although grammatical terms are helpful in explaining and in turn conceptually organizing the material, neither the SAT nor the ACT will ever explicitly test your familiarity with the terms. (Keep that fact – that grammatical terms will never appear on the SAT or ACT – in mind as you decide what method for studying the following material works best for you.)

For these reasons, students often find that, once the underlying grammatical knowledge and skills have been learned, improving on the Writing section is merely a matter of taking some practice tests to get good at applying that foundation. The results are quickly rewarding both for their performance on the SAT and ACT and for the general communication of their thoughts.

Before we get started – and consistent with our goal of providing a rigorous but understandable guide to the English sections – we will provide an overview of the error concepts we discuss to whet your appetite for mastery of the material. Hopefully, this helps clarify the organization, too. In parentheses we note the label we have assigned to that error; underlined are the parts of the sentences most relevant to the respective errors.

1. Pronoun Errors

> **(1A)** Shifts in Person: An inappropriate, mid-sentence change in a pronoun's relationship to the writer.
>> Erroneous: When <u>you</u> brush <u>your</u> teeth, <u>one</u> must be circumspect.
>> Fixed: When <u>one</u> brushes <u>his or her</u> teeth, <u>he or she</u> must be circumspect.
> **(1B)** Shifts in Number: Referring to a singular entity with a plural noun or pronoun, or vice-versa.
>> Erroneous: I witnessed the <u>kid</u> swimming quickly across the pond, and <u>they</u> looked like a large fish.
>> Fixed: I witnessed the <u>kid</u> swimming quickly across the pond, and <u>she</u> looked like a large fish.
> **(1C)** Case Errors in Comparisons: Comparing two entities that are written in different cases.
>> Erroneous: <u>She</u> is much scarier than <u>me</u>.
>> Fixed: <u>She</u> is much scarier than <u>I am</u>.

(**1D**) Case Errors with Relative Pronouns: Using subjects *who* or *whoever* instead of objects *whom* or *whomever*, or vice-versa.

Erroneous: <u>Whoever</u> the officer summons must report happily to court.

Fixed: <u>Whomever</u> the officer summons must report happily to court.

(**1E**) Errors in Forming the Possessive Case: Failing to properly punctuate and distinguish between joint and discrete possession.

Erroneous: <u>Bob and Mike's</u> apartments were close to each other.

Fixed: <u>Bob's and Mike's</u> apartments were close to each other.

(**1F**) Case Errors with Compound Nouns: Failing to preserve correct case among each noun within a series of nouns.

Erroneous: <u>The turtle, the frog, and me</u> quickly became friends.

Fixed: <u>The turtle, the frog, and I</u> quickly became friends.

(**1G**) Case Errors with Appositives: Failing to use the same case for an appositive and what the appositive is describing or defining.

Erroneous: <u>Us</u> humans sure are helpful people.

Fixed: <u>We</u> humans sure are helpful people.

(**1H**) Errors with Ambiguous or Nonexistent Pronoun References: Ambiguity of the noun to which a pronoun intends to refer.

Erroneous: Walk to the table with the coffee mug and then clean <u>it</u> thoroughly.

Fixed: Walk to the table with the coffee mug and then clean <u>the mug</u> thoroughly.

2. Adjective Errors

(**2A**) Comparative and Superlative Errors with Adjectives: Failure to distinguish between proper uses for comparative and superlative adjective forms.

Erroneous: Between her and her sister, Samantha was born the <u>earliest</u>.

Fixed: Between her and her sister, Samantha was born <u>earlier</u>.

(**2B**) Diction Errors: Semantic misuse of a word.

Erroneous: <u>All together</u>, the day went pretty well.

Fixed: <u>Altogether</u>, the day went pretty well.

3. Adverb Errors

(**3A**) Adverb Placement Errors: Placing an adverb further away from the intended object of modification than is necessary, yielding semantic distortion.

Erroneous: I <u>only </u>owe them one dollar.

Fixed: I owe them <u>only</u> one dollar.

(3B) Errors in Distinguishing between Adverbs and Adjectives: Failing to modify nouns with adjectives and adverbs, adjectives, and verbs with other adverbs.

> Erroneous: He paddled our canoe very <u>quick</u>.
> Fixed: He paddled our canoe very <u>quickly</u>.

(3C) Redundancy: Semantic repetition.

> Erroneous: The competition is <u>annual</u> and will be held <u>every year</u>.
> Fixed: The competition is <u>annual</u>.

(3D) Comparative and Superlative Errors with Adverbs: Failing to correctly distinguish between proper uses for comparative and superlative adverb forms or failing to form the comparative or superlative correctly.

> Erroneous: She taps the keys <u>softer</u> than she should.
> Fixed: She taps the keys <u>more softly</u> than she should.

4. Preposition Errors

(4A) Idiom Errors: Misuse of customary preposition after an adjective or adverb.

> Erroneous: Gordo was <u>desirous for</u> some money.
> Fixed: Gordo was <u>desirous of</u> some money.

(4B) Case Errors with Prepositional Phrases: Using the subjective case instead of the objective case for prepositional objects.

> Erroneous: Only between <u>she and mom</u> will the battle rage.
> Fixed: Only between <u>her and mom</u> will the battle rage.

5. Verb Errors

(5A) Subject-Verb Disagreement: Failure to preserve consistency of number and person between verb conjugation and subject. There are many ways to mess up subject-verb agreement; you'll learn them all.

> Erroneous: Neither the Smiths nor their butler <u>know</u> the answer to the riddle.
> Fixed: Neither the Smiths nor their butler <u>knows</u> the answer to the riddle.

(5B) Errors with the Subjunctive Mood: Failure to recognize need for the subjunctive mood and form it properly.

> Erroneous: If Bob <u>was</u> here, he would know what to do.
> Fixed: If Bob <u>were</u> here, we would know what to do.

(5C) Using the Wrong Tense: Using a tense to mean something other than the tense may function to mean.

> Erroneous: Since last year, I <u>will have been</u> a great painter.
> Fixed: Since last year, I <u>have been</u> a great painter.

(5D) Past Participle Errors: Failure to recognize need for past participle in perfect tenses and then form it properly.

Erroneous: My frog <u>has swam</u> in the Olympics three times.

Fixed: My frog <u>has swum</u> in the Olympics three times.

(5E) Passive Voice and Wordiness: Excessive wordiness resulting from use of passive voice or other undesirable construction.

Wordy: The avocado sandwich that was eaten by me was thought by me to be decadent.

Fixed: I thought that the avocado sandwich that I ate was decadent.

(**5F**) Inconsistent Tenses: Failing to ensure logical consistency of tense in a sentence.

Wordy: The show began in the morning, and by midday, it <u>had been</u> excellent.

Fixed: The show began in the morning, and by midday, it <u>had become</u> excellent.

6. Verbal Errors

(**6A**) Mismodification: Use of modifiers, like present participles, squinting adverbs, and prepositional phrases, such that ambiguous or wrong modification results.

Erroneous: <u>Having stolen</u> the answer key, the test was easy for me.

Fixed: <u>Having stolen</u> the answer key, <u>I</u> found the test easy.

(**6B**) Believing Myths: Thinking that using split infinitives or ending a sentence with a preposition is wrong.

Correct: <u>To boldly go</u> where few have gone sounds scary.

Also correct: <u>To go boldly</u> where few have gone sounds scary.

(**6C**) Errors in Choosing between Gerund and Infinitive Complements: Not knowing whether a verb takes a gerund or infinitive complement.

Erroneous: The camels <u>dislike to paint</u> the warehouse.

Fixed: The camels <u>dislike painting</u> the warehouse.

7. Conjunction Errors

(**7A**) Illogical Conjunctions: Failure to ensure that conjunctions are used such that their meanings are respected rather than used nonsensically or redundantly.

Erroneous: <u>Because</u> I was ready, I <u>thus</u> commenced the jog.

Fixed: <u>Because</u> I was ready, I commenced the jog.

(**7B**) Errors with Syntax: Fundamental deviation from the standard form of a proper sentence.

Erroneous: Although the art was uninspired and so it also lacked impact on its viewer.

Fixed: The art was uninspired, so it lacked impact on its viewer.

(**7C**) Lack of Parallelism: Structurally relating phrases that are not in consistent grammatical form.

Erroneous: Both <u>to ski</u> and <u>fishing</u> can make a fine weekend.

Fixed: Both <u>skiing</u> and <u>fishing</u> can make a fine weekend.

8. Punctuation Errors

(**8A**) Comma Errors: Using a comma where one does not belong or improperly omitting one.

Erroneous: His best friend Waldo was a sly dog.

Fixed: His best friend, Waldo, was a sly dog.

(8B) Colon Errors: Failing to precede a colon with an independent clause or follow it with an independent clause or list.

    Erroneous: My favorite items are: paint, a ceiling, and a floor.

    Fixed: My favorite items are paint, a ceiling, and a floor.

(8C) Semicolon Errors: Using a semicolon other than to connect two independent clauses or to form a complex list.

    Erroneous: I love it when that happens; always lots of fun.

    Fixed: I love it when that happens; it's always lots of fun.

Grammar

For the most part, we will try to organize the content by what seems to be the most relevant part of speech and define (and sometimes redefine) any technical terms as we go along. Errors will be labeled with a number and letter to make the organization clearer and for reference. As you will see, some parts of speech are relevant to more errors than are others.

Pronoun Errors (1)

A *pronoun* is a word that takes the place of a noun, to which it refers. *She* and *it* are examples of pronouns.

Shifts in Person *(1A)*

In brief, the grammatical *person* refers to the nature of the referent of a pronoun, in context. Fortunately, though, you do not need to really understand the fundamental concept of person; you need merely to be able to recognize what person a pronoun is in.

There are three distinct persons:

> *First-person* pronouns refer at least in part to the speaker or writer. They are *I, me, my, mine, myself, we, us, our, ours,* and *ourselves.*

> *Second-person* pronouns refer at least in part to the listener or reader. They are *you, your, yours, yourself,* and *yourselves.*

> *Third-person* pronouns refer to a person or thing other than the types for first- and second-person pronouns. They are *he, him, himself, his, she, her, herself, hers, her, it, itself, its, one, one's, they, them, themselves, theirs,* and *their.* All non-pronoun nouns, like *hat,* can also be considered third-person.

Pronoun references to the same person or thing should be in the same grammatical person. The tests may shift between persons within a sentence in order to see whether you notice the error.

Note, however, that not all shifts of person are erroneous; logic should drive your consideration here: *Are the pronouns that are in different persons even meaning to refer to the same thing?* If not, the shift is grammatically correct, if it is logically so.

Here is a sentence whose shift is *ungrammatical*:

> If **one** strives to be a great sorter of colorful hats, **you** must spend years in dedicated training at the hat factory.

Through logical inference, we can assume reasonably that the writer of the sentence intends for *one* and *you* to refer to the same hypothetical person who may aspire to sort hats. As indicated earlier, though, *one* is in the third person – unlike *you*, whose person is second. Therefore, the sentence commits an ungrammatical shift in person, from third to second. So it is incorrect.

The shift from *one* to *you* and vice-versa is the most common case of this type of error, particularly as tested on the SAT.

Here is an example of the aforementioned cases in which a shift in person is *acceptable*:

> If **you** do not do the laundry by the time the cake is done, **I** will be forced to melt the cake to spite you.

The subject *I* in the second clause is clearly meant to be a different person than the *you* whom the writer initially addresses, so the shift here is logically sound. Remember that only pronoun references to the same person or thing must be in the same grammatical person.

Another common form of this error type involves shifting from a general noun – that is, a noun that could be any one person or thing – to *you*, as in

> A **speaker** must be well-prepared, but **you** must not be so prepared that the pile of lies that you speak sounds overly calculated to deceive.

It is reasonable to assume that *speaker* and *you* intend to refer similarly to a hypothetical speaker. *Speaker* is in the third person; *you* is in the second person. This disconnect is incorrect. Correct the sentence like so:

> A **speaker** must be well-prepared, but **he or she** must not be so prepared that the pile of lies that he or she speaks sounds overly calculated to deceive.

In addition (but for subtly different reasons), a shift from a general noun to the pronoun *one* is also incorrect. This is due not precisely to a shift in person (both *one* and, for example, *speaker* are in the third person) but to the differing natures of reference: Whereas *speaker* here refers generally to a hypothetical speaker, *one* refers even more generally to any person – whether or not he or she gives speeches.

That logical shift is also incorrect, even though the person is consistent. When a pronoun reference is made to a general noun, such as *speaker* in this context, *you* and *one* must be avoided in favor of the appropriately referential pronoun phrase *his or her*. Here is an example of an incorrect shift:

> The **writer** who rips up **one's** own manuscript spawns a cycle of wasted time.

Corrected, the sentence reads

> The **writer** who rips up **his or her** own manuscript spawns a cycle of wasted time.

Shifts in Number *(1B)*

Grammatical *number* is a clearer concept than *person*: A noun or pronoun is singular when it represents a single person or thing, and a noun or pronoun is plural when it represents more than one person or thing.

As with shifts in person, those in number must be logically consistent. You will likely be able to easily recognize illogical number shifts as errors, as long as you are on the lookout.

The most common manifestation of the need to preserve number occurs with *they* and its inflections: *them, their, themselves,* and *theirs*. Although most people frequently use those words to refer to a singular person, on the SAT and ACT this is considered erroneous; on those tests, ***they* and its inflections are always plural**, so a singular reference using *they* represents an illogical shift in number. This error is frequently tested, so ingrain it in your mind.

Here are some sentences that exemplify *incorrect* shifts in number:

> The acorn-less **squirrels** stopped the squadron of skunks when the skunks stole **his** specially selected acorns. (Change to *their*.)

> **Everybody** needs to consume **their** nutrients in order to live. (Change to *his or her*.)

> The remorseful **boy** returned the hundred dollars that **they** had stolen from **their** teacher. (Change to *he* and *his*, respectively)

---

[136] SAT Word Alert: *Garrulous* (adjective) means "excessively talkative"

The garrulous[136] **sandwich**, after returning from the Panini conference, had much to say about **their** adventure. (Change to *his or her*.)

The **agency** is about to begin **their** evaluation of the nominees. (Change to *its*.)

Now, one may argue that the last two sentences are potentially correct because *they* and *their* could be referring to a group that is not specified within the given sentences. While that is validly a technical possibility, the benefit of the doubt for pronoun references on the SAT and ACT is not to be given: Unless the context makes the reference to plural entities clear, *they* and *there* can be presumed incorrect.

Errors in number need not involve pronouns and are not necessarily even shifts. Again, a keen eye for recognizing illogical number will help you to notice these errors. Here is one such error:

Given the time difference, it was miraculous that all of the world's seven billion **people** woke up from their **bed** at the same moment.

It seems unlikely that the entire world population is cozy enough to share one bed, so this sentence is wrong because *bed* should be pluralized. Here is another example:

Americans everywhere want to have sufficient food and be able to afford a nice **home**.

Each American strives to be able to purchase a nice home; *all* Americans would need multiple homes in totality to be satisfied. We can fix the error in multiple ways; here is one correct rewrite:

Every American wants to have sufficient food and be able to afford a nice **home**.

Case Errors in Comparisons *(1C)*

First, a terminology introduction: Grammatical *case* is determined by a noun's or pronoun's function in a sentence. There are three possible cases:

A pronoun is in the *subjective* (alternatively dubbed *nominative*) case when it is acting as a verb's subject. Think of it as the "subject case." These pronouns may *act* or *be* (in a state). The subjective pronouns are *I, you, he, she, it, was, they, who*, and *whoever*.

A pronoun is in the *objective* (or *accusative*) case when it is a verb's or preposition's object. Think "object case." These pronouns may be *acted upon*. They are *me, you, him, her, it, us, them, whom*, and *whomever*.

A pronoun is in the *possessive* (or *genitive*) case when it modifies a noun. These pronouns are *my, mine, your, yours, his, her, hers, its, our, ours, their, theirs, whose,* and *whosever*.

Being able to recognize the case of a noun is important, because nouns (unlike pronouns) do not visibly inflect; in other words, nouns do not look different for different cases. *Sandwich* is *sandwich,* whether I am eating a sandwich (object case) or a sandwich (subject case) is eating me. (Possessive nouns are easy to recognize, because they should have apostrophes.)

Here are some nouns, followed by indications of their case:

The **water** fell down into a pool of sad, misplaced jellyfish. (subject of *fell*)

Bob ate some ham. (subject of *ate*)

I smashed the glass wall, and **it** broke up into shards. (subject of *smashed,* then *broke*)

The pre-ham pig bit **Bob**. (object of *bit*)

I gave him some **jellyfish jelly** for his sandwich, and he sang. (object of *gave*)

Just in time to catch the scheduling **mistake**, Sid reviewed the **flight plans**. (object of *catch*, then *reviewed*)

Bob's ham tastes good. (possessive modifier of *ham*)

I snagged **her** shoes. (possessive modifier of *shoes*)

Alright, now for the error: case errors in comparisons. In colloquial speech, it is common for us to use the objective case instead of the subjective case in the second part of a comparison, as in

I always knew that you were so much smarter than **him**.

To the ears of most people taking the SAT or ACT, this sentence sounds fine. But technically – as well as for purposes of the SAT and ACT – this sentence is not fine: *Him* should be *he is*.

Why is that? In order to understand why, you must consider what exactly is being compared. Are we comparing, in a strictly grammatical sense, *you* to *him*? No. Instead, we are comparing how smart you are to how smart he is. These are actions or states, for which we use pronouns in the subjective case. Written out fully, the original, incorrect sentence would read

I always knew that you were so much smarter than **him is**.

Now it should be clear that the subjective-case alternative, *he*, is needed: "…than he" or "…than he is" are both acceptable. **In general, the two entities involved in the comparison need to be in the same case.** Consider this sentence:

I like **him** more than **her**.

This time, it may truly be *him* and *her* that are directly, grammatically involved in the comparison, and not some relevant action thereof as before. Therefore, the objective case of *him* and *her* may be correct. The intended meaning may be that the writer likes *him* more than the writer likes *her*. For that meaning, the sentence is correct.

This is not a merely pedantic[137] concern: Sometimes the conveyed meaning can be changed by what case we use. Here is an alternative to the previous example sentence, in which the intended meaning is now apparently different:

I like him more than **she**.

Now we are comparing *I* with *she* in terms of their likes. This sentence means that *I* like him more than *she* does. "Does" may be omitted, as "is" could have been in the example sentence above pertaining to smartness.

Case Errors with Relative Pronouns *(1D)*

A *relative pronoun* is used to link a noun to a clause (called a *relative clause*, which is an adjectival type of dependent clause) that describes that noun. Here is an example of a sentence containing a relative pronoun, which in this case is *that*:

The hat **that I wear** suits me as a cherry suits a photogenic sundae.

The relative clause *that I wear* is describing *hat*; it tells the reader to which particular hat the writer refers. Relative clauses will be discussed further later, but for now the only relevant aspect is the relative pronoun.

Even though relative pronouns serve a linking function (the description to the noun), they still must be in the proper grammatical case themselves. The subjective relative pronouns are *who* and *whoever*; the objective relative pronouns are *whom* and *whomever*; the relative pronouns that can be in either the subjective or objective case without visibly inflecting are *that*, *which*, and *whichever*; and the possessive relative pronouns are *whose* and *whosever*.

One common problem involving case and relative pronouns is that *who* (or *whoever*) is used when, instead, *whom* (or *whomever*) ought to be used.

---

[137] SAT Word Alert: *Pedantic* (adjective) means "overly concerned with formalisms"

Remember that *who* is in the subjective case, meaning that it must be the subject of a verb. If you can't answer the question *What verb (in the relative clause) is this* who *the subject of?*, it probably isn't a subject, so the object *whom* or *whomever* should be substituted. Here are two correct examples of each case:

The person **whom he hugged** soon resembled a blueberry. (Subject is *he*.)

The brother **whom she made fun of** left behind a bitter taste. (Subject is *she*.)

The person **who hugs much** also eats many blueberries. (*Who* is subject of *hugs*.)

The brother **who likes bitter foods** has lots of fun. (*Who* is subject of *likes*.)

What we have thus far referred to as relative pronouns have two functions other than relativizing clauses as above. First, *whoever* and *whomever* can be used to nominalize clauses, which is to say that they can create *noun clauses*. The clause – for example, *She wants to build a snow fort* – can be nominalized by a relative pronoun:

Whoever wants to build a snow fort should join me in the igloo.

In that sentence, the noun clause serves as the subject of *should join*. The second additional use for relative pronouns is interrogative: They can be used to frame questions. For example:

Who is preparing my seafood salad?

Who thinks they have the fortitude to beat me?

As with relative clauses, for both of these additional uses for relative pronouns, care must be taken to ensure the proper case is used. Often, the subjective case is our default. In these sentences, though, the subjective case is incorrect:

Incorrect: **Who** do I need to send this message to?

Correct: **Whom** do I need to send this message to? (*Whom* is object of *send this message to*)

Incorrect: **Who** should I proclaim as my new secretary?

Correct: **Whom** should I proclaim as my new secretary? (*Whom* is object of *proclaim*)

Incorrect: I will send the package to **whoever she selects**.

Correct: I will send the package to **whomever she selects**. (*Whomever* is object of *selects*)

Incorrect: The alligator will consume **whoever it desires**.

Correct: The alligator will consume **whomever it desires**. (*Whomever* is object of *desires*)

Sometimes, though, our ear would suggest the objective case when the subjective case is in fact correct.

This may occur when we have a noun clause, as in the last two example sentences. The analysis to determine whether *whoever* or *whomever* should be used must be done internally within the noun clause rather than be based on whether the noun clause is itself functioning as a subject or object within the sentence. (That in both of the last two example sentences, the noun clauses were objects and the object *whomever* was appropriate is merely incidental.)

An example in which both the noun clause and pronoun are subjects:

Whoever slams the door will be punished. (*Whoever* is subject of *slams*)

An example in which the noun clause is a subject and the pronoun is an object:

Whomever I arrest will face years of solitary confinement. (*Whomever* is object of *arrest*)

An example in which the noun clause is an object and the pronoun is a subject:

The reporter will grant an interview to **whoever wins the lottery**.
(*Whoever* is subject of *wins*)

An example in which the noun clause is an object and the pronoun is an object:

The speakers' quality will shock **whomever they are placed near**.
(*Whomever* is object of *placed near*)

In each case, it is critical to identify whether the nominalizing pronoun is the subject of any verb. If it is, the subject *whoever* is appropriate; otherwise, use the object *whomever*.

To review this error class: The relative pronouns that are case-sensitive are *who, whoever, whom*, and *whomever*. (The case-insensitive relative pronouns are *that, which*, and *whichever*. The possessive relative pronouns are *whose* and *whosever*.) *Who* and *whoever* are subjects of verbs; *whom* and *whomever* are objects.

In interpreting relative clauses (dependent clauses linked to by relative pronouns) and interrogative sentences, ensure proper distinction between *who* and *whom*.

When a relative pronoun nominalizes a clause, careful differentiation within the resulting noun clause as to the role of the pronoun (subject or object) is needed to determine whether *whoever* or *whomever* is correct.

This was our most challenging coverage yet in this chapter, so it is perfectly fine if you need to go back and reread the example sentences to solidify understanding. We hope that you are managing to sludge through this material; we believe it gets more interesting the more you learn along the way.

To sum it up: *who* or *whoever* performs an action or is in a state, so it must be the subject of a verb; *whom* or *whomever* is the object of a verb – some action is performed onto it, one could say.

Errors in Forming the Possessive Case *(1E)*

Typically, formation of the possessive case poses no problems to those who are careful. To form the possessive case of a singular noun that does not end in *s*, such as *manatee*, we add an *s* proceeded by an apostrophe, forming *manatee's*. To render possessive a singular noun that already ends in *s*, simply add an apostrophe to the end of the word. *Means*, for example, becomes *means'*. This rule works for all common nouns (rather than proper nouns); the SAT or ACT will not test your ability to form the possessive case of a proper noun that ends in *s*.

Forming the possessive case with a plural noun that ends in *s* requires that an apostrophe be appended to the end; if the plural noun does not end in *s*, though, an apostrophe and then *s* should be added. So, respectively, *laptops* changes to *laptops'*, and *men* changes to *men's*.

But some people face difficulty when confronted with possession involving *compound nouns*, which are phrases containing two or more joined nouns, such as *Mark and Sally*. When there is possession, should the phrase be *Mark's and Sally's* or *Mark and Sally's*?

The rule to remember is that if the possession is *joint* (that is, all of the noun phrase's constituent nouns are doing the possession together), only the last noun should be in the possessive case. If the possession is *discrete* (in order words, each of the noun phrase's constituent nouns is possessing separately), each of the nouns should be in the possessive case.

Here are a couple examples:

> **Mother and Father's** hotel room is suitable to my rather modest needs and wishes.

> **Mother's and Father's** heads are hurting them.

The first sentence exemplifies joint possession; the latter sentence exhibits discrete possession, in which each parent has his or her own bothersome head.

If the possessed noun is singular, the possession must be joint: There cannot be multiple separate possessors of a single object. If the possessed noun is plural, logic must guide your determination of whether the possession is joint or discrete.

Here are two more examples of joint possession:

David and Amanda's house exists only fictitiously.

America and Canada's troops have begun to fight. (If apparent intention is to convey that a common body of troops fielded jointly by America and Canada is fighting some third party)

And two sentences exemplifying discrete possession:

My, Bob's, and Henry's hats may fall off our heads.

America's and Canada's troops have begun to fight each other.

Case Errors with Compound Nouns (1F)

All of the nouns in a compound noun must be in the same case as each other: Each noun within the series of nouns should be in the case that the noun phrase itself serves in the sentence.

This error manifests in two primary ways. First, in colloquial speech, we often incorrectly use the objective case for pronouns that are in compound nouns serving as subjects, when in fact the subjective case should be used. Here are two such situations:

Incorrect: **Roberto, Juan, and him** decided to construct an invisible shrub sculpture.

Correct: **Roberto, Juan, and he** decided to construct an invisible shrub sculpture.

Incorrect: **My friend and me** really need your help in catching this mongoose.

Correct: **My friend and I** really need your help in catching this mongoose.

The second manifestation is to use the subjective case when the objective case should be used because the noun phrase is the object of a verb or preposition, as in these examples:

Incorrect: Please hand the money to my dishonest **assistant and I**.

Correct: Please hand the money to my dishonest **assistant and me**.

Incorrect: She sang angelically for **he and I**.

Correct: She sang angelically for **him and me**.

I and *he* are not the subjects of any verbs here (neither is performing an action or being in a state), so their objective alternatives should be used.

Case Errors with Appositives *(1G)*

An *appositive* is a noun or noun phrase that is adjacent to another noun, which it describes or defines. Here are some sentences with appositives in them:

My daughter, **Mika**, is a relative of my son, **Gerald**. (Appositives of *daughter* and *son*, respectively)

Barbeque pizza, **his favorite food**, tastes good. (Appositive of *barbeque pizza*)

The relevant rule here is that appositives must be in the same case as the noun that they are describing or defining. Here are some examples of the correct application of this rule:

My spokespeople, **she and he**, are swamped after the scandal. (Appositive of subject *spokespeople*)

They lampooned my spokespeople, **her and him**, after they poorly handled the scandal. (Appositive of object *spokespeople*)

We llamas are helpful in eating food. (Appositive of subject *llamas*)

Give **us** needy people some of your supplies, or else we will be sad. (Appositive of object *needy people*)

Errors with Ambiguous or Nonexistent Pronoun References *(1H)*

A pronoun is a referential unit. It refers to a noun. It must be clear to which noun the pronoun refers; there must also be a noun for the pronoun to refer to within the text (referred to as the requirement for *endophora* over *exophora*, in which the reference is to a noun written outside the text).

Therefore, pronoun references must not be ambiguous or nonexistent. Be wary of giving the benefit of the doubt: **Ask yourself for each of the pronouns that you encounter on the English sections, *What is the referent of this pronoun?*** If there is not a clear referent for any pronoun, the pronoun is considered ungrammatical on the SAT and ACT.

Spotting errors of nonexistent pronoun reference is often no problem for those who are looking out for such a problem. Issues of ambiguity, however, are a bit tougher. Nuance of interpretation is required: The mere presence of multiple technical possibilities for what referent is meant by a pronoun does not imply logical ambiguity. This sentence, for instance, is correct:

> The computer needs a new mouse because the current **one** is too small for my hand.

Grammatically, *one* could be referring to either *computer* or *mouse* since all are singular and in the third person. But logically, the reference is clearly to *mouse*. There is no logical ambiguity, so the sentence is correct.

Perhaps a bit frustratingly, there are no objective, general guidelines for determining whether a pronoun reference is logically apparent and therefore unambiguous. The **process for identifying pronoun ambiguity** is this, though: Identify, using number and person, possible grammatical referents; consider whether a single one stands saliently as the logically correct alternative; if it does, the reference is unambiguous.

With practice, the subjectivity involved in that logical consideration will be reduced, and in its place you will have confidence in what the writers of the SAT and ACT are looking for. (We think their demonstrated subjectivity is reasonable.) Here is one traditional example in which the pronoun reference is ambiguous:

> I want to go to the mall or maybe the beach, because **they** sell great hot dogs **there**.

Neither of the marked pronouns is clear: Does the writer mean the mall or the beach? Also, *who* exactly sell great hot dogs?

Also note that we said that a pronoun ought to refer to a noun; this deliberately excludes clauses. So on the SAT and ACT, this sentence is wrong because the pronoun *that* intends here to refer to the clause *I know he likes her*:

> I know he likes her. **That** makes me, like, jealous.

There is another class of pronouns that we haven't discussed yet, called *demonstrative pronouns*. They are *this, these, that*, and *those*. Demonstrative pronouns can each also function as adjectives when placed to modify a noun. Examples of demonstrative pronouns:

> I need to buy **that**!

> **These** are the greatest manatee trading cards I have ever held.

Examples of demonstrative adjectives:

I need to buy **that** slipper!

Are **those** walrus action figures what you were looking for?

Demonstrative pronouns and adjectives, being referential, must be clear too.

There is one exception to the statement that pronouns must be referential: *Dummy pronouns* (formally called *pleonastic* or *expletive pronouns*) do not need to have clear or even existent referents. This is because they do not intend to refer to anything and serve merely as syntactic placeholders. *It* is sometimes a dummy pronoun, as when describing weather.

Here are a few examples:

What is **it** like outside?

It is a beautiful day today.

It is time for a new tomato crusher.

To identify a dummy pronoun, ask yourself whether a pronoun *intends* to refer to something. If it does not, it is a dummy pronoun and does not need a referent.

Adjective Errors (2)

An *adjective* is a word that modifies a noun or pronoun. *Hungry*, *short*, and *secretive* are adjectives.

Comparative and Superlative Errors *(2A)*

An adjective can take three forms: *positive, comparative,* and *superlative*.

The "standard" form of an adjective is its positive form – *hungry*, for example. The comparative form is most often formed by adding the suffix *–er* and is used for comparing two things. The superlative form is usually formed with the addition of the suffix *–est*; unlike the comparative form, the superlative form is for comparing three or more things.

The SAT and ACT sometimes test your ability to recognize the need to distinguish between the comparative and superlative forms. In doing so, use your knowledge that the comparative form is for comparison between two things and the superlative form is for comparison among three or more things. Some examples:

Incorrect: I can't decide which of my two hands is **strongest**.

Correct: I can't decide which of my two hands is **stronger**. *(Comparative form)*

Incorrect: Among the three children, Sally was **happier**.

Correct: Among the three children, Sally was **happiest**. *(Superlative form)*

Comparative and superlative distinction is another error whose recognition is uncomplicated but which does require you to be mindful.

Diction Errors *(2B)*

Using a word that, in context, conveys a meaning that is clearly in contrast to the intention constitutes an error in usage (also called an error in *diction*). Often, the two words will be *homophones* (words that sound the same but have different meanings and spellings), such as *to* and *too*, though this is not always the case.

Here is an adjectival diction error:

The large ape wielding the baseball bat made the small monkey **fearsome**.

Fearsome means "tending to bring about fears in others"; the more logical word is *fearful*, meaning "in fear." Correction:

The large ape wielding the baseball bat made the small monkey **fearful**.

A diction error with a homophonic gerund:

Incorrect: **Excepting** failure leads inevitably to its reproduction.

Correct: **Accepting** failure leads inevitably to its reproduction.

A particular instance of diction error regarding the aforementioned relative pronouns warrants mention here: It is to use *who* or *whom* when *which* should alternatively be used, or vice-versa. This error requires observing the formal semantic (i.e., meaning-related) purpose of each relative pronoun.

While *that* can liberally be used to link descriptions to either persons or things, *who, whom,* and *which* are more particular in their requirements: *Who* and *whom* refer to people but not things, and *which* refers to things but not people. Therefore, these two sentences are correct:

The people **that I know** are nice.

The people **whom I know** are nice.

These sentences are incorrect:

The people **which I know** are nice.

The table **whom I sat on** boldly supported my weight.

Another notable, particular error that could be considered one of diction (though really it's just improper verb conjugation through omission of the past participle) is to write "of" instead of "have." The ACT has a fondness for testing this.

Incorrect: I **would of** correctly addressed the memo to the bird if I had known!

Correct: I **would have** correctly addressed the memo to the bird if I had known!

Here are some very commonly confused word groups that you want to ensure you have straight:

You are nice. **You're** nice.

Your attitude is nice.

They are nice. **They're** nice.

Their attitude is nice.

Look over **there**!

It is nice outside. **It's** nice outside.

The **dog's** tail wagged nicely. **Its** tail wagged nicely.

Who is coming to fix this? **Who's** coming to fix this?

Whose purple hammer is this?

To elaborate on the remaining diction error potentialities would bulge this chapter beyond your (or our) delight. It is difficult to specifically prepare for questions on diction errors, because there are infinitely many ways to misuse words in the English language. Thankfully, though, errors of this sort are rare on the SAT and ACT, and they are usually simple enough to be spotted by those who are looking for them.

For those who would like to learn some of the more interesting and pervasive errors made by modern English speakers, we recommend *Common Errors in English Usage* by Paul Brians. It may help you out on the occasional SAT or ACT question. Certainly, it will improve the accuracy of your communication.

Adverb Errors (3)

An *adverb*, such as *happily*, *quickly*, or *very*, is a word that modifies another adverb, an adjective, or a verb.

Adverb Placement Errors (3A)

An adverb should generally be placed as close as possible to what it is modifying. A failure to do this is an error when ambiguity of or distortion in meaning results.

An adverb meant to generally modify the predicate of a sentence can usually be placed in myriad ways. All of the following, for example, are acceptable and have essentially identical meanings:

> **Slowly**, I unraveled the mystery around me.

> I **slowly** unraveled the mystery around me.

> I unraveled the mystery around me **slowly**.

A way in which adverb misplacement commonly occurs is to place an adverb (often *often*) before a verb when the actual intention is to modify the object of that verb, as in:

> Your father and I only want you to marry once!

As the sentence reads now, the request is to have *you* do nothing other than marry. The more reasonable intention, however, is to have *you* marry no more than once, which is conveyed by:

> Your father and I want you to marry **only** once!

If we write the following sentence, the communicated meaning is of limitation on the range of activities the writer completes:

> I drove hastily to the store and **only** arrested two perpetrators for shoplifting.

In that sentence the writer conveys that he did not do anything to the perpetrators beyond arresting them; as an intended meaning, this seems unlikely. Consider these rewritten sentences:

> I drove hastily to the store and arrested **just** two perpetrators for shoplifting.

> I drove hastily to the store and arrested two perpetrators **just** for shoplifting.

In the first of these two sentences, the adverb *just* modifies the number of perpetrators, emphasizing that no more than two were acted upon by the writer. In the latter sentence, the conveyance is that the reason for arrest was limited to shoplifting. All three sentences say similar but subtly varied things.

Because in many cases the logically inferable intention differs from the meaning imparted by an adverb's placement in a sentence, the SAT and ACT can test your ability to correct the misplacement.

Errors in Distinguishing between Adverbs and Adjectives *(3B)*

An adjective must modify a noun; modification of adjectives, verbs, and adverbs is under adverbs' purview. The SAT and ACT test whether you can recognize departures from these rules. Here are some problematic sentences:

> You did really **good** on your grammar test.

> I feel **badly** about how I punched you repeatedly.

Incorrectly, the adjective *good* there is meant to modify the verb *did*; it is describing *how* someone did. This better describes adverbial not adjectival modification, so the adverb *well* should be used instead of *good*. You probably find this first sentence rather elementary.

The second sentence is slightly less straightforward. It may seem upon initial glance that *badly* is meant to modify *feel*, thereby justifying the form of adverb-on-verb modification. In reality, though, *feel* is serving as a linking verb between *badly* and *I*; the noun *I* is truly what is being modified. The feeling itself is of badness; *badly* ought not describe how the feeling occurred. *I feel bad* is correct.

In such constructions – those in which a linking verb connects a subject to a modifier meant to describe the subject rather than the action – the descriptive word or phrase is a *predicate adjective*. (*Bad* was a predicate adjective in our example.) If the verb links a subject to a noun or phrase meant to *define* rather than *modify* the subject, the definitive word or phrase is a *predicate nominative*.

Redundancy *(3C)*

We'll group this under "Adverb Errors," because redundancy is often adverbial. But prepositions and adjectives are relevant here too.

Redundancy is incorrect on the SAT and ACT. We operationally define redundancy as repetition of meaning. Here are some examples of the type of redundancy that you should be watchful of:

> I wake up every day at 6 **a.m. in the morning**. (*a.m.* and *in the morning* repeat.)

> We will be having a **weekly** assembly **each week**. (*Weekly* and *each week* repeat.)

He is the **most unique** dog. (*Unique* encompasses the idea of *most* because there can only be one level of uniqueness.)

The third sentence fails to recognize that some adjectives are *absolute adjectives*, which means that they should not be modified in extent. *Unique* is one such word subject to denotative preclusion of mitigation or amplification; binary uniqueness or non-uniqueness is specified by *unique*'s definition as "without equal."

Similarly, differing degrees of one's being *perfect* or *dead*, for example, would be illogical outside a figurative context. Non-magnitudinal modification of absolute adjectives is acceptable, however: One can, for instance, be "possibly unique," if a writer's knowledge is limited.

Colloquially, we sometimes use more prepositions after verbs than we need. This can lead to prepositional redundancy, which is incorrect. The SAT tests this rarely but not never. The possibility is worth becoming familiar with:

Incorrect: Take the milk can **off of** my boat.

Correct: Take the milk can **off** my boat. (In nearly all standard constructions, *off of* is wrong.)

Incorrect: We regularly sort the whites **apart from** the other colors in the laundry.

Correct: We regularly sort the whites **from** the other colors in the laundry.

If a preposition can be omitted without a resultant change in meaning, drop it.

Finally, watch out for redundant double negatives. Most students easily recognize these, but don't let any slip by. An example:

Incorrect: I **hardly** did **nothing** to him.

Correct: I **hardly** did **anything** to him. *or* I did **almost nothing** to him.

Comparative and Superlative Errors with Adverbs (3D)

Recall the concept of comparative and superlative adjectives and that, for example, *better* is a comparative adjective (comparing between two people or things) and *best* is a superlative adjective (comparing among three or more people or things). Time for Comparative and Superlative Errors: Adverb Edition!

The concept applies similarly to adverbs, which can also be in a comparative or superlative form. Mistakes in forming the comparative or superlative form of an adverb arise when the adjective form of the adverb, incorrectly, is used instead of adding *more* or *most* to the adverb in order to modify it for the comparative or superlative form, respectively.

An example should clarify that guideline. Consider the adverb *quickly*. Is *quicker* the comparative form of that adverb? No, that's the comparative *adjective*. (And it's certainly not *more quicker* because that is redundant.) Instead, we ought add *more* to form the correct comparative adverb: *more quickly*. Likewise, the superlative adverb is not the adjective *quickest* or the redundant *most quickest* but rather *most quickly*. Check out these sentence pairs:

Incorrect: He eats **quickest** among the eight of us.

Correct: He eats **most quickly** among the eight of us. (Adverbial superlative form)

Incorrect: I run **speedier** than you do.

Correct: I run **more speedily** than you do. (Adverbial comparative form)

Preposition Errors (4)

Prepositions link words and phrases. Some prepositions are *in, on, above, within, before, among,* and *at.*

Idiom Errors *(4A)*

There are certain verbs that, in most constructions, must be followed by particular prepositions. Often, there is no generally applicable set of guidelines for deciding which preposition is appropriate. For example, one would have difficulty deducing that *partake in* is incorrect but that *partake of* is correct. For this reason, these so-called *phrasal verbs* (combination of verb and succeeding preposition, called a particle) can be considered *idiomatic*: They must simply be memorized.

To make this list completely clear, elaboration on other possible, rare alternatives and explanations of when which should be used would be necessary. That would consume far too much real estate for this book, though, so any curiosity in learning more about the use of a phrasal verb should be satiated via an Internet search. But illustrative of the difficult nature of idiomatic phrases, you may find conflicting accounts of what is correct.

Taking the time to read through this list several times – perhaps saying it aloud to facilitate better, more organic retention – should prepare you well for assessments of idiom errors on the SAT and ACT. Thankfully, such questions appear relatively infrequently. (Notice, too, that many of these are adjective phrases. To complete the phrasal verb, imagine a conjugation of the verb *to be* in front of the adjective.)

abide by   absent from

accuse of
accustomed to
agree on / agree upon / agree with /
agree to
afflicted with
afraid of
angry about
annoyed with / annoyed by
apologize for
apply for
approve of
argue with / argue about / argue for
arise from
arrive at
associated with
aware of
believe in
belong to
blame for

came into use
capable of
care about / care for
cater to
characteristic of
charge of
cite as
committed to
compare to / compare with / compare
against
compensation for
comply with
composed of
comprise (not comprised by or
comprised of)
concerned about
condemn as
confidence in
conform with / conform to
connected to
conscious of
consider to be (not consider as)
consist of
consistent with

contrast with
contribute to / contribute toward
convince of / convince to
count on

debate over / debate about
dedicated to
define as
depart for / depart from
depend on / depend upon
depict as
desirous of
differ from
disagree with
discriminate against / discriminate
between / discriminate among
to the dismay of
dispute over / dispute about
distinguish from
divergent from

emphasis on
enamored of
endeavor to
enter / enter into
escape from / escape to
excuse for / excuse from
at the expense of

familiar with
fascination with
fire from
fond of

guilty of
hide from
hint at
hope for / hope to / in the hope of

impose on / impose upon
inconsistent with
indebted to
indifferent to
insight into

insist on / insist upon
instrumental in
intend to
interested in
involved in / involved with

jealous of

lead to
limited to

mistrust of

object to
oblivious to
obsessed with / obsessed about
obtain from
opposed to
opposition to / opposition toward
originate in

partake of
participate in
plan on / plan to
proclaim as
pray for / pray to
predate by
preoccupation with
prepare for
prevent from
prohibit from
proud of
provide for / provide with

qualify for / qualify as

react to
reason for
recover from
regard as

related to
rely on / rely upon
resentful of / resentful toward
resort to
respond to
responsible for
result in

satisfied with / satisfied by
search for / in search of
see as
separate from
similar to
stare at
stop from
stumble upon / stumble on
subscribe to
succeed in
suffer from
superior to
suspect of
suspicious of
sympathize with

tamper with
thank for
think of
tired of
transition from / transition to
trust in
turn to / turn around

upset with / upset over

vote for / vote against

wait for
went about
work with / work for
worry about

Case Errors with Prepositional Phrases *(4B)*

Prepositional phrases comprise a preposition and its objects. Here are a couple prepositional phrases; the preposition is **bold**, and its objects are *italicized*:

Look **under** *the table* before you are eaten!

I looked **at** *her* to decide whether she would eat me.

Naturally, the objects of a prepositional phrase must be in the objective case; to use the subjective case, as in the following sentences, is *incorrect*:

I want to have a race **between** *you and I*.

I looked intently **at** *Bob and he*.

He gave the book **to** *I*.

With *who* can I share this information?

The objects should, respectively, be *you and me*, *Bob and him*, *me*, and *whom*.

Verb Errors (5)

A *verb* expresses a state or action; its *subject* is in that state or performs that action. For example, in *I split the banana*, *split* is the verb and *I* is its subject. (*Banana* is the object.)

Subject-Verb Disagreement *(5A)*

Subject-verb agreement, a topic tested highly frequently on the SAT and ACT, is founded on the idea that a verb's form should reflect the number and person of its subject. That's why the verb in *I am hungry* is different from that in *He is hungry*, despite the common singularity of subject; it's also why, despite the common first person, the verb in *I am hungry* is different from that in *We are hungry*.

Although plural subjects generally take plural verbs, there are multiple topics that are relevant to attaining a more nuanced understanding of subject-verb agreement:

Amounts are singular. Sometimes, even subjects that seem plural in form are to be treated as singular because of their precise meaning. This is the case with *amounts*, which in grammar contrast with *numbers*.

There are a couple questions to ask that will help you to distinguish between amounts and numbers: *Am I referring to specific units of something (a number) or to a general mass or concept (an amount)? Can I count the idea expressed by the noun (a number), or is the noun referring to something that is practically indiscrete (an amount)?*

A singular number and a singular amount will always take singular verbs. However, whereas a plural number will take a plural verb, an amount that is plural in form should take a singular verb. Here are some examples, in which the plural verbs' subjects are numbers and the singular verbs' subjects are amounts:

Llamas like to graze. *(number)*

Fewer beds are needed so that we have enough space. *(number)*

Five-dollar bills are nice to have. *(number)*

Five dollars is not enough to buy this hamburger. *(amount)*

Less than two hours remains in the online auction to buy a watch. *(amount)*

Nine inches is too short for this ruler. *(amount)*

Consistent with the concept of amounts, in the last three sentences we are not referring to individual units but to the singular concepts of, respectively, money, time, and length; therefore, we use singular verbs. *Five-dollar bills* is plural because we are referring not to the abstract monetary valuation but to the physical currency.

(You may have also noticed that *fewer* is used for plural numbers and that *less* is used for amounts.)

Sentences' subjects are not within prepositional phrases. It is a very common error to conjugate a verb to the plural form when a singular subject is modified by a prepositional phrase with a plural object, as in

The **color** of the trees **are** wonderfully green!

The intervening prepositional phrase *of the trees*, because the plural object *trees* is nearest to the verb *are*, confuses some students into thinking that a plural verb is appropriate. Actually, however, *of the trees* is not the subject: *Color* is and it is singular. Therefore, this sentence is instead correct:

The **color** of the trees **is** wonderfully green!

Here are some more examples of correct subject-verb agreement in sentences that contain prepositional phrases, which appear in brackets to clarify the syntax of the sentence:

The **planet** [with three moons] **has** captivated astrophysicists' interest.

The **two turtles** [under the umbrella] **are** shielded from the hail.

The **number** [of stellar grades on this transcript] **makes** me proud.

The **president**, [in addition to his close advisors], **wields** great power.

However, prepositional phrases do sometimes affect subject-verb agreement. Although the guideline that a sentence's subject is not in the prepositional phrase is correct, there are some subjects for which the prepositional phrase *is* relevant to subject-verb agreement. The subject is still not in the prepositional phrase, but in such cases the singularity or plurality of the subject is indicated by the singularity or plurality of the object of the intervening prepositional phrase. This example should clarify:

Half [of my pie] **is** gone.

Half [of my pies] **are** gone.

In both sentences, the subject is *half*. But *half* can be either singular or plural, so we must look at the object of the prepositional phrase to determine how the subject should be conjugated in any particular case. The singular *pie* yields the singular *is*; the plural *pies* yields the correspondingly plural *are*.

Other fractions and percentages fit this pattern, as in

Five percent [of birds] **lack** impressive flying skills.

Five percent [of the bird population] **takes** issue with my claim.

Some indefinite pronouns are also affected by this rule. This is discussed soon.

Collective nouns can be singular or plural. A *collective noun* is a noun that appears singular in form but that refers to multiple people or things – sometimes grouped, sometimes ungrouped. The word *group* itself is an example of a collective noun.

If the people or things are meant to be thought of as a cohesive group, the collective noun is singular. If the intention is to convey the people or things as discrete, however, the collective noun is plural. Some examples:

The team has been winning all of its games. *(singular: cohesive group)*

The team keep fighting each other. *(plural: separate team members)*

The group needs a new strategy to fight evil. *(singular: cohesive group)*

The group need to get along better. *(plural: separate group members)*

On the SAT and ACT, you should use context to inform your decision on whether the collective noun ought to be singular or plural. Singularity emphasizes the wholeness, the collectiveness, of a group; plurality suggests separateness.

Compound subjects require special attention. *Conjunctive compound nouns* are two or more nouns joined by *and*. They are usually plural, as in

The tabletop and **the table's legs** are of the same color.

The **sun** and **earth** are not of the same size.

The one circumstance that makes a conjunctive compound noun singular is to mean for the compound noun to refer to a single idea. For example:

Macaroni and cheese is a good food for eating.

Indiana Jones and the Last Crusade is not about his last crusade.

Disjunctive compound nouns are two or more nouns connected by *or*. The singularity or plurality of the verb of which the disjunctive compound noun is the subject is determined only by the noun closest to the verb. So these sentences are correct:

My boat or **the water** is malfunctioning.

My boats or **the water** is malfunctioning.

The water or **my boats** are malfunctioning.

You or **I** am needed to fix the toilet.

I or **you** are needed to fix the toilet.

The last two sentences reaffirm the idea that subject-verb agreement has two components: number as well as person. *I* agrees with *am* and *you* with *are*.

Inverted verb structures can throw you off. Verbs must agree with their subjects, even if the verb precedes the subject. Examples of *failing* to apply this rule with expletive pronouns (such as *there* and *here*) and prepositional phrases:

There **is** three things you need to know.

There **seems** to be new sheriffs in town.

Here **is** those papers.

Around the turn **is** three camels that need feeding.

On top of my house **is** children who have little sense.

The *correct* versions of these sentences:

There **are** three things you need to know.

There **seem** to be new sheriffs in town.

Here **are** those papers.

Around the turn **are** three camels that need feeding.

On top of my house **are** children who have little sense.

Memorize the correlative conjunctions. The three primary correlative conjunctions are *both...and*, *either...or*, and *neither...nor*, exampled below:

Both my client **and** his brother are crooks.

Either Chloe **or** her representative has to be present at the signing.

Neither the dog **nor** the cat has proper speech etiquette.

Both...and is always plural. As with disjunctive compound nouns, the singularity or plurality of *either...or* is determined by the singularity or plurality of the noun closest to the verb. The same is true for *neither...nor*. And – as was also the case with disjunctive compound nouns – the agreement must match in not only number but person, too. Examples:

Either the zebra **or** bears look quite cute.

Either the bears **or** the zebra looks quite cute.

Either you **or** I am rather thirsty.

Either I or you **are** rather thirsty.

The sentences would be formed similarly if *neither...nor* were used instead of *either...or*.

Learn the three categories of indefinite pronouns. For the purposes of subject-verb agreement (and that's all we really care about 'round these parts), there are three categories of indefinite pronouns.

Category One's indefinite pronouns are always *singular*, and they are *each, either, neither, much, anyone, someone, somebody, anybody, anything*, and *something*. Any intervening prepositional phrases are irrelevant. Examples:

Each of you **is** a liberally sovereign human.

Neither of the options **is** acceptable.

Something needs to be put into the spice mix.

Much of the movie **is** contrived.

Category Two's indefinite pronouns are always *plural*, and they are *few, others, many, both,* and *several.* As before, any intervening prepositional phrases do not affect subject-verb agreement. Examples:

Many of the dogs **want** to bark.

Others are on the way to reinforce the front line.

Category Three's indefinite pronouns can be singular or plural, depending on the singularity or plurality of the prepositional phrase. They are *some, any, all, most,* and *none.* Examples with *all*:

All of the show **was** pleasantly shocking.

All of the foods **were** delectable.

Errors with the Subjunctive Mood *(5B)*

Verbs can take three moods: *indicative,* which is used for questions and most statements, *imperative,* which is used to make commands, and *subjunctive.*

Clearly explaining the uses of the subjunctive mood in a general way is challenging. But in an approximate way, it is used to convey wishes, possibility, requests, and requirements; it expresses things that do not necessarily exist yet in reality.

Verbs conjugated in the subjunctive mood are often preceded by *that* or are in dependent clauses beginning in *if* when the main, independent clause contains *would.* Looking at some examples of the subjunctive should impart some understanding:

You would be a stronger person if you **were** to have more muscle.

You would have been a stronger person if you **had** had more muscle.

It almost seems as if she **were** a mean person.

It also seemed as if she **had** been a mean person.

I wish that you **be** at the movie tomorrow tonight.

I wish that you **had** been there to see the fight.

Using the Wrong Tense *(5C)*

A brief coverage of the various verb tenses is worthwhile. Following this to the letter is inadvisable, though; try instead to garner an internalized *sense* for the tenses' roles. But first, here is the verb *give* conjugated to all of the tenses:

Simple present: *I give*
Present progressive: *I am giving*
Present perfect: *I have given*
Present perfect progressive: *I have been giving*

Simple past: *I gave*
Past progressive: *I was giving*
Past perfect: *I had given*
Past perfect progressive: *I had been giving*

Simple future: *I will give*
Future progressive: *I will be giving*
Future perfect: *I will have given*
Future perfect progressive: *I will have been giving*

Present Tenses

Simple present: Refers to habitual actions (*I eat everyday*) or being *(This is my house)*. It may also be used to refer to scheduled future events *(The concert is next month)*.

Present progressive: Refers to ongoing actions *(I am working on the project right now)*. Can also refer to some future actions *(I am rewriting the composition tomorrow)*.

Present perfect: Used to refer to past actions with effects on the present and actions that occur in both the past and present. *Since* and *for* often signal the present perfect tense *(For three years, I have been an accountant; since last week, I have fasted)*.

Present perfect progressive: Refers to an action that occurs in both the past and present, with an emphasis on the ongoing nature of the action *(I have been running for over an hour)*.

Past Tenses

Simple past: Refers to past completed actions *(I ate lots of fat yesterday)*.

Past progressive: Refers to past completed actions while emphasizing the continuous nature of the actions *(I was painting the house)*.

Past perfect: Refers to a past action that occurred before another, specified past action *(He told me that he had taken the test)*. The past perfect tense is sometimes signaled by *by* *(By the time the movie came out, interest had waned)*. In constructions involving *before*, the simple past is used for the earlier action, because the relationship is encompassed by *before* *(Before we came home, we covered up the mark on the car* rather than *Before we came home, we had covered up the mark on the car)*.

Past perfect progressive: Like the past perfect tense, except with an emphasis on the ongoing nature of an action.

Future Tenses

Simple future: Refers to future actions.

Future progressive: Refers to future actions, with an emphasis on their continuity.

Future perfect: Refers to an action that, by a certain future moment in time, will be completed. Often signaled by *by (By noon tomorrow, I will have grown)*.

Future perfect progressive: Similar to future progressive, except indicates with emphasis that the action occurred prior to the specific time.

Past Participle Errors *(5D)*

The past participle is used in forming the perfect tenses. In those constructions, it follows a conjugation of *to have*, which functions as an *auxiliary* or *helping verb*:

My fish has **given** me much grief with its yelling.

Some verbs' past participles look the same as their simple past tense forms, as in

I **walked**.

I have **walked**.

The SAT and ACT test that you can recognize when the past participle should be used – which is when you have a perfect tense. This also requires knowledge of verbs' past participles. Here are some that you should know. The format is base form; simple past tense; past participle:

arise; arose; arisen

become; became; become

begin; began; begun

blow; blew; blown

break; broke; broken

choose; chose; chosen

come; came; come

dive; dived/dove; dived

do; did; done

draw; drew; drawn

drink; drank; drunk

drive; drove; driven

drown; drowned; drowned

dwell; dwelt/dwelled; dwelt/dwelled

eat; ate; eaten

fall; fell; fallen

fight; fought; fought

flee; fled; fled

fling; flung; flung

fly; flew; flown

forget; forgot; forgotten

freeze; froze; frozen
get; got; gotten

give; gave; given

go; went; gone

grow; grew; grown

hang (a thing); hung; hung

hang (a person); hanged; hanged

know; knew; known

lay; laid; laid   lead; led; led

lie (to recline); lay; lain

lie (say untruths); lied; lied

put; put; put

ride; rode; ridden

ring; rang; rung

rise; rose; risen

run; ran; run

see; saw; seen

set; set; set

shine; shone; shone

shake; shook; shaken

shrink; shrank; shrunk

shut; shut; shut

sing; sang; sung
sink; sank; sunk

sit; sat; sat

speak; spoke; spoken

spring; sprang; sprung

sting; stung; stung

strive; strove/strived; striven/strived

swear; swore; swore

swim; swam; swum
swing; swung; swung

take; took; taken

tear; tore; torn

throw; threw; thrown

wake; woke; woken

wear; wore; worn

write; wrote; written

Passive Voice and Wordiness *(5E)*

The *passive voice*, as contrasted with the *active voice*, is used when the logical subject that is performing the action of the verb is not the grammatical subject of the verb. Consider this sentence:

The fish was eaten by the sailor.

The grammatical subject for the action of eating is *the fish*. However, the person doing the eating is *the sailor*. This disconnect indicates that the sentence is in the passive voice. The true, logical subject of the action in a passive construction is either omitted or signaled by *by*.

Contrary to the claims of some, the passive voice is not ungrammatical, and the SAT and ACT do not consider use of the passive voice to be technically incorrect. But the SAT and ACT do consider ambiguity and wordiness to be incorrect. Since the passive voice often results in a lack of clarity on the verb's logical subject and in verbosity, only rarely will an acceptable sentence use the passive voice.

So your ability to recognize the passive voice should be used as a trigger for questioning the correctness of an option or sentence. If the passive voice is correct, it must be used with specific stylistic intentions to emphasize the logical object of an action.

We will cover the different question types later, but to preview with specific application: On the SAT's Identifying Errors questions, you are to select only what is incorrect. The passive voice would probably not appear in the best choice for a question type that gives you multiple options from which to pick, but don't select it as an explicit error on the error identification questions.

Inconsistent Tenses *(5F)*

This is one of those rules that are not generalizable in a meaningful way: Tenses do not always have to be the same throughout a sentence. However, the preservation of logic is necessary.

Spotting inconsistent or otherwise illogically changing tenses is dependent upon your understanding of what tenses are and having an eye for what the sentence is meaning to say.

Real-life context matters too: World War I, for example, already happened; it cannot be referred to in the future tense. These two sentences exhibit inconsistent or otherwise illogical tenses:

> Tomorrow, I **fed** my dog.

> After the movie ended, I **will begin** to restock the refrigerator.

Verbal Errors (6)

The three primary verbals – which are formally verbs but which function as other parts of speech – are participles, gerunds, and infinitives.

Mismodification *(6A)*

Present participles generally have the suffix *–ing* and function as adjectives. As such, they must modify nouns. In the phrase *walking dog*, for example, the participle *walking* is modifying the noun *dog*.

Participles and participial phrases should be placed as closely as possible to the nouns or noun phrases that they modify. So when a prepositional phrase appears at the beginning of a sentence, it should modify the subject of the sentence.

Here are some *(incorrect)* examples of a failure to observe that rule (the participle is highlighted):

> While **eating**, care should be taken to chew.

> **Considering** the budget deficit, economic pessimism is understandable.

Possible corrections:

> While **eating**, **one** should take care to chew.

> **Considering** the budget deficit, **I** understand the economic pessimism.

There are two other types of mismodification, which result in ambiguity: squinting modifiers and prepositional mismodifiers.

Squinting modifiers are adverbs placed between a subject and a verb and that could modify either of the two, so ambiguity results. An example:

Walking **slowly** results in fatigue.

Does this sentence mean to suggest that walking at a slow pace leads to fatigue or that walking (at whatever pace) leads slowly to fatigue? Clarifying corrections:

Slowly walking results in fatigue.

Walking results **slowly** in fatigue.

Prepositional mismodification results when a prepositional phrase can serve to modify more than one aspect of a sentence. Again, there is resultant ambiguity, which we don't want. An example:

I went to destroy the wall **with my car**.

Is the suggestion that *I* used his or her car to get to the location of the wall or that the car was used to destroy to the wall?

Non-Errors: Myths *(6B)*

An *infinitive* is the base form of a verb preceded by *to* – *to walk*, for example. Some hold that it is incorrect to break apart the base form and *to* with an adverb, as in *to briskly walk*. This form, called a *split infinitive*, is not actually incorrect.

Another non-error is to end a sentence with a preposition. For instance, it's fine to ask, "What sauce does this food come with?" "With what sauce does this food come" is also acceptable, though it risks emitting pretentiousness.

Take care not to fall into a real error in trying to avoid ending with a preposition. Some people repeat the preposition, using it earlier in the sentence as an apparent attempt to sound more grammatically correct but then still putting it at the end of the sentence, as in the incorrect sentence

To whom should I deliver this glorious parcel **to**?

Errors in Choosing between Gerund and Infinitive Complements *(6C)*

A gerund often looks similar to a participle because it has the suffix *–ing*. However, gerunds do not modify nouns as adjectival participles do; instead, they themselves function as nouns. In the following sentence, *sleeping* is a gerund:

Sleeping is a proven means of reducing one's tired feelings.

An infinitive or gerund that is used as the object of a verb is called a complement to that verb. An example of an infinitive complement:

I like **to stare** at cows.

And a gerund complement:

I practice **staring** at cows.

Some of the verbs that take infinitive complements have another, intervening object, as in

I forbid **you to ignore** me.

Here are some verbs that take infinitive complements, as in *agree to surrender* (words that appear on both the infinitive and gerund lists are marked with asterisks):

agree

aim

appear

arrange

ask

attempt*

be able

beg

begin*

care

choose

condescend

consent

continue*

dare

decide

deserve

detest

dislike

expect

fail

forget*

get

happen

have

hate*

hesitate

hope

hurry

intend

leap

leave

like*

long

love*

mean

neglect*

offer

ought

plan

prefer*

prepare

proceed

promise

propose

refuse

regret*

remember

say

shoot

stand*

start*

stop*

strive

swear

threaten

try

use

wait

want

wish

Verbs that take gerund complements, as in *admit stealing*:

admit	like*
advise	love*
anticipate	mind
appreciate	miss
attempt*	neglect*
avoid	permit
begin*	postpone
can't help	practice
cease	prefer*
complete	quit
consider	recall
continue*	recommend
delay	regret*
deny	remember*
detest	report
dislike	resent
enjoy	resist
escape	resume
excuse	risk
finish	spend time
forbid	stand*
forget*	start*
get through	stop*
have	suggest
hate*	tolerate
imagine	waste time

Verbs that take an infinitive and another object, as in *advise you to help*:

advise	expect
allow	forbid
ask	force
beg	have
bring	hire
build	instruct
buy	invite lead
challenge	leave
choose	let
command	like
dare	love
direct	motivate
encourage	order

pay	send
permit	teach
persuade	tell
prepare	urge
promise	want
remind	warn
require	

Attempt to develop a sense for which type of complement these verbs call for by committing it to implicit memory. Reading them aloud with a sample infinitive or gerund is helpful.

Conjunction Errors (7)

Conjunctions are in the business of hooking up words, phrases, and clauses. There are three main branches of conjunctions: *coordinating, subordinating,* and *correlative.*

The coordinating conjunctions are *and, or, nor, but, yet,* and *so.* Some subordinating conjunctions are *unless, because, although,* and *if.* Some correlative conjunctions, as previously mentioned, are *either…or, neither…nor,* and *both…and*; some others are *whether…or* and *not only…but also.* (Variations on the latter, like *not only…but,* are also acceptable.)

Illogical Conjunctions *(7A)*

Understanding the various coordinating and subordinating conjunctions' semantic implications – that is, their meanings – is important: The SAT and ACT sometimes test your ability to recognize errors in the usage of conjunctions.

Since speakers of English are familiar with all of the major conjunctions, recognizing illogicality of conjunction is merely a matter of looking for it. Some examples of *incorrect,* illogical conjunction:

> I want to get dog food, **but** I'm on my way to the pet store to get some right now.

> **Although** the man was large, he had trouble fitting in his seat.

> **Because** I am low on money, I spent lots on the car.

Possible corrections:

> I want to get dog food, **and** I'm on my way to the pet store to get some right now.

> **Because** the man was large, he had trouble fitting in his seat.

I am low on money **because** I spent lots on the car.

Redundancy is also illogical. Redundancy with conjunctions is most often due to using a *conjunctive adverb* (such as *however*, *nevertheless*, and *thus*) that means the same thing as an also used subordinating conjunction. An example:

Although he was hungry, he **nonetheless** chose to wait to eat.

I thought I needed a new computer, **but** I found out that I didn't, **however**.

Nonetheless and *however* should be omitted.

Errors with Syntax *(7B)*

Sometimes, sentences simply won't make sense on a broad grammatical level – a sentence's *syntax*, or its arrangement of phrases and clauses, will be off, often because of a misuse of conjunctions, as in

Because he wants to be a doctor and would like receive a good education.

The movie, which has lots of gory scenes, but it was praised by many conservative critics.

The first sentence is merely an introductory adverbial clause, one that cannot stand independently. It is a fragment. The second sentence begins with a noun phrase that never ends up being the subject of any verb, followed by a relative clause, which is connected improperly with a conjunction to an independent clause. Both sentences clearly ring as wrong in the ear. Possible corrections:

Because he wants to be a doctor, he wants to receive a good education.

The movie, which has lots of gory scenes, was nonetheless praised by many conservative critics.

A fluency in English should suffice for recognition of fundamentally faulty syntax. Just watch for it.

Lack of Parallelism *(7C)*

Parallelism refers to the need for phrases that are used in similar structural ways to be parallel, or balanced, in form.

There is no meaningful way to speak generally of when parallelism is needed and what exactly constitutes a breach of parallelism. That does not, however, stop the SAT and ACT from testing knowledge of parallelism. In order to help you to form a good general sense of the concept, we will go through some specific cases.

Just to justify organizing parallelism under conjunctions, we'll first cover parallelism as it applies to correlative conjunctions: The phrase that appears after the trigger for the correlative conjunction pair (such as *either* or *not only*) must be parallel with the phrase that appears after the coordinating conjunction. A few examples of a *lack of parallelism*:

People should not only **eat less** but **they should exercise more**.

I want both **to walk** and **run**.

I like neither **falling** nor **to get hurt**.

I don't know whether they will **fail** or **if success is in their future**.

The first sentence is incorrect because the subject *they* appears in the second phrase but not the first: The latter is a clause and the former only a predicate, which is not parallel. Similarly, the second sentence is incorrect, because *to* appears in the first phrase but not the second. That the third sentence is incorrect demonstrates that infinitives are not parallel to gerunds. Corrections:

People should not only **eat less** but also **exercise more**. *or*

Not only **should people eat less** but **they should exercise more**.

I want to both **walk** and **run**. *or*

I want both **to walk** and **to run**.

I like neither **falling** nor **getting hurt**. *or*

I like neither **to fall** nor **to get hurt**.

I don't know whether they will **fail** or **succeed**.

The other major application of parallelism is to lists – most commonly of adverbs, verbs, clauses, and verbals (gerunds or infinitives). Examples that are *not parallel*:

He ran **quickly**, **swiftly**, and **without much effort**.

She **started** the project, **worked** on it for hours, and **it was finished** by 10:00 p.m.

I know that **you need to breathe**, that **you should probably eat**, and **to think**.

I like **fixing**, **to repair**, and **reworking**.

Corrections:

He ran **quickly**, **swiftly**, and **effortlessly**.

She **started** the project, **worked** on it for hours, and **finished** it by 10:00 p.m.

I know that **you need to breathe**, that **you should probably eat**, and that **you should think**.

I like **fixing**, **repairing**, and **reworking**.

Logical parallelism must also be preserved in comparisons. Only grammatically alike things may be compared, and the nature of the comparison should make sense. Two *incorrect* examples:

Salad is better than any food in the whole world.

Salad's taste is superior to any other food.

On the first sentence: Salad is a food, and it cannot be better than a composite of which it is a constituent; so the phrase should be *any other food* instead of merely *any food*. The comparison in the second sentence is illogical because a taste cannot be compared to a food – only to other tastes. Corrections:

Salad is better than any **other** food in the whole world.

Salad's taste is superior to **that of** any other food. *Or*

Salad's taste is superior to any other **food's**.

One more example, in which both errors – redundancy by category comparison and lack of logically parallel comparison – show up:

Incorrect: Those in the Martian army were more zealous than **any army in the galaxy**.

Correct: Those in the Martian army were more zealous than **those in any other army in the galaxy**.

Punctuation Errors (8)

Punctuation, such as commas and periods, is more important to know for the ACT than for the SAT, though an understanding of punctuation will help you to eliminate some choices on the SAT's Improving Sentences questions. (Punctuation will not be tested on the SAT's Identifying Errors questions.)

Comma Errors *(8A)*

Commas (,) serve many purposes, the most commonly tested of which are

Connecting items in a list. Contrary to some people's practice, the SAT and ACT require that a comma be placed before the *and* preceding the final item of the list, as in

I possess apples, sandwiches**,** and pasta.

This is known as the Oxford comma.

Connecting independent clauses when there is a coordinating conjunction. An independent clause is one that can stand alone. *Because he is hungry*, for example, is a dependent clause because it cannot stand alone, but the independent clause *He is hungry* can.

When you have two independent clauses and would like to join them in one sentence, connect them with a coordinating conjunction and a comma, as in

He is hungry**, and** she needs water.

The comma is necessary in such constructions, as is a coordinating conjunction. Failure to use a coordinating conjunction results in a *comma splice*. An (*incorrect*) example of a comma splice:

Bob runs**,** he wins.

(Some authors use comma splices for stylistic effect, but the SAT and ACT afford you no such liberties.)

If the coordinating conjunction is connecting what are not complete clauses, the comma should be omitted, as in

He is hungry **and** needs water.

If we were to repeat the subject, creating a second independent clause, the comma would again be required:

He is hungry**, and** he needs water.

Following an introductory dependent clause. When a dependent clause appears before an independent clause, a comma must connect the dependent clause to the independent clause. If the independent clause comes before the dependent clause, the comma is optional. So you need a comma here:

If you need more cans of jelly**,** go steal some.

But you don't need one here:

Go steal some cans of jelly if you need more.

Another example:

Correct: After I unhinged the door₂ I thrust it toward the beast.

Also correct: I thrust the door toward the beast after I unhinged it.

Enclosing nonrestrictive appositives and clauses. A phrase or clause is *restrictive* when it, in its description or definition of a noun, narrows the meaning of that noun. An example of a restrictive appositive (described under error type 1G) and a restrictive clause:

My friend **Patrick** lives under the sea.

The planet **that I live on** is inhabited by many other beings similar to me.

The punctuation of the first sentence suggests that *Patrick* restricts *friend*; it indicates to which friend you are referring. If the modification were nonrestrictive – conveyed by flanking *Patrick* with commas – the implication would be that you have only one friend. Similarly, the lack of commas around the clause *that I live on* implies correctly that more than one planet exists, so the descriptive clause narrows (or *restricts*) the possibilities.

If you had only one friend and there were only one planet, the sentences would be alternatively punctuated thus:

My friend₂ Patrick₂ lives under the sea.

The planet₂ which I live on₂ is inhabited by many other beings similar to me.

Here are three situations in which the nonrestrictive modification is more logical:

My mother₂ Olga₂ has a unique name in our neighborhood.

Earth₂ which is covered mostly by water₂ is populated by many thirsty people.

My first book₂ *How to Walk while Running*₂ was a smashing success.

There is but one earth, and the typical person has only one person whom he or she considers his or her mother. Finally, it is possible to have only one first book. One more example in which non-restrictive modification is correct, meaning that commas are required:

One of my fish₂ Gills₂ is an elegant swimmer.

Errors can result from following the advice that commas should be placed wherever someone pauses in reading. That advice is far too shaky for our liking. Here are some cases in which you **should not use commas**, some of which review the previous coverage:

Before a parenthetical phrase

Incorrect: I grabbed the bag, (which was lavishly filled) and skipped home.

Correct: I grabbed the bag (which was lavishly filled) and skipped home.

Correct: I grabbed the bag, which was lavishly filled, and skipped home.

Around the word *that*

Incorrect: They took the sodas, that looked the freshest.

Incorrect: They took the sodas that, looked the freshest.

Correct: They took the sodas that looked the freshest.

Correct: They took the freshest soda, which looked tasty.

Between a noun and its modifying adjective

Incorrect: The sad, short, man limped to the finish line.

Correct: The sad, short man limped to the finish line.

To intervene between a verb and its subject, even when a compound noun is used

Incorrect: Joe, Monica, and Monica's dog, are all really great buddies.

Correct: Joe, Monica, and Monica's dog are all really great buddies.

When the modification is restrictive – that is, when it narrows the adjacent noun

Incorrect: My mother, Sue, is a bit taller than my father Robert.

Correct: My mother Sue is a bit taller than my father, Robert.

Correct: My mother, Sue, is a bit taller than my father, Robert.

When connecting two clauses when there is only one, unrepeated subject

Incorrect: My face has been itching lately**, but** is getting better.

Correct: My face has been itching lately **but** is getting better.

Correct: My face has been itching lately**, but it** is getting better.

<u>Before prepositional phrases or within a prepositional phrase that is not a list</u>

Incorrect: I woke up**,** in the beginning of the day.

Incorrect: I woke up in the beginning**,** of the day.

Incorrect: I woke up in**,** the beginning of the day.

Correct: I woke up in the beginning of the day.

Correct: In the beginning of the day**,** I woke up.

Colon Errors *(8B)*

A colon (:) introduces a list or an explanation or example of the clause before the colon. The explanation or example must be an independent clause; the list does not need to be, but the clause before the colon must still be independent. Correct examples:

I have three pens**:** a blue one, a green one, and an invisible one. *(list)*

He turned in his homework early**:** He had spent the entire night working on it. *(clause)*

In formal writing and for purposes of the SAT and ACT, the clause before the comma must be complete:

Incorrect: First: We went to the store.

Correct: First, we went to the store.

Incorrect: I want: some records, a stereo system, and a nice couch.

Correct: I want some records, a stereo system, and a nice couch.

Also correct: I want a lot of things: some records, a stereo system, and a nice couch.

Semicolon Errors *(8C)*

A semicolon (;) separates two independent clauses that are related, as in

The municipality was massacred with many millions of missiles; thus, it is in ruins.

It is wrong to separate an independent clause and a dependent clause with a semicolon. This is *incorrect* because *because it was delayed* is a dependent clause:

The movie comes out tomorrow; because it was delayed.

Another example in which the semicolon is inappropriate (the second phrase lacks a subject):

The man was always very hungry; and sometimes even starving.

The one situation in which a semicolon can be used in another way is to separate items in a *complex list*, which is a list at least one of whose items contains an internal comma, as in

He has lived in Chicago, Illinois; New York, New York; and Mexico City, Mexico.

Such a construction helps to clarify structure.

And this marks the end of our lightning tour through grammar. Congratulations on making it through!

SAT Question Types

On **Improving Sentences questions**, you will be given a sentence, part or all of which will be underlined. The five choices offer four possible ways to rewrite the underlined portion and one choice – always option (A) – for sticking with the original. Example:

Neither of the twin llamas' curators were willing to feed them.

(A) Neither of the twin llamas' curators were
(B) Neither of the twin llama's curators was
(C) Neither of the twin llamas curators was
(D) Neither of the twin llama's curators were
(E) Neither of the twin llamas' curators was

Your job is to identify which choice represents the best way to convey the intended meaning. In this example, Choice (E) is best, because it correctly punctuates the possession of the plural *llamas* and uses a singular verb, *was*, to agree with the singular *neither*.

No answer will be the "best" one if it contains a grammatical error. Therefore, the first step in your consideration of which answer to choose should be a scan of the choices for ungrammaticality. If you see an error, rule out the choice that contains it.

If two or more grammatically sound choices remain, check next for clarity: Are any of the choices ambiguous? Perhaps a conjunction will not make much sense, or the pronouns' references will be unclear.

Your final tool is to rule out wordy choices. Disregarding the ambiguous, illogical, and ungrammatical phrasings, the correct answer is always the most concise one – and the most concise choice is usually the shortest.

To review the hierarchy of answers to rule out: ungrammatical ones, then ambiguous ones, then wordy ones. Finding need to resort to the third level – in which the more concise answer is chosen – is quite rare. Frequently, the first level will take care of all the choices except one (the correct one), as in our example above.

An **Identifying Errors question** presents a sentence with four underlined words or phrases, each of which corresponds to a possible answer choice; choose option (E) if none of the other choices seem to be the answer.

> <u>Walking</u> (A) down the road from school, the group of ice cream and candy trucks <u>was</u> (B) an <u>attractive option</u> (C) in the <u>students'</u> (D) eyes.

The *correct answer* to an Identifying Errors question is the underlined word or phrase that features *incorrect grammar*. Each sentence will contain merely one error at most, so choosing option (E) means that the sentence is completely correct.

In the given example question, the five possible choices are *Walking* (A), *was* (B), *attractive option* (C), *students'* (D), and no error (E). (A) is the correct answer, because it results in mismodification, as described under error 6A. Here is a possible correction:

> Walking down the road from school, the students found the group of ice cream and candy trucks to be an attractive option.

If ever you put your narrow-minded grammar hat on, it should be on the Identifying Errors questions: You are on the hunt for grammatical errors. Beyond the naturally acquired nuances that characterize any College Board question (which you will pick up as you practice), there is little more to these questions than a smart application of the rules of grammar, which have been covered so far with enough depth and breadth to make outstanding success on these questions realistically feasible.

One effective strategy to extinguish any errors you do find yourself making on Identifying Errors questions is to employ a tactic we discussed in Chapter 5 to deal with tough math problems: "Think Like a Test-Maker." This works for English questions, too: Write out some questions that test the concept you're having trouble with. The new perspective you gain when you turn the tables helps you to more quickly solidify your understanding.

Grammar will not come up as often on the **Improving Paragraphs questions**, whose focuses are clarity and sentence-level and paragraph organization.

You'll be asked, for example, to consider what the most logical locations of sentences are, how best to connect those sentences using the appropriate subordinating conjunctions, and what order of paragraphs works best. You may also need to rephrase sentences or rearrange the clauses in them.

Reading the paragraphs with an eye for what they are trying to say is integral to your ability to make intelligent choices for how best to phrase and organize the content. The subjectivity that comes into play on these questions can be overcome with some use of the official practice questions and keen application of commonsensical logic.

ACT Question Type

The ACT features just one English question type. You will be given five prose passages, parts of which are underlined. Much like the SAT's Improving Sentences questions, you will be given four choices for each question corresponding to an underlined phrase: three possible changes to the underlined phrase and one choice – again choice (A) – that offers no change.

The ACT's question type is indeed similar in format to the Improving Sentences questions, but its content pulls from all three of the SAT's question types, as you'll need to be on the constant watch for grammatical, stylistic, and organizational errors and lacks of clarity or conciseness. The ACT's questions test punctuation more often than do the SAT's, but the grammatical concepts on the ACT are generally more straightforward.

The Essay

Always the first section on the SAT and the last on the ACT, the essay is the only part of either test that is graded subjectively. Your essay will cross the (slightly) discerning eyes of two graders, who will independently score the essay from 1 to 6 – though scores of 0 can be awarded for off-topic essays – summing to a total out of 12. If the graders agree on the score, your result will be an even number. If they disagree by 1, your score will be odd: scores of 4 and 5, for example, yield 9 out of 12. If the graders' scores disagree by 2 or more points (it happens more often than you might expect), a third, supervisory grader is brought in to settle the matter.

Clearly, there is no surefire formulaic recipe for ensuring a 12, given that the graders are given a rubric that each will apply differently. Against this unfortunate reality there are two countervailing reasons for optimism: First, the essay score is not terribly influential, carrying less weight than the multiple-choice questions on the SAT in factoring into your overall Writing score and not even being factored into the ACT's Composite Score. Second, all SAT and ACT writers look for a general set of rather simple criteria.

To internalize these criteria as goals for what to achieve and focus on with your essay clarifies what you have to do. The successful achievement of these goals, even if the essay has multiple points of weakness, tends to earn its writer at least 10 out of 12, which is good enough for an 800 on the SAT if you do well on the multiple-choice questions. (Even 9 out of 12 can cut it for that purpose on most administrations.) These guidelines should form your essay-writing mentality and process:

Skip immediately to the heart of the prompt – the question. Prior to sharing the meat that you're really interested in, the SAT and ACT offer a casual mix of discussion and quotations on the general topic at hand before working their way to the question. You care about only the question. The rest of the prompt is meant to arouse your mind and initiate brainstorming. These are unconvincing reasons to read the introductory material.

You have 30 minutes on the ACT essay and only 25 minutes for the SAT essay; don't waste it reading what the SAT and ACT think you should find interesting about the topic. Any ideas for arguments they give you will, moreover, be plainly obvious ones that every other student will be writing about. You don't want to be average on the essay; you want to stand out with fresh ideas. Don't get bogged down – time-wise or creatively – by the prompts. Jump straight into the question, where things actually get a bit interesting.

Opinions vary on which test – the SAT or ACT – offers more interesting prompts. The ACT's prompts are certainly more relevant to the practical lives of most high school students, since they invariably revolve around some education-related topic. The SAT's prompts, on the other hand, usually touch upon a more philosophical, profound matter, such as is the proper role of an individual in society or differing perspectives on how to achieve happiness.

Upon first reading the question, briskly brainstorm ideas for both sides. The question you are posed will always be binary, of a form that calls upon one of two stances. Your job is to decide which of these positions you prefer and defend it. Most students approach this decision with the wrong mentality, thinking that before writing, they need to figure out which position is the "correct" one. They are both correct. A successful essay can always be written on either.

To determine which side you would prefer to write about, understand that the essay is all about defending your position: The better position for you is the one that you can more easily defend. Defense on the SAT and ACT comes in the form of explaining examples and how they prove that your side is the right side.

Because of this, you should dedicate an ever-so-brief period of time immediately after reading the question to trying to think up examples for each side. We're talking spending no more than 30 seconds or so on this process. Pick the side for which better examples seem to occur in your mind. If you can't decide which side you like more, it's fine to just pick one side randomly. Remember, neither side is inherently superior; it's all about how cogently you make the case for it. You should know which side you are defending within a minute (maybe two) of the start of the essay section.

Take a couple minutes to outline your essay. Everyone has a different method that he or she employs in planning an essay for school. Some students loathe mapping out their essay in any prescribed detail, preferring instead to just start writing and seeing where their ideas take them; antithetically, others meticulously outline every detail, blurring the line between that outline and the essay itself. There is similarly variegated[138] sentiment when it comes to planning the SAT and ACT essays.

Pragmatically, we'll come out somewhere in the middle. It is simply too easy to lose track of organization and topic if no plan is formed prior to writing to make that a recommendable approach for anyone. An off-topic essay is scored 0; this must be avoided at all costs. Recognizing also that time is a limited commodity on the SAT and ACT, we think there is great risk in allotting much time to writing out examples and sorting out the organization of your paragraphs. We think a range of 2 to 3 minutes is an ideal sweet spot for most students: It should give you sufficient time to think up umbrella points that you will make as well as brief sketches of the associated examples for support.

We won't dictate how exactly your outline should look, but it shouldn't be anything fancy. The graders will never read it; it's merely to get your general ideas on paper so you know what you are doing and where you are headed when you begin to write.

Don't feel pressured into any particular organization. Your goal is to write a persuasive essay. Persuasion is contingent upon clarity; how can we be convinced of what we don't quite understand? An integral component to clear written communication is organization. But organization ought be a function of what you're writing about rather than some patterned structure set in stone.

Upon beginning to plan their essays on the SAT and ACT, most students can still hear their middle school teachers admonishing them to write an introductory

---

[138] SAT Word Alert: *Variegated* (adjective) means "varied or diverse"

paragraph, three body paragraphs, and a conclusion. Anything else was wrong. Well, that's no longer true: Three body paragraphs are most definitely not needed. In fact, we usually recommend that students try for two. We have found that writing about two main arguments works better for students, because they support them more fully and feel more confidence in the points. The third body paragraph often receives less attention, is more poorly developed, and generally feels like a third wheel.

Essays with only two body paragraphs can and often do receive high scores – as long as two compelling, on-topic arguments are presented, developed (i.e., explained), and supported with examples.

Cut to the chase. Taking too long to arrive at your thesis fatally dooms an essay. The graders want to know immediately where you stand on the prompt and what you're going to do to prove that you're right. There should be no lollygagging; tell the readers your stance in one terse, crystal-clear, and plain sentence before you do anything else. This sentence, your thesis, binds you for the rest of the essay: You will not veer from the topic or jump ship to the other side.

Whatever the marks of a great essay introduction are in the literary world – exciting hooks and eloquent, flowing progression toward a position – they don't apply to the SAT and ACT essay. Favor clarity over eloquence. The graders will spend so little time on your essay that any subtlety will surely be lost on them. An excellent, general-purpose introduction is a short thesis statement followed by one to two sentences previewing the supportive arguments you will proffer[139]. When you begin the body paragraphs containing those arguments, the focus on clarity remains: Begin each paragraph with explication as to what your point is for that paragraph and how it serves to prove your thesis.

Shun ambivalence and flip-flopping. Politicians would make terrible SAT and ACT essay writers, because there is no room on these tests' essay sections for the safe middle ground or for pandering to evanescent whims by changing your position. Rather than democratic appeasement, buoying the credibility of your one-sided thesis is your one task on the essay. Keep any mid-essay regrets as to your selection out of your mind: Both sides to every prompt have plenty of viable argumentative support and in turn infinitely many example possibilities.

This task poses some problems for the more contemplative students, to whom so many possible arguments for both sides occur that tuning out half of them is challenging. Just remember that you are not mounting a scholarly discussion or comprehensive philosophical analysis here; you are writing in less than half an hour a draft that will be read in a couple minutes. Fair and balanced this essay should not be. Argue boldly (but with support)!

---

[139] SAT Word Alert: *Proffer* (verb) means "to put before a person for acceptance"

Just about any example can do the trick, but some tend to lead to higher scores. Almost anything you can think of could theoretically be used as an example to support one of your arguments: a movie you saw, a conversation you overheard, a book or short story you read, a personal experience, an historical event, etc. Most students tend to use primarily personal experiences. These usually work sufficiently well for writing a good but not very high-scoring essay, because the student is familiar with all the details but the example itself is boring and does not sound intellectual.

In order to distinguish yourself on the SAT and ACT essay and thereby achieve a score of 10 or higher, you must sound insightful. Relating a personal experience about, for instance, the time you felt really tired in school to your argument that starting school later would give students more energy is appropriate, but it is predictable and straightforward. High-scoring essays make less obvious connections.

History and literature usually provide better opportunities than most personal experiences to facilitate insightful discussion of an argument. For this reason, we recommend that students rely primarily on supporting their points with examples drawn from books or history. The less obvious the connection, the better; but clarity is still important. You must unambiguously demonstrate that the cited example truly proves what you claim it does. Using particularly well-suited, unusual personal experiences is fine; just don't bring up the same experiences every other student will. Citing statistics occasionally is all right, too, but don't make your essay all about numbers; you want to show off your writing skills.

Some students find it helpful to think up a set of generally applicable examples ahead of time that they can put to use on any prompt they encounter. We don't think this is necessary for most students, but it can certainly reduce the stress of needing to pull examples out of your head when you have thought them over beforehand.

Invent. It can be difficult to clearly remember historical or literary examples, so as long as you are positive that the argument makes sense feel free to fill in the gaps. Chances are you remember what you're writing about better than your reader. The SAT and ACT essays are about practicing rhetoric and persuasion, not factual memorization and recall. Do not force your readers to suspend disbelief, however: All examples must be plausible, or else your essay lacks any force to convince its readers.

Write a lot. The graders' analysis of your essay is superficial because they have to get through so many in little time. They know that longer essays tend to be more fully developed and supported – and therefore better. They seem to have internalized this correlation, and longer essays are quite significantly better received by graders than are shorter essays. Fill up as much space as you can without significantly compromising quality. General markers of quality writing – like logical organization, a clear and consistent thesis, well-selected arguments, and convincingly explained examples – trump any attempts at complexity or nuance. Your time is better spent getting lots of words on paper than ensuring you say the ideal stuff in the ideal way.

Write legibly. Given our last advice, it is worth pointing out that you shouldn't write so quickly that your essay cannot be read. Unreadable essays are, unfortunately, not given the benefit of the doubt. They receive scores of 0. Thankfully, though, SAT and ACT graders read so many essays written by those with poor handwriting that they develop impressive skill for discerning words. But don't stretch your luck too far.

Write well. Even though the time constraints are rigorous and the review superficial, the common qualities that characterize effective writing style apply here as well. Write with interesting, precise vocabulary, but don't use words that you don't understand just because you have seen them in a dictionary or an SAT word list. Avoid stilted, excessively formal language, yet, of course, don't use slang. Observe the rules of grammar, which you hopefully learned rather well in the preceding pages. Don't obsess over proper spelling but do ensure that blatant misspellings are corrected. In order to accomplish that, we recommend a quick proofread of about one minute right before time is called.

Vary your sentence lengths and structures: A repetition of short, simple sentences sounds elementary; inexorable series of long sentences, too, usually lead to wordiness and lack maximum persuasive effect. Graders also particularly like to read fluid essays. Fluidity marks mature, controlled writing and is an essential component for high-scoring essays; choppy essays are a pain to read. Ensuring the logical flow and connectedness of your ideas is vital, and, rhetorically, the varied use of appropriate transitional words and phrases helps to achieve that organic flow in your writing.

Use counter-examples responsibly. We wrote that insightfulness is a criterion for great essay scores. One of the most effective ways to convey that capacity is to demonstrate that your perspective is not limited; you are aware of the objections that could be made to your arguments and possess the skill to explain them.

Being the open-minded people we are, we recognize that you could be objecting to what we just wrote. *Didn't we say that you are to defend only one side, with no waffling?* Yes. The difference in our advocacy here is that we recommend that you very carefully, responsibly express the counter-examples while never conceding to them; the point is to bring them up to tear them down. For example, if one of your examples suggests that gun restriction would help reduce violence, you can cite the potential objection that such restrictions would infringe on liberty. In response to this counter-argument, you can note that in all domains of government, certain abridgments of liberty in one sense are acceptable to support the general welfare and liberty in another sense.

Do not distract from your primary argument by overusing counter-examples. We recommend that if you do decide to include a couple, bring them up near the end of your essays, perhaps even in the conclusion before hitting home your thesis. Note also that the ACT essay's graders seem to particularly value counter-examples.

Practice! Writers of all skill levels would benefit from applying the tips we've shared to see what specific approaches work best for them and to gain experience applying them. The more you practice, the better and more quickly you will be able to pick a side, develop examples, and draft your essay. In the official guides published by the College Board and ACT, you can also find real students' scored essays to get a rough sense of the standards used to score the essays.

CHAPTER 8
SURMOUNTING THE SCIENCE SECTION

Science has made us gods even before we are worthy of being men.

Jean Rostand (1894-1997)
French Biologist & Philosopher

Overview

Unique to the ACT, the Science test assumes that your high school requires you to take three years of science and that by the time you take the ACT, you have been exposed to the biological and physical sciences. In this section, we will go directly to the source to make sure you know what to expect when you take the Science test. As the famous Chinese general and military strategist, Sun Tzu (544 B.C. – 496 B.C.), wrote in *The Art of War*:

> *"It is said that if you know your enemies and know yourself, you will not be imperiled in a hundred battles; if you do not know your enemies but do know yourself, you will win one and lose one; if you do not know your enemies nor yourself, you will be imperiled in every single battle."*

Thus, in this book we will help you know your "enemy" – the test (in actuality a friend: remember *Why You Should Care*) – as well as yourself, through ample[140] and deliberate practice. In this way you will win "a hundred battles," or at least achieve a high score on the test and, more importantly, literacy when it comes to reading scientific material.

Without further ado, the ACT Science section consists of 40 questions that need to be answered within 35 minutes[141]. Do the math (hopefully without a calculator, since you do not get one on the Science test) and figure out how many seconds, on average, you have per question[142]. Because of the limited time per question and how involved each of the passages *appears to be*[143], students often grouse[144] about being under time pressure. We will discuss later in this chapter how you can relieve some of this pressure and feel comfortable about finishing in time.

---

[140] SAT Word Alert: *Ample* (adjective) means "abundant"

[141] That means the test will take less time and probably be less painful than watching an episode of *Jersey Shore*.

[142] 35 minutes / 40 questions = .875 minutes per question, or about 52.5 seconds.

[143] Note the emphasis on "appears to be," because the ACT Science section appears to be more complex than it actually is.

[144] SAT Word Alert: *Grouse* (verb) means "to complain"

So what is actually covered in the ACT Science test? According to the official ACT student website (http://www.actstudent.org):

> *"The content of the Science Test includes biology, chemistry, physics, and the Earth/space sciences (for example, geology, astronomy, and meteorology). Advanced knowledge in these subjects is not required, but background knowledge acquired in general, introductory science courses is needed to answer some of the questions. **The test emphasizes scientific reasoning skills over recall of scientific content, skill in mathematics, or reading ability.***"

Read that last sentence again, because it is important. The ACT Science test is trying to gauge your reasoning skills, *not* your math and reading abilities – there are already sections devoted to those – or your memorization of scientific facts like the speed of light and Avogadro's number[145]. We will emphasize this point again below. So how exactly does the ACT test your scientific reasoning skills? As with other sections, the ACT precisely summarizes the passage and question formats you can expect:

- *"**Data Representation (38%).** This format presents graphic and tabular material similar to that found in science journals and texts. The questions associated with this format measure skills such as graph reading, interpretation of scatterplots, and interpretation of information presented in tables, diagrams, and figures.*

- ***Research Summaries (45%).** This format provides descriptions of one or more related experiments. The questions focus on the design of experiments and the interpretation of experimental results.*

- ***Conflicting Viewpoints (17%).** This format presents expressions of several hypotheses or views that, being based on differing premises or on incomplete data, are inconsistent with one another. The questions focus on the understanding, analysis, and comparison of alternative viewpoints or hypotheses."*

Wow, there is a lot of jargon in the description above. Better get used to it, because one essential skill you will develop on your journey to ace the ACT is how to excavate the true meaning of a figure, table, and passage, even if it is buried under tons of jargon. Get your shovel ready, because we're about to do some digging.

---

[145] Good to know anyways, at least for Tuesday Trivia. The speed of light is roughly 300 million meters per second and Avogadro's number is about $6.022 * 10^{24}$, and represents how many atoms or molecules are in a mole.

Outstandingly Effective Science Strategies

Science is a way of thinking much more than it is a body of knowledge.

Carl Sagan (1934-1996)
Astrophysicist & Author

The science reasoning section on the ACT is like the Wizard of Oz (warning: spoiler alert). In the movie, Dorothy and her friends are terrified by what appears to be an intimidating wizard. However, they discover that, behind a curtain, the giant wizard is actually being controlled by an ordinary old man. The same goes for the questions in the science reasoning section. Do not let the ACT passages intimidate you, because behind the tables, graphs, plots, and formulae is a very straightforward and surmountable section.

One of the differences between the Science and math sections is your score improvement profiles. In the latter you will make gradual gains as you begin learning how to solve particular problem types, such as in geometry, algebra, trigonometry, etc. On the contrary, your performance on the Science section will likely be characterized by sudden, punctuated improvements. The trigger for these spikes of improvement will be your transition to thinking scientifically. Fortunately for us, one does not have to be a Nobel Laureate to get a 36 on the ACT Science section. However you will be more likely to get a 36 if you begin thinking like a Nobel Laureate – that is, thinking critically and scientifically. Thus, the first few outstandingly effective strategies are aimed at helping you think this way.

Do Not Get Caught Up with Jargon

More so than most fields, science is filled with jargon. A recent article in a well-read science magazine explains this phenomenon:

> *"Scientists typically fail to craft simple, clear messages and repeat them often. They commonly overdo the level of detail, and people can have difficulty sorting out what is important. In short, the more you say, the less they hear. And scientists tend to speak in code. We encourage them to speak in plain language and choose their words with care. Many words that seem perfectly normal to scientists are incomprehensible jargon to the wider world. And there are usually simpler substitutes.* "[146]

There are two primary ways students respond to jargon. Forgive the analogy, but say a student trying to ace the ACT Science test is like a cow trying to cross a road at night to get to greener pastures. Complicated-looking jargon is like a car that comes out of nowhere and is only feet away from hitting the cow. Upon encountering jargon, some students will be like the cow that freezes in its tracks,

---

[146] Somerville RCJ and Hassol SJ (2011). Communicating the science of climate change. *Physics Today* 64(10): 48-53

stares into the headlights, and winds up on a McDonald's menu. Other students will be like the cow that dodges the car – recognizing that it is a danger associated with crossing any road – and moves on to greener pastures. Which cow do you want to be like?

The key to not getting caught up with jargon is to expose yourself to many practice passages, tables, graphs, and scatterplots and to remember that, as with the reading comprehension section, all of the answers to the ACT Science questions can be found in the information provided.

Any time you see a word that you are not familiar with, simply circle it and try to figure out what the text is saying using context clues. After you have finished a practice test, go back through and look up any words you circled, write down the definitions, and review them occasionally. In surprisingly short order, you will have mastered most of the "intimidating" science words the test will throw at you.

Practice, Practice, Practice

This applies to all of the sections but warrants special emphasis for the ACT Science test. Your goal is to start thinking systematically and critically about the information you are provided. There is no magic pill to develop this thought process – you simply need to practice it deliberately, and over time it will develop.

A side benefit of practicing is that the more passages, graphs, tables, and figures that you expose yourself to, the greater the chance that you will encounter similar topics on the actual test. If not on the test, you will certainly encounter this type of material in college and your career. For example, maybe a bar graph comparing the average rainfall between cities does not interest you, but a similar-looking bar graph comparing your company's market share with that of other companies assuredly will.

Where do you find practice material? The most obvious place to start is ACT practice test books, as we recommended earlier. There are also many free resources online with example passages that describe experiments and contain figures and tables that you can practice interpreting. If you want to raise the bar on yourself and make turn the ACT Science section into "child's play," you may consider visiting research journals and reading about cutting-edge experiments being done by researchers. One particularly good journal is the Public Library of Science (PLoS: http://www.plos.org/) because it is freely accessible and contains top-notch, peer-reviewed research with figures and tables galore.

As you read through a real research journal, you will be struck by the relevance of the ACT Science's format: graphs, tables, and jargon abound! If you try to make up questions about the research articles and critically analyze the ones you read, the ACT passages will be a walk in the park.

Read the Information Provided, Then Look at the Questions

The saddest aspect of life right now is that science gathers knowledge faster than society gathers wisdom.

Isaac Asimov (1920-1992)
Russian-American Biochemist & Author

This is similar to the strategy that we recommend for the reading comprehension and critical reading passages, in which scanning the questions before beginning the passage is useful only for marking line references. If you jump straight to the questions and spend time reading them without taking the time to at least skim the information provided, you will not be able to see the forest for the trees; in other words, you will get caught up in details and not see the big picture. While you read, it is important to ask yourself, "What is the main point of this information, and why are they providing it?" In this way, you will be able to know which excerpt, figure, or table to refer to once you actually reach the questions. Oftentimes, the passage will give you too much information, so the ability to separate the relevant from the irrelevant is critical if you want to complete the section in time and, more importantly, if you want to become a critical reader and thinker.

The types of information that will be pertinent to each question will quickly become intuitive after you have completed enough practice tests. Based on the nature of the question and a prior read of the passage, you will know right away whether a question calls upon you to, for example, compare data points on a graph or synthesize two facts from the text.

Use a System When Approaching Tables and Figures

Even if you have no interest in pursuing a career in science, technology, engineering, or math, the importance of being able to interpret tables and figures cannot be understated. Whether you are an entry-level employee or the CEO, you will need to be able to make sense of the performance data of your unit, department, or company. This skill is becoming even more important in this age of "Big Data." In 2011 approximately 1.8 zettabytes (10^{21}) of data were created or replicated, which is enough to fill 57.5 billion iPads[147] (enough iPads to make a mountain 25 times higher than Mt. Fuji). Figures and tables make it easier to spot patterns and trends within this mountain of data, which is one reason infographics have become so popular. Your goal on the ACT Science section is to learn to interpret those tables and figures.

The first step is to describe what you see in the table or figure. Pay attention to the title, the axes (which often tell you which variable is independent, usually the x-

---

[147] Source: *Mashable Social Media*. "How much data will humans create & store this year?" Available: mashable.com/2011/06/28/data-infographic/

axis, and which is dependent, the y-axis), the legend, the range of values, and the units. As you practice, get in the habit of going through that checklist in your mind and fully trying to understand what is being shown. The next step is to actually interpret the table or figure. There are many questions that you can ask yourself, such as: *Are there patterns or trends that stand out?* and *Do some bars/lines/values differ from the other bars/lines/values in the table or figure?*

Using a consistent set of questions to frame your analysis of the table or figure will make you faster and more comfortable. Develop a mental checklist of the essential elements of each table or figure that you must consider. Each new graphic need not be a novel experience; once you've worked with several dozen tables and mastered your checklist, it will feel as though each "new" table is a familiar friend.

Our coverage of the Science section may seem relatively brief in comparison, but we believe you will be very pleasantly surprised by the benefits you will experience by applying those simple principles and strategies. Success on the Science section is a matter of thinking analytically about data and the visual representation of that data, a skill that is essential to making sense of our physical world and society today.

CHAPTER 9
AP AND SAT SUBJECT TESTS

by Christian Fong

Christian comes from Elk Grove, California, and graduated as the valedictorian of Franklin High School in 2010. He scored 2400 on the SAT (after a 2380 on the first attempt), 35 on the ACT (twice), and 800 on seven SAT Subject Tests. He took 20 AP Tests and scored 5 on all of them. In 2010, the College Board selected Christian as California's male AP State Scholar for passing more AP Tests than any other male student in California.

Christian enjoyed only one thing more than tests in high school: academic competition. He scored first in Sacramento County in Academic Decathlon, and his score was the third highest in the country for that round. His teams took second place in the Northern California Science Olympiad, first place in the SACMATH competition, and first in the Gordon D. Schaber Moot Court Competition, where he was awarded Best Speaker four years consecutively. In addition, he was Chief Justice and twice the Conservative Party Chairman for the Northern California region of the Junior Statesmen of America, where he won eight Best Speaker awards, as well as Head Delegate for his school's Model United Nations.

He is now a senior at Princeton University, where he studies Operations Research and Financial Engineering with certificates in Applied Mathematics, Computer Science, and Statistics and Machine Learning. He won the Shapiro Prize for Academic Excellence and was elected to the Tau Beta Pi engineering honor society. In his free time, he helps develop statistical methods for answering difficult social science questions. He plans to pursue a PhD in political economy at Stanford University.

We are excited that Christian has contributed his insights in this chapter!

What to Expect from This Section

If you are planning on applying to selective colleges, you will probably take a number of AP and SAT Subject Tests in high school. This section will explain what these tests are and will also provide high-level insights into the "personalities" of these tests that should help you efficiently prepare for them.

What Not to Expect From This Section

This is not a review book for particular AP and SAT Subject Tests, and it therefore will not explain any of the facts and concepts you will need to do well on these exams. Sorry, but you will have to go out and get test-specific books.

Although this section will attempt to give you an idea of what preparing for each test entails and their importance in the admissions process, it also will not tell you exactly how many or which tests *you* should take. You must consider the courses available to you at your school, the time you are willing to allot for preparing for these exams, and your motivation to learn the material.

What Are These Tests, and Why Should I Take Them?

Before getting into the gory details of the personalities of particular tests and approaches for preparing for them, you should take some time to understand what these tests are and why (or if) you should take them. The first section is about the technical, verifiable facts about these tests – a kind of brochure. I will offer lots of my opinions in the later sections.

AP Tests

Strictly speaking, the Advanced Placement Tests (hereafter referred to as APs) are a set of standardized examinations administered by the College Board – the same company that administers the SAT, PSAT, and SAT Subject Tests – every May. They are subject-specific and are designed to test understanding of their respective subjects at an introductory college level. While the number fluctuates, there are usually about 30 different AP Tests you can take. Every AP (with the exception of AP Studio Art) has both a multiple-choice and a free response section. Most tests are three hours long.

Most (but not all) students prepare for their APs, at least in part, by taking corresponding AP courses in their high schools. Some students prepare on their own without taking any formal AP course; this guide will later provide tips on how to "self-study" for AP Tests.

American colleges (as well as some colleges abroad) provide a variety of incentives to do well on these tests. You will often hear that students who "pass" an AP Test get "college credit." The terms "pass" and "college credit" are both more ambiguous than they at first seem and mean different things to different colleges.

The material benefits of doing well on APs can, depending on the college, include any of the following:

1. Improved odds in the college admissions process (more on the specifics of this particular benefit later).

2. The ability to place out of introductory-level courses. While high school students tend to fixate on the first advantage, college students tend to enjoy this one the most. If you don't have to clutter your freshman class schedule with introductory courses, you will be able to spend more time exploring courses from departments outside your major and have the opportunity to

take advanced courses earlier. The latter option could help you in finding a summer internship or getting involved in research with a professor. More importantly, the advanced courses tend to be more fun.

3. The option to graduate from college in fewer than four years. Many students who earn this option choose not to exercise it. After all, if you are going to put a lot of effort into getting into a great college for your undergraduate degree, why rush to get out? However, in some contexts, graduating early can be quite an attractive option – for example, if you are going to have to spend a lot of time in graduate school (as you will if you go to medical school or get a PhD) or if the costs of attending college place a significant burden on you and your family.

4. The ability to take a higher "class standing." Many universities allow seniors to select their courses first, followed by juniors, then sophomores, and finally freshmen. Most courses have a limit on enrollment, and if the upperclassmen take all of the spots, you're out of luck. If you had "sophomore standing" as a freshman, you would be allowed to select your courses during the sophomore enrollment period. Some universities (for example, the University of California, Berkeley) allow students who have enough AP credits to take a higher class standing.

Of course, the score you need on your APs to get these benefits will vary by college as well. AP Tests are scored on a scale from 1 to 5, where 1 is the lowest and 5 is the highest. In the vernacular, a 3 is the minimum score required to "pass" the AP. However, many selective colleges require a 4 or even a 5 to skip introductory courses or take a year of advanced standing, and it goes without saying that the most selective colleges will not be terribly impressed by a 3.

SAT Subject Tests

Like the AP Tests, SAT Subject Tests (hereafter called by their old name, SAT IIs) are subject-specific standardized tests administered by the College Board. Both your SAT IIs and – to a lesser extent – your APs, along with a host of other factors, are considered by the admissions committee during the application process. Beyond these few similarities, SAT IIs are almost fully characterized by their differences from AP Tests:

- While APs are administered only once a year, the College Board offers sittings for the SAT IIs every month or two – usually at the same time as the SAT.

- Many selective colleges require applicants to take at least two (and sometimes three) SAT II's, although the applicants can usually choose which ones. On the other hand, colleges will never explicitly require students to take a certain number of APs.

- While you get about 30 APs to choose from, you have about half as many choices for the SAT II – and many of these are foreign language tests.

- SAT IIs are only infrequently used to place out of introductory courses in college and are almost never used for advanced standing.

- SAT IIs are scored on a scale from 200-800 (although on most tests it is impossible to get a 200 even if you get every question wrong). You can only get scores divisible by 10: 590 is a possible score; 595 is not.

- SAT IIs are only an hour long.

- SAT IIs are exclusively multiple-choice.

What Do APs and SAT IIs Really Mean?

Now that you have the objective facts of these test – most of which you probably could have gotten for free from the College Board's website – you are probably hoping for something more prescriptive. How important are these tests, *really*? How many should I take, which ones, and when? I will give you the information you need to make an informed choice about which AP Tests you should take in the next section.

When an admissions officer looks at your application, he or she will see four quantitative measures of your application.

1. GPA (and possibly a class rank)

2. SAT score

3. SAT Subject Test scores

4. AP scores

Grades and rank provide a good idea of how well you did compared to the other students in your classes but are not very good for comparing you to a pool of applicants from across the world who went to wildly different high schools. In some schools, smart kids can easily get A's sleeping through class, turning in their homework, and reading the book the night before the test. At others, the smart kids engage in cutthroat competition for a limited number of A's. Simply put, GPAs are not directly comparable across different high schools.

On the other hand, everyone takes the SAT – it is a quick and easy way to compare students from different schools. Unfortunately, unless you plan to major in reading passages of less than two pages, correcting other people's sentences, or arithmetic, the SAT doesn't provide a very good indication of how good you are at what you *like*.

APs and SAT IIs provide you with an opportunity to strut your stuff at subjects that you might actually like – be it history, physics, literature, or French.[148] Scoring well on an AP or SAT II says that your commitment to a subject is more than just talk – you've tried it and you're actually fairly good at it, too.

Moreover, as standardized tests, APs and SAT IIs provide a convenient and objective way of comparing you to students who went to different schools.

With that said, these tests have significant limitations. While the SAT is, for the most part, not closely related to the sorts of material you cover in your courses and your score is therefore relatively insensitive to the quality of your teachers, most AP courses will try to approximate what is on their respective AP exams. Accordingly, student outcomes on tests are highly sensitive to the quality of their teachers and classes. In some schools, only the top few students will earn 5's, while at elite high schools, the majority of the class gets the top score.

The SAT IIs and the APs suffer a further defect in that, from the perspective of the most selective colleges, the maximum score does not indicate true excellence. You have to be quite good at a subject to get a 5 on the AP exam or an 800 on the SAT II, but at the very best universities, many of the applicants are very good at almost every subject. Thus, at that level, the APs and SAT IIs fail to serve as meaningful differentiators of specialization.

All told, your scores on the SAT IIs will be an important part of your application – although a decidedly less important part than your GPA and class rank, your extracurricular activities, and (usually) your SAT score. AP scores factor into the process but are primarily for class placement and credit, unless you vigorously self-study them. Low scores on these tests coupled with high grades will imply that your classes were easy, and high scores in a diverse array of subjects will show that you have an agile mind and are able to master large bodies of information.

Preparing for the AP and SAT Subject Tests

Test Psychology and Scoring

The APs and SAT IIs are probably significantly "harder" than any test you have taken in the classroom. APs will not allow you a cushion of high grades on assignments, projects, and unit tests throughout the semester to buoy your grade at the end. Your teacher will (typically) test only the material covered in class or in the readings; AP exams are designed by people who have no idea what your teacher covered.

Most importantly, APs have a radically different definition of an excellent performance. In most exams in most classrooms, you need to get more than 90

---

[148] Unless, of course, you really like anthropology or geology, in which case you're out of luck.

percent correct to score an A. Scoring on the AP is significantly more complicated. While the exact number varies among subjects and years, you typically need to score only 65-75 percent of the points on an AP to get a 5.[149] That is, getting a 5 on an AP Test *feels* like getting a C or D on a regular test.

Many students find this adjustment challenging, to say the least. Even if you "know" that you need only 65-75 percent of the points to get a 5, you will probably still find the AP a rather jarring experience if you have never actually taken a test on which you won't know a third of the questions. You will not perform as well if you are demoralized by not knowing a significant proportion of the questions. You might even panic and miss questions that you could have gotten if you had calmed down.

The best way to avoid this is to take full-length practice tests for your first year of AP Tests. After your first batch of AP exams, you probably won't run into this problem.

One final note on scoring: Neither APs nor SAT IIs are "curved" in the strict sense. By that, I mean that the College Board does not decide in advance that the top 20 percent of students will get 5's (or the top 3 percent will get 800's). Rather, they decide in advance how many points you should be able to score if you know your stuff. The College Board calibrates their expectations using the performance of students in past years.

I will, sometimes, talk about the "curve" of a test. *Curve* is an unfortunate multiple-meaning word. While it was originally used to describe the quota system I described above, it has also come to mean the number of questions you must get right to get a good score.[150] Thus, when I say that a test has a generous or an unforgiving curve, I mean that you need to score a relatively small or large percentage of the points to get a high score, respectively.

The Personalities of the Tests

Although APs and SAT IIs ostensibly test your mastery over a variety of subjects, virtually all of these exams test two broad skill sets.[151] The first is memory, which, unsurprisingly, is your ability to recall large bodies of information quickly. The

---

[149] If you are curious about how exactly the College Board decides this number, they consider a variety of factors. First, when they write the exam, they have a pretty good idea of how many points you should get if you know the material. They calibrate this by checking against student performances from past years.

[150] Statistics aficionados will know that "curve" derives from the Gaussian distribution, or "bell curve." Teachers expected test scores to follow a normal distribution and assigned grades based on where students fell relative to their classmates.

[151] There are notable and important exceptions, and I will discuss these at length.

second is process application – your ability to master and apply algorithms, or rules for solving problems.

Of course, every exam tests memory to some degree – after all, you have to remember algorithms in order to apply them. Likewise, most memory-based exams will have an essay component that requires some minimum process aptitude, if only to know how to arrange the facts you remember in a coherent way.

Nevertheless, as I describe and characterize the individual APs and SAT IIs, I will talk about the degree to which they are memory- or process-focused. Be sure to take the time to learn your own strengths, knowing whether you are quick to memorize massive sheets of facts or can easily pick up new problem-solving techniques. This will give you a better idea of which tests you will find easy and which tests you'll find hard.

When Should I Start Studying for APs?

While you should pay attention and keep up in your classes throughout the year, you can probably safely put off studying for the AP Tests themselves until March. If you start much earlier than March, you will probably forget a lot of what you learn by the time you take the tests in May, and starting in March gives you enough time to learn the material for most classes in time to take the test. If you are feeling pretty good about your classes and just need to brush up on things from earlier in the semester, you can even put off studying until April.

This is not a hard and fast rule. If you are completely lost in an AP class, you will want to start catching up before March. If you have a truly exceptional teacher, you might not need to study outside of class at all. The March start is simply a rule of thumb. Be sure to use your head and assess how much studying you need to do and how long it will probably take you to do it.

How Should I Study?

As a general rule, review books are the best way to study for APs – especially the memory-based tests. They have many of the facts that could be tested and, more importantly, several practice tests with answer keys. While reading these review books, it is extremely important to make sure you actually *remember* what you read. You don't get extra credit for poring over these books if the moment you stand up (or roll over to go to sleep, depending on how you study), you forget 80 percent of what you read. As you read, you should periodically stop and ask yourself questions like *What was going on two pages ago?* and *What kind of essay prompts would this information be useful for answering?*[152]

---

[152] As you ask yourselves these questions, be sure to also answer them.

For the memory tests, the practice exams at the back of the book are useful for making sure you remember everything you have read and pointing you to the parts of the material you need to review. For process-oriented tests, the review is sometimes a helpful refresher, but the practice exams are *essential.* The best way to master algorithms is to apply them over and over again to practice problems, and the practice exams will allow you to do just that.

Now, you are probably wondering which books you should buy and for which tests. Barrons, The Princeton Review, Kaplan, REA, and McGraw-Hill are all names you should keep in mind for every test, but I will not recommend specific books for specific tests. As someone who owns (literally) a closet full of AP books, I can tell you the majority of review books that these companies publish are terrible.

The great majority of these review books are written for students trying to hit a score of 3 or 4. Those that are *not* often make their tests excessively difficult and spend a lot of time on details that are both uninteresting and untested.[153] The review sections often miss or do not adequately explain important concepts. The tests often have answer keys with wrong answers or will tell you the answer is B and then explain why the answer is D. They even have typos all over the place.[154]

Even though these review books are not very good, they are pretty much all you've got to prepare for the AP exams. The best solution I have found is to buy several review books for each test you are taking. While individual books might have glaring omissions or bad tests, if you combine several, you will usually get a pretty good review and find some reasonable tests.

Self-Studying

Some top students decide they want to take AP Tests without taking AP classes to prepare for them. This is called "self-studying" the test. In some communities – notably CollegeConfidential.com – self-studying an AP Test is a badge of honor. It shows that you are proactive and can pick up new subjects quickly without relying on others for support.[155]

---

[153] If you are the gung-ho kind of student, you're probably thinking that you want the hard book, because it is better to be over-prepared than underprepared. Just wait until April rolls around. When you are trying to study for seven tests at once, you will not at all appreciate a review book wasting your time with irrelevant details or tests that do not accurately reproduce what you will see on the AP.

[154] And I don't mean putting "you're" instead of "your." I remember one well-known publisher's book which – I'm not kidding – had a paragraph that ended with "aaaaaaa###aaaaaa." I am pretty confident that some of these books do not have editors.

[155] The notable exception here is "self-studying" tests for foreign languages you speak at home. While this is a good way to demonstrate your proficiency in a foreign language, don't expect admissions officers to be very impressed with your 5 on Spanish if you speak Spanish at home.

There is unquestionably a certain allure to self-studying tests. If you go to a high school where this has not happened before, you will almost certainly generate some buzz if you take an AP exam without taking the corresponding class. However, the admissions benefit for self-studying APs is marginal; you will almost certainly get more bang for your buck if you start a successful club or significantly improve your performance in one of your existing extracurricular activities. If you are the kind of person who enjoys teaching yourself new things, then you will probably enjoy self-studying APs, and you should do it. If you want to improve your application, there are more efficient ways to spend your time.

If you want to self-study, the approach is fairly similar across tests. Buy several review books, read through each of them (and make sure you have a strong understanding of what you read), and then take the practice tests. Sometimes, you will want to get a supplemental textbook that will treat important topics in more detail than you can get in the review books.

Some APs are more conducive to self-studying than others for a variety of reasons: Perhaps the available review books are good or the exam covers a reasonably narrow set of facts or algorithms. But for the most part, deciding which, if any, APs you should self-study will depend on what kind of learner you are. If you are extremely good at memorization, you might find Art History or Biology a breeze. If you are an excellent writer, Language and Composition is a good bet. If you have already taken Calculus AB, Calculus BC is probably doable.

However, there are some tests that are, for the strength of the available review books and their relatively small curricula, considered "easy" self-studies. These are Psychology and Environmental Science (and sometimes Human Geography). If you want to self-study and aren't quite sure what to do, these are a safe bet.

When Should I Take My SAT IIs?

You can take the SAT IIs almost any time you can take the SAT. However, if your SAT II maps to an AP Test you are taking, you shouldn't let all of that cramming you do in April and May go to waste. In that case, I strongly recommend you take your SAT IIs in June. You will still remember most of what you have learned from studying for the AP, and you will have a couple of weeks to catch your breath and review material specifically for the SAT II.

Generally speaking, preparing for the AP helps with the SAT II more than preparing for the SAT II helps with the AP. SAT IIs tend to be more detail-oriented, while APs tend to be more conceptual, and, usually, learning the concepts helps you remember the details more than memorizing the details helps you grasp the concepts.

Breaking Down the AP and SAT Subject Tests

I will deal with the tests by subject group and compare the AP and SAT II directly. Without further ado:

The History Tests

If, for a moment, you play a little mental video of a stereotypical history classroom, the imaginary class is probably memorizing events and dates. Sure enough, the history exams are very memory-focused exams – at least on the surface. Fortunately, you won't have to waste very much time memorizing dates. While knowing the dates for important events can provide important context for inferring the answers to questions you don't know, it is unlikely that any question on a history AP or SAT II will flatly ask you for the date a certain event happened.

You will, on the other hand, be asked to recall the significance of important historical developments and the relationship between particular events and broader historical trends.[156] Therefore, while history is a "memory test" in that you could conceivably memorize every such development and relationship, approaching the test in this way is highly inefficient (not to mention boring). Instead, you should try to understand the "narrative of history" and grasp why things are happening and why they are important for what happened later. If you have a strong understanding of the broad strokes of history, you will be able to place the people and events you study in context and will therefore be able to better remember them.

To put that in more concrete terms, let me analogize this to navigating when you're learning how to drive – something many of you are probably learning right now or will be learning soon. If you simply print directions from Google Maps, it will probably take you quite a while to remember the specific sequence of turns you're supposed to make. However, if you have a thorough understanding of the major roads and highways and where they intersect, you will find remembering directions to particular places much easier. Likewise, in history, if you understand on a high level what important changes are happening, you will have an easier time remembering the events and the people that go with them.

The SAT IIs

There are only two history SAT IIs: US History and World History. Both tests cover the same scope in both time and space as their corresponding AP Tests (except World History can sometimes include some European History, because there is no SAT II in European History). As a general rule, the questions on the SAT II will be more specific than the questions on the APs and are more likely to

---

[156] For those of you that go on to study history in college, you will quickly find that these relationships and significances which were treated as facts in high school are open to interpretation, to say the least. There is a "standard" or "textbook" interpretation of history (American history in particular) that will be presumed for these standardized tests. Fortunately, the multiple-choice questions will have only one reasonable answer, no matter how you want to interpret history.

test your ability to recall certain events and names rather than their significance. If you ever find a question about dates, it will be on an SAT II.

Document-Based Questions

All of the history APs with the exception of Art History will have a free response component called the Document-Based Question (DBQ). The Document-Based Question will present you with a set of sources – first-hand accounts of some development, historical records (possibly political cartoons, tickets, posters, among all kinds of other things), and sometimes commentary from people who came later. These documents will be fairly short. You must construct an essay to answer a given question using the documents.

While the DBQ can be intimidating, with proper training, it essentially becomes free points. The documents give you everything you need to infer a reasonable answer to the prompt, and the DBQ is scored according to a rigid rubric that you can find on the College Board's website. Make sure you go into AP Test with the rubric memorized, so you can make sure you put some points on the board without thinking too hard.

And now for the advice on the specific tests:

World History (AP and SAT II). Many find World History intimidating. After all, for US History, you essentially have to remember what happened in only one country – so it seems like remembering what happened for all of them must be harder.

Luckily, that's just not the case. World History compensates for its breadth by sacrificing a lot of depth. More than any other history test, World History lets you get away with just remembering the most important people, the most significant events, and the most widespread and long-lasting developments. You will study wildly different civilizations that developed at different times and in different ways and you will have to be prepared to compare and contrast these civilizations. The essays will likely ask you about very broad subjects, like the development of trade routes or oppressive governments. Some essays will prompt you to compare two regions; others will ask you to trace developments in a single region over time.

Note that because European History covers Europe from the Renaissance onward and US History picks up around the arrival of Columbus, World History will give very little attention to these region-time pairings. Geographically speaking, World History will focus on Latin America, Africa, and Asia (the whole continent, including India and the Middle East). Questions about Europe will typically cover either the period before the Renaissance or during the Cold War.

European History (AP). Whereas World History is characterized by an emphasis on understanding history on a very large scale, European History focuses on the details. Obviously, European History covers less ground in both time and space (it starts with the Renaissance). The countries you will spend most of your time studying developed along similar trajectories; drawing the connections between these countries will be much easier than for World History. However, the cast of characters you will need to remember is much larger, and the list of events that you will need to know is much longer – and you will have to be able to comment on those events in much greater detail for the essays. The essay prompts will be fairly specific: Check out some of the prompts on the College Board's website and think hard about whether you could write several pages on the subject. Fortunately, to compensate for the increased specificity of the prompts, you have to respond only to your choices out of a longer list of prompts.

US History (AP and SAT II). US History is decidedly more similar to European History than it is to World History. You will have to remember many people and events in detail. Moreover, there is a stronger "narrative" to US History than there is to European History and certainly World History (as they are taught at the AP level). For those two tests, events are related and reflect underlying trends; you can think of them as rivers with a current. US History is treated more like a line of dominoes. Events in AP US History are not just related; one causes another to happen. If you can master this chain of events, you will do very well on the test.

One quick note on this test: I have heard that some AP US History courses use Howard Zinn's *A People's History of the United States* as a textbook. While it is an interesting book and you should definitely give it a read if you are interested in history, it does not teach the standard textbook interpretation of American history that you will see on the AP Test. If you find yourself in a class taught with this book, be sure to supplement with several AP review books and possibly another textbook (Kennedy's *The American Pageant* teaches fairly close to the test).

Art History (AP). Art History is the black sheep of the history tests: While the other three are reasonably closely related, Art History really does its own thing. I would go as far as to say that it is really more closely related to Biology than the other history APs, because it is very memory-intensive. Success in Art History depends on memorizing a massive body of facts – works of art and their artists, which periods they belong to, and the general characteristics of each period. Although, as with the other history tests, there is some room to infer answers you don't know if you have a strong grasp of the traits of the period, a number of the questions will be brutally specific.

Note that, even though it has "art" in the name, Art History does not require anything in the way of artistic inclination. It is a test of memory, not creativity. Don't be scared away from this test if you are not an artist yourself.

The Math Tests

Students, as a whole, tend to do well on the math tests. In fact, in most years, a higher proportion of students scored a 5's on Calculus BC than on any other test. Of course, as you will learn in Statistics, some of this can be attributed to selection bias. While anyone can sign up for US History, you have to complete the entire high school math sequence before you can take Calculus. Thus, the students taking these math tests tend to be at a higher level.[157]

However, these tests are also structurally different from the other AP Tests. While most of the other tests rely, to at least some degree, on memorizing a bucketful of facts, the math exams require mastery of a relatively small set of algorithms. Since that set of algorithms is fairly small, you will probably see and practice every one of them in your course – whereas even a very good history course would have a very hard time teaching you the answer to every conceivable question from American history.

Calculus AB and BC (AP). Most of the high school math you do before calculus is essentially algebra-based. If you figured out how to divide on both sides of the equation and graph functions, you were pretty much golden. Calculus will throw in a number of new operations that you will have to understand – in particular, derivatives and integration.

Some students make this transition seamlessly and do not find calculus any harder than their previous math courses; others see it as a quantum leap. If you are in the first group, you will probably find this test a breeze. If you are in the second group, get help (from your teacher, a review book, or a tutor) and get it fast. The good news is that, if you can master the material in your class, the AP Test won't throw you many curveballs. The questions you will see on the AP Test are very similar to the questions you will see in standard calculus textbooks.

Calculus AB and Calculus BC share both "Calculus" and the B. There's a lot more in that than you might think. A fair share of the Calculus BC curriculum is really the second half of Calculus AB; you even get an AB sub-score to see how you did on the AB-based portion. The C part of the curriculum is decidedly harder than the A part you leave behind, but you're also older, smarter, and more practiced in math.[158]

Statistics (AP). A lot of students make a mistake by approaching Statistics in the wrong way. Statistics is a math test, mostly because it definitely isn't anything else. However, the focus in Statistics is not just getting the numbers to come out right. In that regard, it is fundamentally different from either of the Calculus tests, and, for that matter, most of the high school level math you have seen. Because of the

---

[157] No, math supremacists, I am not saying that math is harder than social sciences. I'm saying it has more prerequisites.

[158] Except, in some high schools, students skip AB and go straight to BC. If you are in that kind of high school, I wouldn't worry too much about AP Calculus.

pervasive use of statistics in the social sciences and journalism, Statistics emphasizes understanding what these numbers actually mean. You must understand what sorts of inferences you can make from your statistical procedures as well as what sorts of inferences you cannot.

While, of course, you must understand the numerical procedures in statistics, take some time to make sure that you are very precise when answering the free response questions. Use the language from your textbook as a model.

Also note that Statistics allows you to bring a calculator, including a programmable calculator such as a TI-89.

Math I (SAT II). Top students often neglect Math I, and with good reason. Math I presumes that you have only successfully completed Algebra II. It will test basic trigonometric functions, but you will probably remember seeing these in your geometry class. Some people take Math I because it requires virtually no preparation. If you have done well in your high school math classes and are a solid test-taker, you should have no trouble getting a high score in Math I. The trouble is that getting an 800 requires precision; you are often permitted to miss only one question, if any. The curve remains steep, and missing only a few questions will be very detrimental to your score. Furthermore, most top colleges prefer Math II, which has a much more forgiving curve and is therefore widely considered the "easier" test.

Math II (SAT II). Whereas Math I is often neglected, the majority of top students take Math II. Unlike Math I, Math II has a very generous curve. If it were a test in school, getting an A would usually be enough to get an 800. Students who have done well in high school math through pre-calculus and are strong test-takers will find this a manageable test. It is especially appealing because it requires relatively little preparation. You might have to review some of the finer points, such as matrices, but there is usually very little – if any – material that you haven't seen before. Of course, you should practice, but you probably will not need a lot of review.

The Science Tests

The science tests are a diverse bunch, ranging from deeply memory-based tests (like Biology) to deeply process-based tests (like Chemistry). They require varying degrees of quantitative aptitude. None of the tests require a particularly strong understanding of experimental design, including Biology, which explicitly requires understanding of a certain set of experiments; you can get away with a thorough understanding of the concepts behind the experiments.

For the many of you who plan to become doctors someday, Biology and Chemistry will provide you with a taste of what you can expect in your pre-med curriculum. You should use these tastes as a harbinger for other tests to come, i.e. the MCAT.

Biology (AP and SAT II). As far as AP is concerned, biology is the science of facts – lots and lots of facts. More than any test with the possible exception of Art History, Biology demands an excellent memory or a very good work ethic and patience for memorization. For the most part, you will not have to do anything except regurgitate information you learned from your textbook. For some, this is easy; for others, this is a nightmare. Fortunately, the questions on Biology are significantly more predictable than they are for any of the history tests. While biology as a field is every bit as wide as history, the portion of Biology covered by the AP Test is much better defined than the portion of US History covered on its AP.

SAT II Bio comes in two flavors, Ecological and Molecular. The difference between Bio-E and Bio-M is the last 20 questions. The first 60 are the same for both tests. Much of what can be said of SAT II Chemistry can also be said of SAT II Biology: The material is similar to that on the AP Test, but you should still review, because SAT II allows for finer differentiation of high scores than the AP Tests do.

As to whether you should take E or M, Bio-E tends to have a slightly easier curve, but the difference is so small that you should simply choose whichever subject you like better. More people tend to choose Bio-M, simply because most people with a strong enough interest in biology to take the test are pre-med types and M is more relevant to their interests. However, ecology usually comes late in the biology curriculum and accordingly might be fresher in your memory.

Chemistry (AP and SAT II). Unlike Biology or any of the social sciences, Chemistry is a process-based test in the spirit of Physics, Calculus, and English. Yes, I realize it is weird to say that Chemistry has more in common with English or Calculus than its fellow sciences Biology and Environmental Science, but it really does. There actually isn't a lot of memorization required in AP Chemistry. You can probably condense AP Chem into a glossary of ten pages. However, you have to not only memorize what those concepts are but also understand how to apply them. You learn what properties make a substance have a lower boiling point and the properties of elements separately. You may well never hear in your class that methane has a lower boiling point than water, but you will learn everything you need to know in order to deduce that. For precisely this reason, a lot of students find Chemistry one of the harder APs.

The material covered in SAT II Chemistry is similar to the material covered in AP Chemistry, but I recommend that you review some even if you are fresh off the AP Test. A lot of the material you crammed in April/May has probably left you. Scoring very highly will require not only a solid grasp of the concepts but also knowledge of the details.

SAT II Chemistry includes the infamous True/False questions. These are not your run of the mill 50/50 guess extravaganzas. For these questions, you must decide whether A is true, whether B is true, and whether B is true *because* A is true – all in one question. Your ordinary multiple-choice reasoning completely dissolves here, so you have to really know your material intimately to get these questions right.

Physics B (AP and SAT II). Physics B, like Chemistry, is a concept test, only with more math, although it won't require anything above algebra and a little basic trigonometry. While most of the multiple-choice questions will be straightforward and look like questions you see in any physics textbook or review book, the free-response questions (FRQs) love to string simple operations together so that it is easy to slip.

Accordingly, there are two approaches to Physics B. You can either thoroughly understand the concepts, so you can "see" how any given problem fits together, or you can practice the heck out of the test until there are very few things you haven't seen before. A healthy mix of both would, of course, be best.

SAT II Physics maps to AP Physics B. It is fundamentally different from Biology and Chemistry, because its curve is so much more forgiving. While students strong in Chemistry or Biology are occasionally tripped up by esoteric or poorly worded questions, students who are strong in Physics succeed consistently. The generous curve allows you to miss a few "off" questions, so scoring an 800 is easier. If you did well on the AP Physics B multiple-choice section, you shouldn't have much of a problem with SAT II Physics. However, if you just completed AP Physics C, you should probably review pretty thoroughly. You would be surprised how much simple algebra you can forget during your calculus-based odyssey in Physics C.

Physics C (AP). Physics C consists of two tests – Mechanics and Electromagnetism. They are unique in that each test is the length of half a standard AP. Each covers most of the same concepts as half of Physics B but incorporates concepts from calculus at the AP Calculus AB level rather than from merely algebra and trigonometry. As in Physics B, the multiple-choice questions are typically straightforward formula applications, and the FRQs can be downright nasty.

The consequences of transitioning from an algebra-based physics to Physics C cannot be overstated. You will need a thorough grounding in calculus to succeed in this test; you want to be thinking about the physical concepts rather than getting hung up in the calculations. Even then, Physics C will challenge your understanding of concepts in physics and calculus alike. Some questions will deal with physical relationships that are not explained explicitly but only implied by the relationships of formulas to their derivatives or integrals.

Environmental Science (AP). Along with AP Psych, AP Environmental Science is considered one of the easiest AP Tests. In terms of the types and emphases of the questions, it is more like Human Geography and Psychology than it is like any other science. You must understand a healthy mix of facts and concepts, but if the facts were the size of a pool of water and the concepts were the depth, Environmental Science would be both small and shallow. You can easily pick up everything you need to know for the test from reading a couple review books. If you must self-study a test, Environmental Science would be a good choice.

The Social Science Tests

Like their cousins in the natural sciences, the social science APs are diverse. While most other tests include at least some things you have seen before (you heard about things like atoms and the American Revolution way back in elementary school), most material you encounter in the social sciences will be entirely new and self-contained.[159] The social science APs map to a number of very popular college majors (economics, government, and psychology are among the largest departments at many universities), so these APs can help you decide if those majors make sense for you or not.

Economics (AP). Economics consists of two full-length tests: Microeconomics and Macroeconomics. You can take either or both of these tests. But because both essentially test "economic thinking," if you take one, you should probably take both. Unlike any other two tests (with the exception of the two Physics Cs) there is no effective difference between the two except the obvious one. Macroeconomics tests the economy as a whole; microeconomics tests the firm itself. Both tests assess theory primarily, with some simple applications that will require a little arithmetic, as well as a few relatively well-known historical examples. Much of this theory is derived from a strong understanding of supply and demand curves, so if you can master these, you should be able to master much of the tests.

However, these are not purely memory tests. Economics wants you to not only be able to regurgitate the theory, but also apply it to new (relatively basic) situations. The FRQs, which work a lot like the ones from US Government, are very similar from year to year, so you should be sure to check them out on the College Board's website.

Government (AP). AP Government comes in two flavors: US Government and Comparative Government. Unlike Econ, these tests have material differences beyond their subject matter.

US Government is exactly what it sounds like. You must be familiar with both the institutions of American government and American political history. Background knowledge is helpful, but the history-type questions are very predictable, so you can probably pick them up from your textbook or a review book. FRQs are straightforward – you simply explain concepts and give examples.

[159] With the notable exception of US Government.

Most find Comparative Government a somewhat more difficult test. First of all, most students are less familiar with the political institutions of a country like Nigeria than they are with their American counterparts. Furthermore, unlike US Government, where you only have to remember whether something is true, Comparative requires you to remember whether a statement is true for a given country. Luckily, the bulk of Comparative Government questions assume that students look at American government as "normal" and focus on the effects of American-style institutions (or the lack thereof). You essentially see how American institutions in other countries lead to different outcomes, or how the lack of American-style institutions contributes to each country's unique characteristics.

Psychology (AP). Psychology is a memory test, albeit a test of memorizing the definitions of concepts from psychology. The base of material is fairly narrow; you can study from your textbook and the review books and expect to know just about everything on the test. Many students find the material in psychology enjoyable, because they can easily connect it to their daily lives.

The test itself is quite straightforward. Multiple-choice questions will test whether you can recall important psychological concepts, and the FRQs, for the most part, require only regurgitation of theories. Like Environmental Science, this test is a good choice for self-study.

Human Geography (AP). To clarify, this is not a test about geography; it is a test of *human* geography. You don't need to know the capital of Azerbaijan or which mountain range separates Iraq from Saudi Arabia.[160] Instead, you will study how human beings arrange themselves in space and how their interaction with their environment (both natural and man-made) influences their ways of life.

As far as the AP Test goes, Human Geography is a strange one. On the one hand, the theoretical material covered is pretty intuitive. There are very few things you will need to read twice, and the FRQs – which mostly cover the theory – should accordingly be pretty easy. On the other hand, unless you have a penchant for memorizing long lists of statistics, there are going to be oddball questions that you just do not know. As in the AP histories, you can often reason out the answer if you have a solid base of geographical knowledge.

The English Tests

English tests are a whole different beast from the others. They are nice, because you have likely taken an English-like course every year since kindergarten. You have had plenty of time to hone the critical reading and writing skills you use on these tests. On the other hand, these tests will draw on skills many years in the making; if

---

[160] Baku is the capital of Azerbaijan. The second statement is a trick! Those of you who know geography very well will note that Saudi Arabia and Iraq are not separated by a mountain range.

you have trouble with writing or literary analysis, it is a steeper climb to go from bad to great in just one semester.

Literature (SAT II). Besides foreign languages, Literature is widely considered the hardest of the SAT IIs. The curve is harsh, the questions can be tricky, and it can be frustrating for the literary-minded to bend their thinking to the demands of a multiple-choice test. This is not SAT I Critical Reading: The passages are far more difficult, and the depth of analysis called for is much greater.

Many choose to take Literature without preparing at all; they look at it as more of an IQ test than anything else and therefore find it appealing. Indeed, if you have an analytical mind well-suited to the purpose of divining the College Board's way of thinking, you can do well on this test without any additional preparation. If not, you can expect this to be a hard test. Familiarity with pre-20th century English is a huge asset.

English Language and Literature (AP). AP English Literature's multiple-choice questions are very similar to SAT II Literature. It can be frustrating trying to figure out not what the passages mean to you, but what they mean to the test writers. To be fair, these questions are multiple-choice. Even though they are to some degree subjective, there is a definitive "best" answer for the vast majority of questions. They are simply not as clear as questions from the natural or social sciences.

Luckily for those of you English-minded people who despise literary interpretation multiple-choice questions, the AP Literature essays give you a chance to shine. You will be given works to analyze for two of the essays and will get to use works of your choice for the final essay. And by works of your choice, I really mean works of literary merit. In some cases, the line of literary merit is clear. *The Great Gatsby* and *Hamlet* are works of literary merit. *Harry Potter* and *The Hunger Games* are not.[161] There is a gray area in between, but it is safest to read off the suggested works list in past AP prompts, so you have a bank of works that are assuredly of literary merit.

English Language and Composition (AP). The English Language free response is quite simply a prose-writing test. You have two plain-and-simple essays and one DBQ-like essay. Whereas the AP Literature essays try to emulate what you will see in college if you major in English or the literature of another culture, the Language essays are more like what you will write if you study the social sciences. The Language multiple-choice section is basically SAT Critical Reading on steroids; it focuses on understanding the structure of papers and how the pieces of the argument fit together over the symbolism of the text.

---

[161] I'm not saying these are inferior books, or even that, objectively, they lack the depth of the books of "literary merit." By literary merit, I mean only that your test graders will find them acceptable subjects for a serious essay.

For those of you with analytical minds who are naturally gifted in expository writing, this test is a cinch. You can probably score a 5 with absolutely no preparation outside reading the rubric for the DBQ-like essay. Regardless of your current writing skills, preparing for this test will be a great way to improve your abilities.

The Language Tests (AP and SAT II). The College Board faces a dilemma with its language tests. On the one hand, it wants to make a test that serves as a meaningful indicator of language development for those students who speak a foreign language at home. Do they only know how to shoot the breeze with family and friends, or are they genuinely proficient in the language? Against that interest, College Board does not want to make the test impossibly difficult for those who picked up the language in school.

The College Board has, in my opinion, not been able to balance these interests. The majority of native-speakers get 800's and 5's, while those who learned the language in school usually find these tests exceedingly difficult. With preparation, you can probably manage the verb tenses and be able to understand most of the passages enough to answer the questions. Unfortunately, unless you have an exceptional high school program or have lived abroad for a while, you will run into a fair chunk of idioms and vocabulary that you just don't know. However, a good score on a language test is probably the most impressive and meaningful accomplishment as far as colleges are concerned.

For the SAT II, if your ear is well trained to your language (especially if you have lived abroad), it would be to your advantage to take the listening test to score some easy points. If your school program is not so good and you are responsible for most of your own preparation, you would probably do better on the Reading test.

The APs add a layer of complexity with the speaking section. Unlike the SAT IIs, on which you can answer the questions at your own pace, the APs will force you to answer the speaking section immediately after hearing the question.

Takeaways

If you just read this section from front to back, you've covered a lot of material. If you read it in pieces, you probably forgot bits between your reading sessions. If you didn't read it at all, now would be a good time to start paying attention. Here is a summary of the main things you should keep in mind:

- APs give you a head start in college, while SAT IIs are useful primarily for your application. Both are significant, but not all-important, parts of your application. Keep this in mind when deciding which tests to take.

- Prepare, at least in part, by reading through a few review books and doing the practice tests.

- Self-studying can be fun but is probably not the most efficient way to improve your college application.

- Don't panic! You don't need to get 90 percent of the questions right to get a 5 on any AP.

- If you are going to take an AP and the corresponding SAT II, sign up for the June SAT II to avoid forgetting important material in between the exams.

Most importantly, keep a sense of perspective about the whole process. High school students worried about their admissions chances often spend time preparing for – and, worse, worrying about – their APs and SAT IIs way out of proportion with how important they actually are for the purposes of college admissions. If you enjoy these tests, then go crazy, but don't let them take over your life if you don't want them to. If you have important things going on outside of the classroom, admissions officers will understand that you are more than your test scores.

CHAPTER 10
THE ART OF COLLEGE ADMISSIONS

Admission at some universities is simply a matter of entering your GPA, rank, and class size into fields and letting an algorithm decide whether you will be accepted. These colleges practice a formulaic approach to admissions, in which almost only objective factors are combined in a similarly objective way to yield an admissions decision: Anyone whose admissions index x is above some threshold y is accepted, where x does not include your extracurriculars, awards, or anything else of the subjective sort and where y is usually immutable[162].

At most schools, however, this is not the case. Most public universities, even the very large ones, will take your non-academic pursuits and your essays into account when they are evaluating your application. Many private universities give far more sensitive attention to each applicant's circumstances, and they read your essays and recommendations with an eye for abstract concepts like personality and fit.

In the pursuit of seeing applicants not as collections of numbers – *this applicant is a 2330-3.87, and that one is a 2180-3.6, though with all 5's on AP Tests* – but instead as people with interests and strengths and weaknesses and contributions to make and resources to appreciate, many colleges and universities, particularly the more selective private colleges, have adopted holistic admissions policies.

Holistic admissions are characterized by subjectivity and unpredictability; they lead to considerations of applicants in nuanced and human ways. As a result, many of the decisions may in comparison seem unfounded, and the process random. But that process, though complicated by a multitude of factors that can be weighed and interpreted differently depending on the school and on the particular individual who happens to be reading your application, is nonrandom. Healthy, effective strategizing is feasible.

Admissions officers at schools whose admissions practices are holistic will glean a general sense of you as an applicant from all of the information that they are given. If they think that you are among the set of applicants (the number of whom is determined by how many students the school can accept) who possess the best academic and non-academic fits for the school, they will accept you.

At such schools, there are no cutoffs – no scores below which all hope is technically lost – nor are there scores – not even perfect scores – that can guarantee acceptance. But, naturally, bad scores hurt, and good scores help; the worse or better the score, the more it hurts or helps, respectively. Similarly, no GPA is

---

[162] SAT Word Alert: *Immutable* (adjective) means "unchangeable"

required, and not even perfect grades in the most rigorous classes will ensure you a spot.

In fact, this pattern is true of all of the factors that play into admissions decisions at holistically reviewing schools. Perhaps frighteningly, no award is a free ticket (though, say, an International Mathematical Olympiad gold medal will come close). Comfortingly, no single bad grade is a death blow. No high-school captainship or presidency is needed; no leadership is required, but it helps. You don't have to play the violin because that's what you think colleges want to see – or the harp because you have to be artificially unusual. You should pursue with vigor what interests you, and good things will follow.

Standing out in a positive way is essential, though. And you'll need all the help you can get: With, for example, six US universities (Harvard, Yale, Princeton, Stanford, Brown, and Columbia) that have acceptance rates below 10 percent (and as low as 6 percent), competitive college admissions are tougher than ever.

Here we focus on holistic admissions. Understanding that the synergistic whole that an admissions officer conceives based on an application is primary, we nonetheless want to break the various considerations down. Distillation of the components of the process conveys how to best prepare yourself for admissions, as long as you keep an eye on how the various factors balance against one another.

As we compelled with standardized testing, leverage how to prepare for college admissions as more than a simple means to an end – here, to get into a good or prestigious college. Allow our advice to guide your road toward accomplishment and of personal success. Colleges can reject applications but they cannot negate the achievements of an applicant.

Applying

Before we move element by element through admissions, we have some process information to share. *In short, how exactly does one go about applying to college?*

1. As early as possible in your senior year (or even during the prior summer), request recommendations from the teachers you choose to write on your behalf and have your standardized test scores and high school transcript sent to the schools to which you may apply. As required by the application you use, upload or mail the recommendations as soon as they are ready. If you are taking additional standardized tests during your senior year or retaking some for a higher score, check with each college to ensure they will receive the updated scores in time to consider them in the evaluation.

2. Fill out your applications online. Most schools accept the Common Application, found at commonapp.org. This application becomes available in late summer of the year in which you apply. It calls for all of your

demographic and academic information, a short essay on an extracurricular activity, and a longer personal essay; these are sent to all colleges to which you apply through the Common Application. Supplementally, colleges may request additional information or essays to be completed for them in particular. Thankfully, most universities with holistic admissions accept the Common Application. If the school you are applying to is not a Common Application member, you will need to fill out a full application from scratch on that college's website.

3. Submit the application – with a time buffer for safety – by the application deadline for your desired filing period. Early Decision and Early Action typically have a deadline of November 1, whereas, for Regular Decision, you usually have until January 1. For rolling admission, earliest possible submission (without rushing the crafting of the application) is preferred.

4. Check your admissions decision online, either by e-mail or through a school's admissions portal. Early admissions results most often become available mid-December. For Regular Decision, it's around late March or early April.

You may be confused by all the abbreviations for admissions filing periods. Here is a breakdown of EA, SCEA, REA, ED, and RD.

Early Action (EA), Single-Choice Early Action (SCEA, which is just another name for Restrictive Early Action, or REA), and Regular Decision (RD) are all non-binding, meaning that if accepted, you are not required to attend. Only Early Decision (ED) is binding. The sole circumstance under which you can attend a school other than one to which you were accepted under ED is that you are unable to afford it, which means that you should apply to a school under ED only if you are confident that you want to attend.

You may apply to multiple schools under EA. This is distinguished from SCEA in that under SCEA, you may apply to no other schools early. Some exceptions to this exist, allowing those who apply SCEA to also apply through a school's rolling admissions program or to an in-state public university through EA. In the past, the only schools to offer SCEA as an option were Stanford and Yale; Harvard and Princeton have recently joined them.

Some ED programs allow you to apply EA to other schools. You'll need to check on the regulations of any school that you are interested in applying ED to, so that no accidental violations occur.

There is usually no admissions advantage in applying under early action admissions.

Despite the higher acceptance rates for EA and SCEA programs – which are due merely to the fact that the applicant pools during these periods comprise people who are stronger applicants – there is generally no admissions advantage in applying EA or SCEA. In theory, therefore, those who are accepted EA or SCEA would have been accepted under RD. Applying Early Decision, however, can boost your chances slightly, because you are showing significant interest in the school and are bound to attend, providing a boost to the school's matriculation yield index.

As mentioned, if a school's admissions are rolling (i.e., results may be given out at any time after an applicant has applied), the earlier you apply, the better. The fewer the remaining slots, the tougher the standards.

We also have some advice on how to go about choosing colleges:

Apply to a lot of schools. Upon realizing how difficult and unpredictable admissions at top colleges is, many people adopt the mentality that it is not worthwhile to apply to multiple highly selective colleges. If you are aiming to attend a top school in general – though not indiscriminately, as top colleges vary greatly among each other – it is precisely the unpredictability of admissions that should drive you to cast a wider net. The weapon strong applicants wield against the subjectivity of today's college admissions is the law of large numbers. Use it.

Consider specific departmental strengths. If you are deeply interested in a specific field, finding a school that has a strong program in that field is a good idea. Keep in mind, though, that the majority of students change their major at least once in college, so in most situations this consideration does not need to be very narrowly guiding. If you are open-minded about most majors, colleges with broadly robust departments are smart targets.

Rankings and prestige matter, sometimes. In many careers, students hailing from well-regarded colleges will receive a more significant look from employers. Attending a well-ranked school also generally affords an advantage in graduate school admissions in that the students tend to have more opportunities for meaningful research and for engaging with prominent scholars in their fields. On average, your peers, too, will be more academically interested at schools whose admissions processes are more competitive.

Personal fit and quality of life matter more. Visit the schools; talk to current and past students – do whatever works for you in order to form a sense of the colleges' feels and, more importantly, how you would fit into those environments. If you're debating between a college that's ranked 17 and one ranked 28, making the decision based on subjective feelings of fit is infinitely wiser than putting much stock into that ranking difference. Also be aware, however, that those who fall in love with one school and can see themselves going nowhere else would be pleasantly surprised by their adaptability if they were to give another school an earnest try.

And don't forget that you can be successful regardless of what college you attend: Your personal qualities, which are independent of your alma mater, will affect your future most of all – more than the prestige of your college, the income of your job, and, yes, even your SAT or ACT score. Hopefully, though, one of those personal qualities is dedication (and if it isn't, you do have the power to make it one) so that you earn the meaningful satisfaction of pushing yourself to get into the best college for you. Oh, and to do your best on the SAT and ACT.

Grades: The Foreground of Your Application

Your high school grades, impossible to look past without a serious study for admissions officers, are the most vivid, striking part of your application portrait. They are at the forefront of your application's review.

Your high school transcript is the most important part of your application.

When we refer to your transcript, we mean your grades and the courses in which you received those grades. In admissions, to these factors everything else is subordinate: They are integral in demonstrating your academic qualification, which is decidedly a litmus test in college admissions. No matter how great your essays or other accomplishments outside the classroom are, a failure to do well in your coursework dooms your application to selective colleges.

What of the supposedly circumspect, "holistic" admissions, you say? While it is true that the interplay among all aspects of an application is ultimately determinative of admissions results, grades predominate the consideration of whether you are able to succeed at a particular college, and college is foremost academic. Standardized test scores, as we will discuss later, play into your academic credentials in an important way, too (though you probably wouldn't have picked up this book if you had not realized that).

As we wrote in Chapter 1, the interpretation of art is complex and subjective, but certain fundamental elements are vital. Great grades are number one on that list.

Find a balance between course rigor and your abilities, but err on the side of pushing yourself with academic challenge.

If you are in dogged[163] pursuit of attending one of the nation's highly selective schools (which we would coarsely approximate as schools with acceptances rates below 20 percent), achieving excellent grades is not enough; you must earn those grades in highly demanding classes. While you do not need to have the most rigorous course load that is theoretically possible, you should be taking one of the most rigorous at your school.

---

[163] SAT Word Alert: *Dogged* (adjective) means "persistent"

If even one of the toughest schedules at your high school ends up seeming a bit easier than what someone at, for example, an elite private high school ordinarily takes, don't fret: Here the holistic nature of admissions helps you, as you aren't expected to do more than your high school's curriculum allows you to.

For those applying to less selective colleges, admission requirements vary too much to allow for meaningful generalization. Looking at the average weighted Grade Point Averages (GPAs) and ranks of accepted students, as published by these schools, will give you a helpful indication of how tough your course load needs to be.

Remember, as well, that taking and dedicating yourself to difficult classes in high school is the best way to prepare for the rigors of college, because you are developing another valuable escalator step for self-improvement. Be mindful of your limits, though. A good goal can be a bit scary, but it shouldn't be impossible or crushingly stressful.

Your weighted GPA is generally more important than its unweighted partner.

The weighted GPA – which, unlike the unweighted GPA, does take into account your high school's impression of the difficulty of your classes and adjusts accordingly – is generally a more telling metric if you are applying to holistically reviewing schools, because the rigor of your course load is important. With that said, it is usually the transcript itself, rather than a numerical summary of it, that admissions officers are most interested in.

Some students become excessively interested in their weighted GPAs, taking every opportunity to compare with students from other schools to see how they stack up in the important category of grades. This effort is misguided: Weighted GPA is valuable because it allows for a more complete picture to compare students within a high school but is still too vague to be used for comparing across schools. Admissions officers spend a good deal of time ensuring that they have a panoramic understanding of what your course load and grades mean in the environment you come from.

We have a high standard in mind when we say you need "great grades."

You understand that no certain GPA is required by top schools but that a high one is crucial. What grades should you have in order to stand a good chance?

Grade inflation is increasingly rampant across the country. As A's become more common, admissions officers have an easier time casting aside applications that have a scarcity of this top grade. Perhaps at the risk of encouraging punctilious[164]

---

[164] SAT Word Alert: *Punctilious* (adjective) means "extreme attention to the details of conduct or procedure"

consistency in your classes, the trend of higher GPAs means you as a college applicant don't have much wiggle room for messing up in your classes grade-wise. A bit ironically, grade inflation may make it easier to get an A, but it also means B's sting more potently than they used to.

The short of it is that students who are accepted to top schools will have almost all A's. However, B's – even an isolated C – will not render your application something for elite schools' garbage cans, especially if these lower grades were earned earlier in high school or you come from a very difficult school. Admissions officers have high expectations for course success, but apparently rare mistakes are forgivable.

You are at no disadvantage if your school grades harshly.

Most schools, especially larger public high schools, inflate grades. But what if your school is tougher than most in its grading or its student body is brimming with academic competition?

Because your grades are evaluated within the context of your high school, any grade deflation that your school practices will show through in your nonetheless strong class rank. And if your rank isn't even outstanding (for example, you fall outside the top five percent), rational hope for elite college admissions success can remain if your peers are sufficiently above average. In fact, some high schools across the country consistently send so many students to top colleges that, by mathematical consequence, many of them must come from outside the top ten percent.

It must be said, however, that such high schools mark the exception. Unless your high school has a distinguished "feeder" history of sending students to top colleges, you'll want to aim to be near the very top of your class.

At some high schools, A's are handed out glibly[165]; at others (such as those elite private high schools), C's are the norm, and teachers are widely averse[166] to granting any student an A. Colleges, thankfully, are well aware of these differences, and they take them into account when evaluating their applicants. Worry about doing the best you can, not about whether that will be good enough.

But what if my high school does not rank its students?

Admissions officers will still do their best to understand what your grades mean. If they need to, they will call to speak to your guidance counselor to better understand how your performance fits into your particular educational context.

For a given GPA, an upward grade trend really helps over stagnant performance.

And as a corollary, a downward grade trend really hurts. Colleges look at everything with a predictive mentality: *What does this score or GPA indicate about how the applicant will do at our school?* For that reason, improving grades will help your chances and can serve to mitigate the negative effect of a relatively poor grade if the grade was received in your freshman or sophomore year.

(Of course, however, this does not mean that, for example, having all A's is inferior to having mostly A's with a couple B's during freshman year. Upward trends are preferable over constant grade trends only insofar as good grades in your junior and senior years can limit the harm from poor grades in your freshman and sophomore years.)

---

[165] SAT Word Alert: *Glibly* (adverb) means "easily, often in a superficial or thoughtless way"
[166] SAT Word Alert: *Averse* (adjective) means "in strong opposition to"

Some schools claim to almost completely disregard freshman grades, in fact. Princeton, for instance, gives them very little attention.

Test Scores: Your Objective Technique

A great technique doesn't make real art on its own, but the more objectively skilled the artist, the more fully realized his or her potential can be. Test scores are as close to an index of technical skill as we find in the art of college admissions; don't let a deficiency here hold you back.

Colleges don't have a preference for the SAT over the ACT, or vice-versa.

In contrast to the mythical dissemination that, for admissions, a good SAT score is more helpful than a good ACT score, admissions officers do not favor one test over the other. This has not always been the case, though. Formerly, some elite colleges did give an advantage to those who sent in SAT scores instead of ACT scores.

While any student, regardless of where he or she lives, may take both tests, the SAT is most popular on the east and west coasts of the United States, and the ACT is taken foremost in the Midwest and parts of the South. In fact, a handful of states in those regions (Illinois, Michigan, Colorado, Kentucky, Tennessee, and Wyoming) require that everyone who wishes to graduate from high school take the ACT.

The SAT has become closely associated with the highly selective institutions in the northeastern United States. Compounded by the fact that some schools in that region had indeed preferred the SAT over the ACT, this association has led to the perception that the SAT – and not the ACT – is still what admissions officers at, for example, Ivy League colleges are looking for.

However, this is today a misperception. It is claimed uniformly[167] by the nation's colleges that the tests are considered equally.

Now, even when made aware of this assertion, some hold onto the idea that the SAT continues to be held in higher regard by the elite colleges. They will point to statistical evidence, citing most commonly the relatively high percent of students who submit the SAT compared to the percent who submit the ACT. At Harvard University, for example, historically, over ninety percent of matriculating students have submitted their SAT scores, whereas only about one in four students has sent in his or her ACT score.

But there is no reason to interpret these data as anything more than indicators of the testing makeup of the *applicant pool* instead of as a reflection of admissions practices. The perception itself is a factor here: Some students send SAT scores because they are under the impression that they need to send in SAT scores to these

---

[167] SAT Word Alert: *Uniform* (adjective) means "consistent and without varying"

colleges, which in turn provides statistical ammo to the proponents of the sophism[168] that the SAT is the favored metric in some colleges' eyes.

The more telling data are the interquartile ranges for test scores published by the colleges. These ranges indicate the 25th and 75th percentile scores for the admitted students. (So for a range of 31-35 on the ACT, about half of students fall between 31 and 35, and about half fall somewhere above 35 or below 31.) A comparison of each college's SAT and ACT score ranges reveals no significant evaluative difference on the part of college admissions officers.

This admissions non-distinction between the SAT and ACT, as we advised in Chapter 3, provides you the valuable opportunity to dedicate much of your preparation to the test better suited to your strengths.

Our recommendation is to approach each test with an open mind, giving it a fair shake after familiarizing yourself with its format, which the earlier chapters in this book have been meant to aid. Then try a couple practice tests (slowly and carefully – to learn rather than to score yourself) for each exam. Pursue further preparation in the test you like more; your goal is to have a high score in the SAT *or* ACT to send to colleges.

Send the score for the test that you did better on.

If you have taken both the SAT and ACT, compare them using the concordance chart in Table 5 of Chapter 2. If one is significantly better than the other, there is generally no reason to send both tests' scores. But if the scores are equal or seem so close that a college may concord them in a meaningfully different way from what is indicated on the ACT's table, sending in both is the safer route.

There are two important exceptions to this guideline. If you are applying to one of the few colleges that superscore *across* the SAT and ACT (as opposed to separately superscoring the SAT or the ACT), you will need to consider whether the combined superscore is better than either test on its own. If it is, send both. If you are not sure, send both.

The other exception occurs rarely. If one of the colleges that you are applying to (the University of Pennsylvania is one example) asks to receive all of the testing from both the SAT and ACT, you should respect this request.

Two relevant concepts here are superscoring and Score Choice. Refer back to Chapter 2, "Getting to Know the Tests," for elaboration on those practices.

Assume that the Writing sections matter.

---

[168] SAT Word Alert: *Sophism* (noun) means "a false or deceptive argument"

Many students invest their hope in the rumor that colleges disregard the Writing sections of the SAT and ACT when evaluating applicants. It is true that, at some colleges, these sections are given less weight than the other sections are; these sections are indeed even completely ignored under some circumstances.

This is not the case at most colleges, though, and colleges' policies on whether or how they consider the test are not clear (for example, MIT says that they consider the Writing section of the SAT but weigh it subordinately). Because the reason for some of the lack of adoption of the Writing section of the SAT as an admissions factor is that the section is relatively new (it was added in 2005), it is reasonable to expect that the already few colleges that do not consider the section will reach great paucity[169] in the coming years.

So do not slack on the Writing sections; you do not want to face regrets.

At all but the highly selective colleges, the published SAT and ACT scores ranges are very helpful.

These ranges are the previously mentioned interquartile (25th to 75th percentile) ranges of SAT and ACT scores. Again, about half of students at the school for which the range applies will fall between the extremes, and about half will fall outside those bounds. Here are a few example ACT interquartile ranges:

University of Michigan – 27 to 31

Iowa State University – 22 to 28

Southern Illinois University Carbondale – 18 to 24

At schools that do not practice holistic admissions to a significant degree, these ranges generally give a good idea of where your score should be if you wish to be admitted. At these schools, as long as the rest of your credentials are roughly commensurate with your score, falling in about the middle of the range implies that you have a fair chance of admittance; having a score below the lower end of the range makes admittance unlikely; surpassing the high end of the range often comes close to ensuring acceptance. So, for example, an ACT score of 25 would bode very well for SIU Carbondale and might get you in at Iowa State, but admittance to the University of Michigan would be very challenging.

If the rest of your application is much worse or better than your test scores, however, the ranges become significantly less directly predictive. A score of 28 for SIU Carbondale might be able to compensate for subpar grades (though even a 36 will not recover for an exceedingly poor academic history in high school) because it demonstrates your capacity to do the work there. Similarly, a score of 26 has the

---

[169] SAT Word Alert: *Paucity* (noun) "smallness of number" or "scarcity"

potential to get you into the University of Michigan if your grades and extracurricular involvements are unusually strong.

The SAT and ACT score ranges can be deceptive for highly selective colleges.

These ranges often mislead those who are looking to apply to colleges that practice very rigorous and holistic admissions – especially in the cases of the nation's most selective colleges and universities.

Consider the ACT interquartile range among recent Stanford University matriculants: 31 to 34. Does this imply, as before, that an applicant with an ACT score around 32 or 33 will stand a solid chance of being admitted to Stanford and that, say, a student with higher than 34 with a commensurate application otherwise will very often be accepted? No.

Elite universities like Stanford receive so many applications from students with excellent testing portfolios that these ranges lose meaning. In fact, the interquartile range among the Stanford *applicant* pool is likely very near to the 31-to-34 range for those who ultimately attend. (The occasionally cited thought that top colleges could fill their classes with only perfect scorers is incorrect, but it gets at the right idea.)

Admissions at highly selective colleges is so competitive nowadays that any randomly selected applicant, no matter what his or her ACT score, does not stand a very good chance of admittance.

Brown University's released testing data reveal this more clearly. Although Brown has an ACT interquartile range similar to Stanford's, not only are those with 36's not guaranteed a spot at Brown, but they are in fact accepted at a rate of merely 32 percent. Clearly, important factors beyond test scores are coming into play here.

This is not to say, though, that standardized test scores do not matter at highly selective colleges. In fact, they do: **The higher your score, the better your chance.**

While the holistically subjective and circumstance-sensitive nature of highly selective colleges' admissions practices means that there is no requisite[170] score for admission (students with scores below the interquartile range still have a chance) higher scores are more helpful than lower scores.

The lower your score is than the bottom end of the interquartile range, the more remote your chance; at a sufficiently low point, admittance is, for practical purposes, impossible. The higher your score is above the top end of the possible

---

[170] SAT Word Alert: *Requisite* (adjective) means "necessary for a particular purpose"

score range, the better your chance is, even if scores alone cannot make acceptance *likely* at any of the elite universities. (In both cases, we assume all else to be equal.)

At the very least, your academic credentials – basically a combination of your transcript and standardized testing – must demonstrate to the admissions officers that you are academically qualified, that you can do the work. After you clear that hurdle, your scores become less important, but, contrary to the claims of some, they do not generally cease to matter.

However, at some schools, there do seem to be threshold scores beyond which increases matter very little, if at all. MIT, for instance, claims that all section scores on the SAT that are 750 out of 800 and higher are considered to be the same. That the acceptance rates for those scoring 750-800 and those scoring 700-740 (MIT does not provide finer divisions) are relatively similar to one another is consistent with that claim. At Stanford, as well, the admit rates do not scale up very much in moving from scores in the 700s to a perfect 800, suggesting that some sort of sub-800 "irrelevance threshold" score may exist.

But for most other elite colleges, there is no reason to believe that even small score increases do not hold *some* helpful admissions value. For example, at Brown, at which only 32 percent of applicants scoring 36 on the ACT were accepted, a significantly lower 12.3 percent of applicants scoring 33 to 35 were accepted. That the percentage-point chance differential between these two score ranges is much larger than that for schools that appear to employ relatively low cutoff thresholds (as mentioned, MIT and Stanford) suggests that the causal factor is the score increase and not some confounding variable, such as a positive correlation between test scores and grades or test scores and essay quality, though these correlations likely do exist to a small extent.

Statistical parlance[171] aside, in effect this all amounts to the generalization that, no matter what types of schools you are applying to, you should **aim for as high a score as you can**. Higher scores will never hurt you, and in almost every case they will help to improve your chance of admittance into one of the colleges that you want to attend.

But some moderating comments are needed here. Outlined in this book's PERFECT Approach, our test preparation philosophy that you should aim for a perfect score can be interpreted inappropriately: We are not advocating eternally and exhaustively preparing and retaking until you achieve a perfect score. Practice does not have to make perfect in order to provide you with accomplishment and admissions success. What practicing *with the goal of making perfect* can do, though, is optimize your performance.

---

[171] SAT Word Alert: *Parlance* (noun) means "a way or manner of speaking"

Moreover, sometimes the effort expended in slightly improving an already high score, though modestly helpful in this element of admissions, **may not be worth it**. If college admissions are an art, they are also a balancing act: Your canvas is finite, and your resources are limited. Could the extra SAT or ACT preparation time be better spent completing schoolwork, studying for a Subject Test or AP Test, or more actively applying yourself in an extracurricular activity? In many cases, the answer is *yes*. This is why we've attempted to present you with *efficient* ways to achieve a great score.

The SAT and ACT are not the only standardized tests that a college may require.

Many schools require scores from SAT Subject Tests as well, but some schools, such as Wake Forest University, are even testing-optional for all standardized tests. Most holistically reviewing, selective colleges require scores from two Subject Tests. A couple schools, like Georgetown University, recommend three scores.

Beyond the engineering programs at some schools, which typically require scores from Mathematics Level 2 and a science test, public universities do not generally require or even consider Subject Test scores. Even at more selective private universities, Subject Test requirements – both those for how many tests to take and in which subjects – may be dependent upon your intended course of study.

See the previous chapter for Christian's breakdown on how to pick the best Subject Tests for you and then how to most effectively prepare for them.

For the most part, certain Subject Tests are not intrinsically superior in admissions to others.

Some admissions officers may look down on certain tests, with the most common manifestation of this being a general preference for Mathematics Level 2 over Mathematics Level 1. But you should generally take whichever subjects you think you can do best on.

The tests are not scaled similarly – for example, 750 out of 800 on the Literature Subject Test is at a much higher percentile than that same score on Mathematics Level 2. Most admissions officers don't familiarize themselves with the percentiles, instead relying on their experiential exposure to the scores to gauge how meaningful a high score on one test is. What results is a mitigation of, but not likely a commensurate compensation for, the differential scoring of the various Subject Tests: You may get a bit of leeway on "harder"-scored tests, but aiming to send high scores out of 800 (rather than submit scores with high percentiles) should be your primary strategic goal.

SAT or ACT scores have historically been more important than Subject Test scores, but for some schools this is shifting.

At most schools that consider Subject Test scores, the SAT or ACT scores will be given more weight. Increasingly, though, there is a trend toward emphasizing Subject Test scores alongside SAT or ACT scores, as some schools' internal analyses have shown that Subject Test scores are highly predictive of a student's success at the college.

AP Test scores usually play a smaller role in college admissions.

AP Tests are not designed to be important admissions tools; with a rather imprecise scoring scale (integers from 1 to 5), they would serve as a blunt metric anyways. The primary purpose of AP scores is to give you an idea of where your knowledge would stack up in a comparable introductory college class on the same topic and then, at some schools, to give you college credit or fulfill a prerequisite for a higher class. Additionally, AP scores are entirely self-reported by the applicant until the student matriculates to the college, compromising scores' credibility on the application.

Yet, at some colleges, they can serve a role in contextualizing your grades. An admissions officer may interpret a smattering of 2s and 3s on AP Tests to be a sign of grade inflation at your high school if you received mostly A's in the corresponding classes. Conversely, scores of 5 may reinforce the perception that a pattern of B's is reflective of grade deflation.

Success with independently studying AP classes' content, as demonstrated through a record of 5s and 4s on AP Tests for which you have not taken the relevant classes, can also show your penchant[172] for and skill in learning on your own. An Advanced Placement record with high scores on independently studied exams is particularly helpful in allowing you to stand out if you come from a high school with a limited curriculum.

Subjective Factors: Crafting the Personal Portrait

Possessing compelling, meaningful subjective factors, such as your extracurricular activities and essays, is your intangible but potent tool for transmuting a collection of good academic accomplishments into an intimate, artistic portrait that the viewer simply cannot deny.

Colleges do not require extracurricular activities – technically.

No college as part of its application process specifically mandates that its applicants have participated in extracurricular activities. But even at schools that do not practice admissions very holistically, extracurricular activities are often desired and occasionally compulsory in practice. At schools whose admissions are holistic, extracurricular involvement is all but vital. At holistic and highly selective colleges,

---

[172] SAT Word Alert: *Penchant* (noun) means "a strong liking"

we would not hesitate to deem meaningful participation in out-of-classroom activities a de facto requirement for admission.

When it comes to extracurricular activities, pursue quality over quantity.

There is, of course, no magic number for the appropriate or ideal number of extracurricular activities applicants to highly selective colleges must have to delineate on the application. Despite some students' behavior that would suggest otherwise, there is no general preference for more activities rather than fewer.

So, first, what is an extracurricular activity anyhow? Indeed, many students inquire whether a given activity in which they participate "counts" as an extracurricular activity for college admissions. Your extracurricular activities need not be the traditional clubs and teams that most high schools have (e.g., Spanish club, math team, service club, Model United Nations, etc.), although those are decidedly appropriate ones to participate in. Basically, whatever interests you – whether it's composing music or photographing tall buildings or writing poetry – can be a perfectly valid extracurricular activity.

But since we want to "pursue quality," some extracurriculars have to be better than others, right? Sorry, but there is no cheap and easy answer here, no universally applicable regimen for the ticket into the Ivy League. But we also don't want to cop out with the familiar refrain that vaguely admonishes you to follow your *passions*, as if most high school students have cleanly sorted everything in life into categories of things about which they are passionate and things about which they are not. (Most adults are still discovering their "passions"!) Instead, **extracurricular involvement is about exploration, devotion, responsibility, and service**.

The better extracurricular activities are those that vividly demonstrate a desire to enrich yourself artistically or intellectually or to enrich the community you inhabit. An admissions officer seeks students that will take advantage of the opportunities that attending the college affords them. Such a student explores what is at his or her disposal, moving on from that which does no good for him or others and sticking devotedly to a few meaningful activities.

Leadership in, a long-term commitment to, and success in your extracurriculars are ways for you to convey that idea to the admissions officers who face a regrettably increasing population of applicants who participate in activities not out of interest in the activities themselves but out of a drive to get into a prestigious college. We have written that developing a genuine desire to do well on the SAT or ACT, rather than painfully forcing yourself through preparation, will lead to better scores. A sincere mentality is helpful for extracurricular involvement, too, especially when it can shine through in the application.

The takeaway here should be that colleges want students who will contribute in meaningful, non-academic ways to their campuses. Your extracurriculars should give them the impression that you will do just that.

When you write your extracurricular activities on your application, your job is very much artistic.

Based only on the title of this chapter, it should be clear that we analogize college admissions to art. We think this captures the multifaceted, holistic, and subjective nature of competitive college admissions. This connection bears not only on how what you decide to do – what classes you take, what activities you participate in, what Subject Tests you submit, what essay topics you opt for, and so on – comes together as a compelling package but on how you convey all of this on paper (or on the web application).

On the Common Application, your canvas is somewhat constrained by the boxes they allow for listing your activities. Don't feel, however, that what they label the boxes should preclude you from being able to tell a miniature story with your listing of extracurricular activities. Use up as much of each box as you can without going beyond space limits (confirm compliance with a print preview before submitting). Employ the space as an opportunity to describe in as illustrative a way as possible what you have been up to.

Instead of writing that, for example, you were Vice President of Spanish Club and calling it a day, indicate under your responsibilities (if it's true!) that you were the organizer of various fundraisers and service clinics for non-native area speakers. It is more descriptive and more interesting; it imparts some substance to the plain title.

Earning awards is great, but it's not the only way to show involvement or success.

Awards are excellent signals of your talent in and dedication to the fields that you have extracurricular interests in. For students whose interests are in math and science, there are a number of widely recognized, prestigious, and challenging competitions to try your hand at, such as the International Mathematical Olympiad, the International Biology Olympiad, the International Chemical Olympiad, the International Physics Olympiad, and the Intel Science Talent Search. If you are interested in these competitions, Shiv was the primary author of *Success with Science: The Winners' Guide to High School Research* (www.successwithscience.org), which is the definitive manual for student research.

Success on the national level in these competitions can greatly bolster your extracurricular profile and in turn improve your chance of admittance, not to mention the intrinsic value of accomplishment and learning that accompanies preparing for and succeeding in the events. Particularly extraordinary results in well-known competitions can make a big difference in your admissions chances:

Any college will have a hard time saying, "No, thanks," to a student who wins the Intel competition.

If head-to-head competition doesn't suit your style or you are interested in fields that don't have many competitions, don't fret: Awards are not the sole route of affirming ability and involvement. Recommendations attesting to your demonstration of those qualities do the job, too, as can sending in research or artistic supplements for professors' review. Inquire with each college you are applying to, in order to see what their policies are for these supplemental submissions.

Don't worry about the effect that your race, ethnicity, gender, or socioeconomic status may have on admissions.

Controversially, at schools that practice race-based affirmative action – which is most American colleges and universities – those that belong to underrepresented minority groups (Native Americans, African Americans, and some Hispanic-American populations) may receive an admissions boost in the interest of building a racially diverse student body.

For the most part, your gender is irrelevant to the admissions process. Yet at schools whose students tend disproportionately to be of one gender (for example, males at science and engineering schools and females at liberal arts colleges), the minority gender may receive a modest tip in the admissions process.

If you have financial need, you may be disadvantaged in the admissions process if a school is not financial need-blind, because such colleges prefer to accept students who can afford to pay unassisted. But at the highly selective colleges that practice circumstance-sensitive holistic admissions and that also tend to be financial need-blind, being socioeconomically disadvantaged may help you, because you have succeeded despite facing the obstacle of being in a low-income family.

But you can't really change any of this stuff, and the various advantages and disadvantages that could be further discussed here are generally not as significant as many believe. So don't worry about it.

Briefly, there are a few more factors that may give certain applicants an advantage.

Applicants who are the first generation in their families to attend college may receive a small bump. A legacy applicant (in other words, one whose parent is an alumnus of the college), especially when the parent has donated to the college, is also advantaged. If you are an unusually strong athlete who intends to participate competitively in college, the coach for the sport at the college may recruit you, which is significantly helpful in the admissions process.

How impactful a recommendation is on the admissions decision depends on what it says.

Recommendations have the potential to be very important, but largely they have little effect, partly because many recommenders are often too vaguely positive in their descriptions: *I recommend Marvin because he is a very good student who has succeeded in my class and will do well at your college.* Of course, a recommendation can also become very important in a bad way if it is negative, over which even overly general extolment[173] is decidedly preferable.

A glowing, specific recommendation is ideal. Such a report will complement the rest of your application, highlighting what you have otherwise indicated to be your strengths but providing some more human depth to the picture. The recommenders you choose should be teachers and other (non-parental) adults in positions important for your development and who can unequivocally recommend you as well as explain *why* such a positive appraisal is warranted.

Leave your recommenders ample time to write a recommendation. If they are rushed, your recommendations may suffer from compromises in quality (and even mild annoyance).

The potential for great importance but the commonplace reality of unimportance applies to interviews, too.

If the interview report is unusually glowing, you may be helped much; if it is negative, you will be hurt much. But frequently, the theme here is similar to that for recommendations: Alumni interviewers' reports are positive and vague and thus relatively inconsequential. The interview is actually more valuable as an opportunity for you to ask questions about the college that your interviewer graduated from, especially if he or she is a recent alumnus. Students are often told to relax and treat the interview as a conversation and chance to learn – rather than as one more test. This is good advice.

If a college is unable to offer you an interview, you will not be disadvantaged in any way. However, don't turn down one that is offered to you; this may raise some portentous flags as to your sociability or interest in the college.

College essays matter a lot.

The essays that you submit with your application are among the most important sources of information for admissions officers at schools with competitive and subjective admissions. At other schools, they will still hold some weight, so spending the time to write strong essays is worthwhile, especially if your objective statistics render you a borderline applicant.

---

[173] SAT Word Alert: *Extol* (verb) means "to praise highly"

Spend plenty of time on your essays, respect the length requirement and prompt (unless you are given free rein on what to write, which is an option for the main personal statement of the Common Application), and contemplate introspectively on what you could write that would more cogently go beyond the numbers and communicate your deep qualities.

Tips on the personal statement?

Absolutely! See below:

Proofread your essay. Unlike on the SAT and ACT essays, you do not have a time limit when you are drafting a college essay. There is, therefore, the opportunity to expunge[174] all grammatical and typographical errors – by simply reading your draft over closely several (or many) times. You do not want your intended meaning to be obscured or distorted by a mishap on the keyboard. Depending on the nature and frequency of the errors, admissions officers may question your ability to write grammatically and/or the care you put into the essay. With that said, isolated, minor errors will not significantly affect your admissions chances; they might even go unnoticed.[175]

Make your essay sound natural. When formulating the verbal units and structure that will ultimately constitute one's college essay, he or she must exercise exacting[176] discrimination in the selection of diction and syntax so as to ensure that his or her essay conveys organically and in the most sententious[177] of ways. Or, as said in less ironic words, make the voice of the writing your own and be concise. Take care to avoid ungainly[178] sentence structures and excessively formal word choice.

You are in control of structure. Nope, you do not need to stick to the format of three body paragraphs, an introduction, and a conclusion that you surely learned earlier in your schooling years. Structure is not unimportant, however; the particular structure you employ should be whatever works best to communicate your message.

Use, but don't abuse, the hook. A hook can be used to attract the attention of your fish – readers. At its best, a hook is often a surprising or seemingly paradoxical[179] metaphor or narrative at the beginning of an essay that serves to lead into and provide context for the rest of your writing. Or hooks, relying on illogical conceits, can end up being too labyrinthine[180] and go unexplained for too long. A good hook

---

[174] SAT Word Alert: *Expunge* (verb) means "to wipe out"

[175] We would like at this point to throw out a "Yeah, you got us" flag of surrender in the direction of anyone who finds an unintentional typo or typos somewhere in this book. There were lots of words to review!

[176] SAT Word Alert: *Exacting* (adjective) means "rigid or severe in demands or requirements"

[177] SAT Word Alert: *Sententious* (adjective) means "characterized by or full of aphorisms, terse pithy sayings, or axioms"

[178] SAT Word Alert: *Ungainly* (adjective) means "clumsy or awkward"

[179] SAT Word Alert: *Paradoxical* (adjective) means "relating to a self-contradiction"

calls for reading on, but if it doesn't ultimately make sense, admissions officers' annoyance and dissatisfaction will befall you. The best way to avoid the latter scenario is to have people whose opinions you trust read over your essays and tell you what they think works and what doesn't.

Do not be abstract. A common downfall of even those who are good writers – one often stemming from discomfort with writing about themselves – is to use such disconnected and abstract language and metaphors that your essay means more on a generally philosophical level than it does on a personal level. Which brings us to…

Focus on yourself. Ultimately, the goal of the personal statement is to offer a clear explanation of you, your personality, and your interests so that the admissions officer who is reading your application is compelled to accept you because he or she understands you and how you could contribute to the school. And in the interest of being an *unusually* compelling applicant amid a sea of "good" college essays, strive to paint yourself in the truest way possible; in that way, your uniqueness and idiosyncrasies[181] will shine through, and you'll stand out.

Don't write a boring essay. All people are so inherently interesting and multi-layered that any boring essay is reflective of a failure to observe the previous guideline that the essay should be an illustration of you.

Falling into college essay cliché may not seem intrinsically boring to the writer, who may just find it comfortable, for example, to state in general terms how the Big Game taught him or her about the importance of practice and perseverance. Even if true, a familiar narrative with hackneyed themes disrespects your depth. Blake has read and edited thousands of students' essays; the most enduring learning he has garnered[182] from this experience (aside from the fact that most students could benefit from reading up on the grammar tips earlier in this book) is that a successful essay surmounts the inviting tendency to obscure the self with conformist triteness. You aren't the same as anyone else. Don't let this expression of you suggest that you are.

If you are interested in contacting us for personalized help with your college essays, follow the "Contact" link at k12.osmosis.org.

Scholarships

College is expensive. Although I am sure that you believe us, here are some annual cost figures to give you a concrete sense of just how true that statement is (additional expenses, such as travel, books, entertainment, dining out, and arbitrary fees imposed by the colleges are excluded here):

---

[180] SAT Word Alert: *Labyrinthine* (adjective) means "complicated or tortuous"
[181] SAT Word Alert: *Idiosyncrasy* (noun) means "a characteristic that is particular to an individual"
[182] SAT Word Alert: *Garner* (verb) means "get or acquire"

Yale University

Tuition: $40,500

Room and Board: $12,200

University of Notre Dame

Tuition: $41,420

Room and Board: $11,390

University of Illinois at Urbana-Champaign

Tuition (in-state/out-of-state): $10,204 / $23,470

Room and Board: $9,714

The figures for Yale and Notre Dame are representative of the costs of the majority of private colleges and universities. Most public universities adopt a pricing structure similar to that employed by the University of Illinois, in which non-residents of the state that the university is located in pay significantly higher tuition than those residing within the state. But some public universities are relatively affordable for in-state students, such as:

University of Florida

Tuition: $5,020

Room and Board: $8,640

All told, it is possible to spend somewhere between $200,000 and $250,000 over four years on an education at one of the nation's private colleges. Out-of-state costs for some public universities, such as the University of California, Berkeley, will reach approximately that much, as well.

Many students eventually rack up costs much greater than even those numbers suggest: Most college undergraduates at four-year schools do not graduate within four years, and only about half do so in even six years.

The vast majority of American families cannot possibly afford these costs without incurring crippling amounts of debt through loans and potentially being relegated[183] to near-impecuniousness[184]. While college is still financially burdensome on most families and many find themselves with few options beyond community college

---

[183] SAT Word Alert: *Relegate* (verb) means "to consign to an inferior circumstance"
[184] SAT Word Alert: *Impecunious* (adjective) means "penniless"

(which is often a good option for students who want to transfer to a four-year university after two years), these numbers do not tell the whole story. There is hope.

Colleges offer aid based on the amount of need that students have.

Colleges typically request that applicants provide the government's FAFSA (Free Application for Federal Student Aid, which also helps to determine eligibility for federal grants) and/or the College Board's CSS PROFILE (College Scholarship Service Profile). Based on the information revealed by those forms, each college will determine the amount of financial need that an applicant has by subtracting the EFC (Expected Family Contribution) from the college's cost of attendance.

Some colleges will then cover that difference in full through loans, which must be paid back; grants, which are need-based scholarships in the typical sense and need not be paid back; or some combination thereof. Other colleges are able to provide aid to offset only part of that financial need.

It is important to note that the EFC as determined by colleges is rarely consistent with the family's own sense of the need – and usually not in the family's favor. Indeed, even at colleges that claim to provide aid for 100 percent of demonstrated financial need, many families find themselves unable to afford the college, aid included.

But some universities, typically the most selective ones, are particularly generous. At Harvard, for instance, families whose combined household incomes are under $60,000 are expected to pay nothing toward the cost of attendance, and families whose household incomes fall between $60,000 and $180,000 will, on average, pay roughly 10% of that income, although special circumstances not taken into account by the single income figure are considered also. (Some aid for those making over $180,000 a year is not unheard of.)

Because of their multi-billion-dollar endowments, other top schools, such as Princeton, Stanford, and Yale, have similarly generous need-based aid programs.

Colleges and private organizations offer aid based on the merit of the applicant.

Many private colleges and almost all public universities, whose need-based aid is generally less significant than private colleges', offer merit-based financial aid. Having to look through thousands of applications to find the ones to be deemed worthy of merit aid, admissions officers at large schools find themselves relying largely on objective, quantitative factors to determine merit aid. (At smaller schools, essays become more important during merit-aid consideration.)

In such cases, having an unusually high SAT or ACT score is enormously helpful, often necessary, in earning merit-based aid. Some schools have scaling aid programs in which a combination of your GPA or rank and standardized testing score will predictably determine how much aid you receive. Other colleges automatically offer near- or full-tuition and fee waivers to students earning very high scores, as long as the rest of their respective applications are strong.

Some of these scholarship programs require applications separate from those for general admission to the university, but some are awarded merely through the identification of applicants who are outstandingly academically promising. Scores are an important factor in that consideration.

Outside scholarships are offered, as well. These sources of aid, which are granted not by the university but by private organizations, are often geared toward a specific group (for example, those whose ancestors fought in a given war or whose parents work for a specific company) and are determined through "softer," less objective factors, such as applicants' essays. Nonetheless, high scores frequently play a role and are an excellent way to beneficially quantitatively distinguish you from a field of applicants.

Your PSAT score can earn you money.

The College Board, the administrators of the SAT, also offers the PSAT (Preliminary SAT), a shorter version of the SAT taken primarily by juniors to practice for the SAT.

By taking the PSAT and fulfilling the eligibility requirements – such as being in your junior year of high school when you take it and a citizen or lawful permanent resident of the United States – you are automatically registered in the National Merit Scholarship Program, a competition run by the National Merit Scholarship Corporation. You might even occasionally see the PSAT called the National Merit Scholarship Qualifying Test, or NMSQT.

A student's progress toward being named a National Merit Scholar follows these steps:

In October of the student's junior year of high school, he or she will take the PSAT. Around April of that student's junior year, he or she may be notified through the mail of having earned a PSAT score that puts him or her among the 50,000 top-scoring high school juniors who took the PSAT that year. The cutoff score is thus around the 96.5th percentile and has historically been near 201 out of 240.

Early in senior year, a student who has qualified to be one of those 50,000 will be notified of whether he or she is Commended (a distinction earned by 34,000 that means that he or she will not progress further in the competition) or a Semifinalist, which is awarded to the remaining 16,000 based on another, higher score cutoff. Whereas the cutoff for becoming Commended is national (again, typically about 201), that for Semifinalist qualification varies from state to state in order to ensure roughly proportionate geographic representation. These state cutoffs also vary from year to year, but these numbers should give you a close idea of where the score for your state will fall in any given year:

Alabama - 208
Alaska - 211
Arizona - 210
Arkansas - 203
California - 218
Colorado - 215
Connecticut - 218
Delaware - 219
District of Columbia - 221
Florida - 211
Georgia - 214
Hawaii - 214
Idaho - 209
Illinois - 214
Indiana - 211
Iowa - 209
Kansas - 211
Kentucky - 209
Louisiana - 207
Maine - 213
Maryland - 221
Massachusetts - 221
Michigan - 209
Minnesota - 215
Mississippi - 203
Missouri - 211
Montana - 204
Nebraska - 207
Nevada - 202
New Hampshire - 213
New Jersey - 221
New Mexico - 208
New York - 218
North Carolina - 214
North Dakota - 202
Ohio - 211
Oklahoma - 207
Oregon - 213
Pennsylvania - 214
Rhode Island - 217
South Carolina - 211

South Dakota - 205
Tennessee - 213
Texas - 216
Utah - 206
Vermont - 213
Virginia - 218
Washington - 217
West Virginia - 203
Wisconsin - 207
Wyoming - 201

The 16,000 seniors who qualify as National Merit Semifinalists are then asked to submit additional application materials (thus far in the outlined steps, only the PSAT score has mattered), including an essay and a high school transcript. Students must also submit an SAT score, which is something occasionally overlooked by Midwestern applicants – and is, in fact, another reason for all students to consider taking both the SAT and ACT. As long as a student sends in these materials and satisfies the SAT-score cutoff (which is approximately, compared to the PSAT cutoffs, a relatively modest 1950 out of 2400), he or she will be named a Finalist. 15,000 of the 16,000 who are Semifinalists become Finalists.

Among those 15,000 Finalists, 8,000 National Merit Scholars are selected, based on a review of the extra application materials. Each of these Scholars is awarded one of the $2,500 National Merit Scholarship Corporation scholarships or one of the usually more generous corporate scholarships, which are given to students whose parents work for one of the participating institutions.

But being a National Merit Scholar, Finalist, or Semifinalist can be much more lucrative than that amount suggests: Many universities offer guaranteed scholarships to such students. The University of Alabama, for example, offers a full tuition and fees scholarship plus a monetary stipend and laptop to National Merit Finalists and Scholars!

Paying for college is a pain.

It is beyond the scope of our coverage to attempt to become your financial adviser or even offer a comprehensive guide to college scholarships. There are many thousands of different scholarship funds out there, some of which are highly competitive and scarce but others of which go largely neglected. Do your research; find potential scholarships that complement a particular niche you occupy, so that competitors for the money are fewer.

If it comes to it, consider very seriously how much debt you are willing to incur in order to attend a particular college. Sometimes, good schools that don't have aid programs as generous as their elite peers do are just too expensive, even after all the merit aid, need-based aid, and outside scholarships are tallied up. Don't be romantically caught up in attending a "better" college if it means years of financial anxiety thereafter. College is an investment in your future, but some forms of that investment are wiser than others.

CHAPTER 11
10 (ESCALATOR) STEPS TO SUCCEEDING IN HIGH SCHOOL, COLLEGE, AND BEYOND

Congratulations on making it this far! If you have adhered[185] to the advice and strategies we inculcated[186] in the previous chapters, you are well on your way to SAT and ACT glory. However, more important than the test scores you earn, which are just snapshots of your current skill set, you have strengthened your abilities in mathematics, reading, English, and science reasoning. Rest assured that these aptitudes will serve you well as you progress in academics and eventually your career.

As we near the dénouement[187] of the book, we think it would be prudent[188] to share ten steps we have taken (and seen our peers take) that have been invaluable for succeeding in high school, college, and beyond. These steps are in no particular order, and they range from extremely practical (things that you can implement today) to slightly idealistic (things that you should strive towards, though they may take more time). We have also provided resources that will help you implement many of the steps.

Just as we are certain that the outstandingly effective strategies in the previous chapters will help you ace the SAT and ACT, we are positive that the steps below will help you get more out of your academic, and even extracurricular, experiences. Without further ado, let's start climbing.

Step 1: Avoid the Stepping Stone Myth

We discussed the Stepping Stone Myth early in the first chapter and feel so strongly about debunking[189] it that we made it into the first step. You may recall that the flaw in the Stepping Stone Myth is not that impressive extracurriculars, test scores, and grades (ETGs) would not help you get into college; they will. Rather, the problem is in viewing those achievements as means to an end rather than ends in themselves. Furthermore, *stepping stone* implies that each stone is independent and does not build upon the others. We have shown you that this is not the case; as an example, improving your vocabulary for the SAT will increase your ability to

---

[185] SAT Word Alert: *Adhere* (verb) means "to stay attached, to hold closely"

[186] SAT Word Alert: *Inculcate* (verb) can also mean "to teach persistently and earnestly" (we used this word in Chapter 6)

[187] SAT Word Alert: *Dénouement* (noun) means "the outcome or resolution"

[188] SAT Word Alert: *Prudent* (adjective) means "wise or judicious"

[189] SAT Word Alert: *Debunk* (verb) means "to expose or excoriate as false or exaggerated"

understand and write more advanced essays, which in turn will improve your GPA and eventually your career prospects. Knowing this, you have devoted more energy to actually learning vocabulary rather than gaming the system through gimmicky testing strategies. Even more meaningfully, you may even – gasp – *enjoy* deepening your knowledge of the English language by finding out new names for ideas; that cannot be mistaken as a mere stepping stone.

This applies not just to academic skills, but also to extracurricular activities. In the eyes of teachers, competition judges, and college admissions staff, there is a world of difference between the students who do activities like science research because they are genuinely interested in them and those who do the activities merely to list on their résumés.

Note that the steps presented in this chapter are not independent, like stones, but rather connected, like those of an escalator. They do not read like a checklist because one would be hard-pressed to put a check of completion next to any of them. As long as you continually strive towards these steps, you will improve your chances of succeeding and, most importantly, improving yourself.

In brief, the sooner you banish the Stepping Stone Myth from your mind and from the minds of your parents, siblings, teachers, and other influences, the sooner you will start getting more out of your activities. But how do you know what activities to pursue in the first place? Proceed to the next step.

Step 2: Seek Inspiration

The best way to have a good idea is to have lots of ideas.

Linus Pauling (1901-1994)
Dual Nobel Laureate, Chemistry and Peace

"What inspires you?"

It is a simple yet rarely asked question that frequently results in not-so-simple answers.

Chances are you've been asked more tepid[190] versions of this question, such as "What interests you?" and "What do you like to do?" When asked these questions, many students will predictably shift their gazes, let out low groans, and mumble, "I don't know" (or worse, "Nothing"). The purpose of step two is to make sure that you don't do this.

Students who answer in the aforementioned way are seldom completely undecided or apathetic[191]. Virtually everyone has interests, ranging from computers to Chinese

---

[190] SAT Word Alert: *Tepid* (adjective) means "lukewarm, characterized by lack of force or enthusiasm"

history, French to fashion, math to music, and paintball to pop culture. However, many students are not necessarily *inspired* by these interests and activities, at least not to the point that they *act* on them. Many of the steps below explain how to raise the bar and act on these interests. For example, the student learning French could begin a blog in which he or she writes posts only in French, the student passionate about math could do a research project or teach younger students after school, and the student who plays music could work towards recording an album.

The quote at the beginning of this step hits the nail on the head. There is a corollary to it: *The best way to have lots of ideas is to expose yourself to many ideas* – that is, to seek inspiration. Interests are just one source (albeit a major source) from which inspiration comes. Other sources of inspiration include one's surroundings, circumstances, and influences. We've included below a list of resources that may help you seek inspiration, come up with lots of ideas, and eventually have some good ideas that you can then act upon.

Resources for Seeking Inspiration

- TED Talks –www.ted.com

- Big Think –www.bigthink.com

- Life Hacker –www.lifehacker.com

- The 99 Percent – www.the99percent.com

- Google Scholar –scholar.google.com

And for those interested specifically in research, below are two helpful resources Shiv has been involved with:

- Success with Science –www.successwithscience.org
- The Archimedes Initiative –www.archimedesinitiative.org

Step 3: Become a Journalist (Or, At Least, Write)

Earlier in this book, we emphasized the importance of reading often and widely in order to improve your reading comprehension skills. Well, step three raises the bar and is based on the observation that one of the best ways to write better is to write often. And the best way to make yourself write often is to make writing a job (at least part-time) – that is, to become a journalist. This doesn't mean that you need to become a reporter for the *New York Times* tomorrow; rather, there are thousands of publications and blogs, covering virtually every topic, that are constantly searching

---

[191] SAT Word Alert: *Apathetic* (adjective) means "not interested or concerned, indifferent or unresponsive"

for interesting content. Many would be happy to accept your contributions. Some of them even pay![192] However, at your stage, that's not the primary reason to write.

In the book *The Shallows: What the Internet is Doing to Our Brains*, Nicholas Carr presents evidence that our habits of Internet browsing and multi-tasking are adversely[193] affecting our abilities to concentrate and engage in critical analysis. As our eyes quickly dart from tab to tab and search result to search result, we've become accustomed to picking up bits and pieces of information without having to synthesize them in a coherent format. The first reason for step three – becoming or at least thinking like a journalist – is that writing forces one to stop to actually consider and amalgamate[194] what he or she has read. This is an invaluable exercise, because one quickly realizes that many of the purported[195] facts and ideas on the Internet conflict or are blatantly[196] incorrect. Paraphrasing the late Dean of Harvard Jeremy Knowles, the main – if not only – purpose of a liberal arts education is to know when someone is "talking rot."

A second reason for writing frequently and in a structured venue is to develop a portfolio early on. For example, Shiv began writing for the teen section of the *Florida Today* as a freshman in high school, and many of his articles helped him as he applied for college admissions and other opportunities. The one caveat to building a portfolio is that you want to make sure what you're writing is high-quality (e.g. free of typos, grammatical mistakes, improper language, etc.) and something you feel comfortable sharing with the world. Use judgment when expressing opinions publicly, especially if a potential recruiter or interviewer could easily find those viewpoints via Google.

Another benefit of writing is that you may have the opportunity to review books or products, interview cool people, and attend space-limited events with press passes. Before providing any examples of these, it is important to note that there are professional standards that you should adhere to. Many a journalist who did not has ruined his or her reputation. Specifically, you must avoid plagiarism at all costs, be honest with and fair to your interviewees, and disclose potential conflicts of interest or altogether avoid such situations. That being said, even if you blog for a fairly niche publication, you can be presented with amazing opportunities. As an example, by writing for the popular medical technology blog *Medgadget*, Shiv has been able to review cutting-edge devices, interview Dr. Oz, and attend TEDMED and the Consumer Electronics Show.

---

[192] Remember those dreaded 500-word essays? Those don't seem so bad when you get paid upwards of $0.25 *per word.* Imagine if each of those essays you turned in was worth $125!

[193] SAT Word Alert: *Adverse* (adjective) means "unfavorable or antagonistic in purpose or effect"

[194] SAT Word Alert: *Amalgamate* (verb) means "to mix or merge, blend, unite, combine"

[195] SAT Word Alert: *Purport* (verb) means "profess or claim, often falsely"

[196] SAT Word Alert: *Blatant* (adjective) means "brazenly obvious, flagrant"

The final reason for becoming a journalist that we will discuss is that writing helps you meet people and make connections. This is related to the next step on building your network. Most high school students have limited networks of peers, family, teachers, neighbors, employers, and, if they're lucky, people they meet at summer programs. As mentioned above, writing can present opportunities such as interviewing people in fields you are interested in. For example, maybe you are interested in learning about Professor Awesome's research at University of My Dreams. As a journalist, you can easily contact Professor Awesome for an interview for your blog or publication and thus expand your network.

Now that you are itching to become a journalist and begin writing in a frequent and structured manner, how do you actually do it? Here's a short list that will get you started:

- Figure out what fields and types of material you'd like to write about (see Step 2: Seek Inspiration).

- Use Google and other search engines to find existing blogs and publications that cover these fields.

- Read a number of the articles and posts at those blogs and publications that really interest you.

- Write a sample post/article or two, or at least generate a list of ideas of topics that you would like to cover if you were writing for that publication.

- Contact the blogs and publications to professionally introduce yourself and enthusiastically express your desire to contribute, perhaps even sharing a few of the ideas you came up with. Though it's important to be honest in your introduction, you should let your ideas and writing samples speak for themselves. To that end, it may not be necessary to immediately volunteer that you are in high school. There is precedent for this: The history and literature buffs among you may remember that some of the most famous female authors used male pen names in order to ensure their works were taken seriously (e.g. Mary Ann Evans, aka George Eliot, and the Brontë Sisters, aka the Bell Brothers).

- Hopefully you'll receive at least one positive reply that will likely ask for a sample post, which you can send in right away. Quick turnaround from writers is highly valued by editors, who are often under time pressure to meet deadlines.

- If no blogs or publications reply in a reasonable time frame, you should persist or even consider starting your own blog! This may have the positive side effect of teaching you how to create a website and, hopefully, even code.

Step 4: Build Your Network (Then Learn from It!)

As a high school student, you may not yet realize how important this step is or what types of opportunities may present themselves if you take the time to build and strengthen your network. Consider the following personal example. During Shiv's junior year at Harvard, he wrote an essay about the large number of science and math majors who wind up going into the financial services sector as opposed to the research and development industry. The conclusion was that, for the sake of our economy, universities needed to do a better job of pairing bright students with R&D companies to plug the exacerbating[197] brain drain to Wall Street. Shiv sent this essay to a few friends and mentors for feedback. One of his classmates happened to know an economist at the National Bureau for Economics Research, and the next thing Shiv knew, he was invited on an expenses-paid trip to Washington, DC to present his views to congressional staffers. The moral of the story is that if you cast a wide and strong net, you're more likely to catch a fish (or something you didn't even expect, like a lobster!).

If you like meeting people, this step should be no problem. Even if you are more on the reserved side of the introvert-extrovert spectrum, online social networking has made it really easy to meet people without sticking your neck out an uncomfortable distance. Becoming a journalist (step 3) and building your reputation (step 8) are really helpful ways to connect with people around the world who may be willing to help you achieve your goals.

Now for a practical question: Who are these people that you should be connecting with? First and foremost, your family. Though we'd like to think that our meritocratic society is devoid of nepotism[198], family remains a strong influence on one's trajectory. Even if Bill Gates isn't your uncle or Mark Zuckerberg isn't your cousin, you can learn a lot and draw strength from your family, who more often than not will be supportive of your initiatives and goals. Next are your friends, who will often go out of their way to help you. Though there will likely be diaspora[199] following your high school graduation, it is a good idea to keep in touch with at least your closest friends. Fortunately, Facebook, Google Hangout, and other social networking sites are here to help you.

Note that your network should include not only peers in your grade level, but also older students whom you may have met through courses, activities like sports teams or orchestras, and at other events. These peers are an invaluable resource when it comes to applying to and deciding on college as well as transitioning to post-high school life. Also, don't be shy to reach out to an older peer (probably via Facebook or e-mail) whom you may never have met in person but who you know attends a

---

[197] SAT Word Alert: *Exacerbate* (verb) means "to increase the severity, aggravate"

[198] SAT Word Alert: *Nepotism* (noun) means "favoritism shown on the basis of family relationship"

[199] SAT Word Alert: *Diaspora* (noun) means "dispersion, dissemination, scattering"

college or studies a major that you are interested in. They will often be more than willing to help. Then, when you become an "older peer," be sure to help younger peers in the same way. Finally, a fourth group for you to build into your network should be mentors such as teachers, professors, employers, coaches, and other professionals. These mentors will be able to write recommendations as you transition to college and beyond, and more importantly they will pass on knowledge and skills that took them years of experience to obtain. It is worthwhile to consider connecting with these people via more professional networking sites, like LinkedIn or Twitter.

Step 5: Teach Yourself (Definitely Coding)

We learn more by looking for the answer to a question and not finding it than we do from learning the answer itself.

Lloyd Alexander (1924-2007)
American Author & Newbery Medal Recipient

This is an unprecedented time in the history of human opportunity. Modern society has become so technologically advanced and interconnected that the only prerequisite to learning virtually anything is a computer with an Internet connection. Less than one generation ago, the collective knowledge of mankind was, for the most part, available only on slowly disintegrating pages that were tucked away deep inside of book fortresses. One had to physically travel and gain access to the oasis to learn anything not already known by teachers, family, or friends.

The advent[200] of the digital revolution liberated human knowledge from tangible[201] books accessible only to the fortunate. Over the course of the past two decades, thousands of websites – and, more recently, videos and interactive apps – have emerged that are devoted to teaching everything from algebra to Zen Buddhism. Many of these are completely free, only requiring a little motivation and discipline. One of the most exciting developments has been the open access to top-notch courses given by excellent professors through platforms such as Coursera (pioneered by Stanford, Princeton, UPenn, and UMichigan) and edX (led by Harvard, MIT) – a phenomenon known as Massive Open Online Courses (MOOCs).

As the quote above expresses, the experience of finding something out for oneself is both invaluable and memorable.[202] If you do not understand something from a course, there is simply no excuse to not learn it. Many topics covered in high school and college textbooks are explained on the Internet in dozens of different ways by

---

[200] SAT Word Alert: *Advent* (noun) means "arrival"

[201] SAT Word Alert: *Tangible* (adjective) means "capable of being touched, definite, real or actual"

[202] There is a great xkcd comic about teaching oneself titled "11th-Grade Activities." xkcd.com/519/

hundreds or thousands of teachers and peers. You can take your pick: this teacher or that teacher, discussion forum or static webpage, image or diagram, YouTube video or animation, practice questions or interactive applet. Next time you have the urge to ask a peer, family member, or teacher something that you think may be explained elsewhere, stop, think, and try to teach yourself. It will turn you into a self-reliant autodidact.

Be sure to learn at least one entirely useful skill, such as how to build a computer, fix a car, balance a checkbook, or use Excel. The job market is at times very difficult, so do not trust your college, especially if it is not pre-professionally oriented, to set you up with marketable skills. One increasingly important skill that you should aim to teach yourself is at least a rudimentary understanding of computers and coding. Developers are always a hot commodity, whether on campus or at a company. Think about how many websites, apps, and electronics you use each day. How many of those are black boxes to you? Regardless of which field you eventually decide upon, a basic literacy and skill set of computers and programming will be helpful. For example, whether you become a fashion designer or set up a private medical practice, you'll need a web and social media presence. Why pay someone else thousands of dollars to set up a basic site when you could learn to do it yourself? We have each taken college programming courses and found them immensely useful, but that's not the only way to gain programming knowledge. Fortunately, it's never been easier to learn how to code, thanks to resources like Codecademy. We've included a number of other resources below that will help you become a self-learning master.

Resources for Teaching Yourself

- Coursera - www.coursera.org/
- edX - www.edxonline.org
- Udemy - www.udemy.com/courses
- Khan Academy - www.khanacademy.org/
- Codecademy - www.codecademy.com/
- LadyAda - www.adafruit.com
- Duolingo - duolingo.com/
- Wikipedia - www.wikipedia.org/
- How Stuff Works –www.howstuffworks.com/
- Google - www.google.com/

Step 6: Teach Others

The best way to learn is to teach.

Frank Oppenheimer (1912-1985)
American Particle Physicist & High School Mentor

If you worked through the earlier parts of this book, you will be intimately familiar with this step. Remember "Think like a Test-Maker, Not a Test-Taker," where we suggested you practice writing questions so you could broaden your perspective? Along with other strategies in the book, this is based on the educational theory that people generally learn better and retain more if they practice doing and then teach others.

The Learning Pyramid is a popular depiction of this notion. Each level of the pyramid represents a style of learning and corresponds to how effective that method is, with the most effective strategies at the base of the pyramid. Thus, simply listening to someone else explain something is at the top, because people purportedly only retain 5-10 percent of what they hear. Discussion of the material improves retention to 50 percent, but the most effective ways are by practicing doing (75 percent) and teaching (90 percent). While the specific values presented in the pyramid are still being researched, the hierarchy intuitively makes sense. Imagine learning algebra without doing any practice problems. Seems difficult, doesn't it? Now think about a time when you taught someone – a friend, sibling, or even parent – a concept. You had to understand that concept pretty well before you could teach it, and chances are that you still remember it.

In addition to learning and retaining more, another benefit of teaching someone is, well, teaching someone. It is a win-win situation, because you will be helping someone understand a challenging concept. That being said, teaching can be frustrating or time-consuming. Therefore, it will be helpful to have (or develop!) patience and compassion – it will serve you well, because eventually you will need to teach someone else, be it your student, employee, child, etc. Another option is to become a paid tutor, especially if you are pressed for time or need another incentive to teach. Many parents and students are willing to pay experienced older students for help, especially when it comes to college admissions exams and GPAs. Also, once you graduate from high school, many colleges have tutoring services through which they pay students to teach other students. For example, at the time of writing this, Harvard's Bureau of Study Counsel (BSC) paid its peer tutors about $15 per hour, which certainly helps defray college expenses or makes for a nice allowance. Peer tutoring is very common; the BSC reports that during the last academic year, 450 peer tutors fulfilled 1,600 requests in over 200 courses. A final note on tutoring for money: Remember that you must always be honest about what you know and fair in terms of fees. It is wise to devote a percentage of your tutoring time to complimentary services. You cannot put a price on goodwill.

Before you post on Facebook that you are available for peer tutoring, here are a few ideas about how to get started teaching others.

- Make a list of the subjects and specific courses that you feel comfortable teaching. Feel free to teach material that you are not the most comfortable with, in order to learn, though you should probably not charge for the tutoring time.

- Talk to your friends or siblings and see if they would like help with any of these subjects. If so, offer to teach them.

- If you start teaching often, try improving your skills by learning from other teachers (see the resources in step five for inspiration). You can also Google "how to teach" and quickly find some good tips that will help you to become more effective.

If you want to venture into paid tutoring, the following tips may also help:

- Start developing a portfolio. That is, make a list of whom you have helped, in what subjects, and how they have performed since. It is a good idea to develop a reputation (see step 8) by asking students you have tutored and their parents to write testimonials or be available as referrals.

- The more you teach and the better you become, the more parents, teachers, and students will come to you asking for help. Most of these people will find out through word-of-mouth, though there are a few ways to let others know about your tutoring services:

  o Tell your teachers and/or guidance counseling office that you are available as a tutor.

  o Announce it on Facebook, LinkedIn, or other social networking sites.

  o Build a website (see resources in step 8, like Weebly) that describes your experience, services, and qualifications (e.g. high grades/test scores, referrals, etc.) and enables people to contact you for help.

  o Consider associating with an official tutoring company. Though the company may take a cut of what you earn, it is usually responsible for finding clients who need help.

- Periodically remind yourself of why you started teaching others, so that you do not lose sight of the main two goals: helping others learn while simultaneously improving your own learning and retention.

Step 7: Create!

Life isn't about finding yourself. Life is about creating yourself.

George Bernard Shaw (1865-1950)
Irish Playwright: Only Person to Receive Both an Oscar & Nobel Prize in Literature

It is better to create than to learn! Creating is the essence of life.

Julius Caesar (100 B.C. – 44 B.C.)
Emperor of Rome

Humans have the unique ability and gift to conceptualize and create. If you take a look around, you will see the creations of countless people: cars, buildings, phones, computers, and this book, to name a few. Knowledge was a prerequisite to each of these creations, which is why we focused steps 5 and 6 on learning. For example, an understanding of Newton's laws of motion and force was necessary before cars and buildings could be created, just as knowledge of Maxwell's equations was essential to the development of phones and computers. However, if it were not for the inspiration and creativity of driven people, the wide gap between theoretical understanding and practical implementation would not have been bridged.

Because of this realization, a personal quote that this author subscribes to is:

> *Work is best spent in one of two ways: either in the acquisition of new skills and knowledge or in the application of those already attained.*

You can find ways to apply any skill or knowledge you possess. The only ingredients necessary are a little creativity and a lot of drive. If you know how to write, try blogging or submitting articles to existing publications (step 3). If you know how to play the guitar, try recording a song or even an album. If you know how to write software, try developing an app. If you have the ability to lead people, try organizing a community service initiative. The point is, try to make use of your skills and knowledge by creating. In the process, you will learn even more and develop a reputation (step 8). A side benefit is that what you create may be viewed favorably when you apply to colleges, scholarships, and jobs. (Who knows – what you create may even lead to a business, in which case you won't have to apply to jobs!) Below are a number of resources that will help you create.

Resources for Creating

- Kickstarter –www.kickstarter.com/

- Make Magazine –makezine.com/

- Instructables –www.instructables.com/

- Life Hacker –lifehacker.com/

- YouTube –youtube.com/

- MakerBot –www.makerbot.com/

- OpenPCR –openpcr.org/

- Various Other Open-Source Platforms

Step 8: Develop a Reputation (A Good One!)

Your reputation can be your best friend or your worst enemy. It may open doors for you or shut them just as quickly. This is why it is important to make sure you develop a good reputation. There are many factors that influence your reputation, especially now that so much of what we say or do can be found on Google.

The most important factor contributing to your reputation is how you behave – both in person and online. That affects how your peers and teachers perceive you, which in turn can affect your reputation, if they are asked about you (e.g., a college recommendation). Hence, it is important to make sure that you sculpt your reputation by behaving appropriately and, as cliché as it sounds, being yourself. In terms of how you behave on sites such as Facebook or Twitter, be careful about putting up compromising pictures or statuses that may come back to haunt you. Nothing on the web is 100 percent private, and it may surprise you by showing up on search engines.

Take a moment to Google your name. If you have a common name, you can narrow the search by adding the name of your high school or city to the query. What comes up in the search and image results? You should be aware of these before you go to college or job interviews, because Googling interviewees has become a common research methodology of interviewers. Obviously, it is better to not have any search results than to have negative ones. Even better, though, is to have positive results.

Fortunately, it is in your power to determine what results come up. In previous steps, we discussed keeping a portfolio (blog) of what you write and create, as well as building your network. If you are a great performer, put up a recording on YouTube (who knows, you may get "discovered"). The same goes if you surf, fly, dance, or do any other type of activity that can be watched on YouTube. If you like to write poetry or editorials, put them up on your blog or website. Then, when people search your name (and they will, whether they are a college admissions counselor or a classmate who likes you), they can learn about your talents and interests.

Resources for Developing a Reputation

- Weebly –weebly.com/

- Facebook –facebook.com/

- LinkedIn –linkedin.com/

- YouTube –youtube.com/

- Google –google.com/

- Gmail –mail.google.com/ (no more AOL, Yahoo, and Hotmail accounts)

Step 9: Keep Your Mind (And Eyes) Open

Chance favors only the prepared mind.

Louis Pasteur (1822 – 1895)
French Chemist & Microbiologist

So much of high school – and school in general, for that matter – has become about following the rules and going through the motions. This has led many students to blindly follow those who came before them and to do no less and no more than what is expected of them. This step is about opening your mind and eyes to unusual opportunities that may very well be life-changing.

For example, listen to your school's news announcements, periodically drop by the guidance office, talk to your teachers and administrators, and use Google frequently. You may find out about many opportunities – competitions, scholarships, summer programs, internships, and many others – that you have a good chance of taking advantage of. There are literally thousands of organizations and philanthropists[203] who provide such opportunities to motivated students in most any field. If you are an athlete, there may be a scholar-athlete award with your name on it. If you are a researcher, there may be an expenses-paid summer program waiting for you to attend. If you are an artist, there may be an opening for you at a local design studio. Remember the analogy from step 4 (building a network): Even if you are casting your net in the hopes of catching a fish, you may inadvertently[204] catch a lobster…and find that you prefer it.

Step 10: Have Fun and Be Grateful

Find something you love to do and you'll never have to work a day in your life.

Harvey MacKay (1932-present)
Best-Selling Author & Businessman

If I have seen further it is because I have stood on the shoulders of giants.

Isaac Newton (1642-1727)
English Physicist, Mathematician, Astronomer, Natural Philosopher, Alchemist, & Theologian

The final step is perhaps the most important in terms of succeeding in high school, college, and beyond. Regardless of what you achieve, it is important to take a step back and do two things.

First, make sure that you are enjoying what you are doing and not doing it for the wrong reasons. This goes back to the Stepping Stone Myth. It is truly the journey and not the destination that is important. Aspire, but live in the present.

---

[203] SAT Word Alert: *Philanthropist* (noun) means "a person who has an altruistic concern for human welfare"
[204] SAT Word Alert: *Inadvertent* (adjective) means "unintentional"

Second, make sure you are grateful to those around you who have made things possible. Even if you disagree with your parents some of the time (or all of the time), they are the reason you are here, so be grateful. Be thankful to your teachers and actually show your appreciation, because, despite high workloads and relatively low salaries, they are there day-in and day-out to make sure that you pass your classes. Take a moment to thank the cafeteria workers and janitors, too, because they are as integral to the functioning of your school as the rest of the staff. Having and showing a genuine appreciation for the contributions of others will keep you grounded and make you a better person. That is one of the most important lessons in this book, along – of course – with how to spot errors in parallelism in correlative conjunctions on the SAT and ACT (kidding).

Conclusion

The steps above are proven lessons for how to succeed in high school, college, and beyond, and we hope that you are able to incorporate even just one or two into your life. Some of them will be easier to accomplish than others. You can start being a journalist (step 3) or teaching yourself (step 5) today, though it may take a little more time to build a network (step 4) or develop a reputation (step 8). To recap, all ten (escalator) steps are listed below. Good luck with your climb!

1. Abandon the Stepping Stone Myth

2. Seek Inspiration

3. Become a Journalist (or, at least, write)

4. Build Your Network (then learn from it!)

5. Teach Yourself (definitely coding!)

6. Teach Others

7. Create!

8. Build a Reputation (a good one!)

9. Keep your Mind (and Eyes) Open

10. Have Fun and Be Grateful

CONCLUDING REMARKS

Congratulations on finishing this book! At this stage we hope you have learned dozens of strategies and hundreds of vocabulary words, grammar rules, and math tools that will get you as close to a perfect score as possible on the SAT, ACT, AP, and any other tests you may take. While you have reached the end of *Standing Out*, the real process of standing out has only just begun. Perhaps you now have the drive to attempt an official practice test Saturday afternoon, or review one you took a month ago with a fresh eye for how to conquer some challenges you faced the first time around.

In the upcoming 2016 revision to the SAT that was announced very shortly before this book was published, we find an affirmation of our philosophy that the best learning is not specific to one test but is instead to prepare oneself to understand and contribute throughout life. The new SAT will focus on bringing the exam further down to Earth and eliminate some of the test's economic bias, for example by eliminating words that would be esoteric to most high school students. The essay will be optional, and the mathematics assessment will be more consistent with a high school curriculum. The guessing penalty will be eliminated, although this won't matter much to readers of this book, as our smart strategic recommendation has been to guess even if you risk a penalty, based on the probability involved. The core preparatory advice of this book remains wholly applicable to the new SAT: gather a sound base of knowledge and follow the wisest, most tested strategies that will allow you to show your true potential, and then hone your craft by taking and carefully analyzing practice tests.

As you finish up high school and enter college, you'll have tremendous experiences and gain additional perspective that should confirm a core message of *Standing Out*: it is more important to develop lifelong skills than it is to game the existing system. If there is one message from this book that we hope you inculcate for life, it is never to forgo genuine self-improvement for short-term success. It is certainly possible to attain good scores through gimmicky strategies or clever guessing, just as it is possible to receive honors and awards as resume padding and still be admitted to selective colleges. However, not only will you reach greater heights if you focus on personal development, but when the curtain has fallen, you will feel a much deeper sense of accomplishment and perhaps a deeper confidence in your genuine abilities. (Oh and one last time: the strategies for the SAT and ACT that promote the most meaningful learning also happen to allow for doing better on those tests, in less time, and more affordably.)

The most amazing people we know walk a path of improvement and generosity every day. It's time to turn theory into practice. Best of luck standing out!

APPENDIX
SETTING A SCHEDULE

We've written a number of strategies to help you prepare for the SAT and ACT with a high level of efficiency so that you can make significant progress without wasted effort and expense. We have one final tool for optimizing your preparation: organizing your time by using a practice schedule.

Haphazardly deciding when and how often to work on SAT and ACT preparation isn't a recipe for success; applying the principles of our PERFECT Approach – such as ensuring understanding of each question before moving on to a new test – is paramount, in our opinion. Nonetheless, we've found that approaching SAT and ACT preparation with a smart plan, even if you don't stick to it entirely, facilitates time management and focus in each practice session – allowing you to reach your goals sooner.

Many students simply set aside some number of months or a whole school year for SAT/ACT preparation, intending to take practice tests once in a while during that period. We don't think effective practice schedules ordinarily need to last longer than a few months, and blowing through whole tests – just hoping that your score is a bit higher than last time – is far from optimal. No one schedule fits every test-taker, but here is our recommendation for how to build a schedule that will work well:

(For this sample timeline, we assume that the student is just over ten weeks out from their first SAT or ACT official administration.)

Diagnostic: Learning Your Starting Place

Anyone who's familiar with typical preparation protocols likely saw this one coming: a diagnostic test to start things off. Many students fear this test; they wonder why they must spend the time and effort to learn their baseline score if the most obvious goal of preparation is to get a good *final* score. In some ways, too, a diagnostic test differs from this book's general advice to hold off on taking full timed tests until a student can confidently answer a test's questions at a comfortably slow pace.

All told, however, we do believe in the value of diagnostic testing, because it informs how you prepare in a number of potentially efficiency-beneficial ways. Therefore, we recommend that you spend a little bit of time at the outset on diagnostics.

You have freedom in how you approach this starting step. For this sample schedule, we assume that you don't yet know which of the SAT and ACT you will take in an official sitting. If this is true for you, your diagnostic testing should include sections from both tests. Don't worry: We're not saying you should spend an entire day taking back-to-back, fully timed SAT and ACT tests.

Instead, spend two or three days (perhaps a weekend) taking sections from the SAT and ACT as you please. These can be taken over several sessions, whenever you have time. Pay attention to which subject each subsection corresponds to (for example, SAT Critical Reading or ACT Science). Time yourself but don't stop when the official time allotment ends; keep a quick pace going but continue until you think you've answered everything you reasonably can.

By the end of that diagnostic testing, you should have completed most of two full tests. It's okay to have skipped a couple subsections on the SAT, as long as you got to some of all three sections. Read over the SAT and ACT essay prompts, though there's not a strong comparative reason to write the essays at this point.

If you already know which test you will be taking, take a full practice test. It can also be over multiple sittings.

What should you learn from this diagnostic experience? Well, first, if you are deciding between the SAT and ACT, reflect on which test you did better and liked more. Did one seem particularly well suited to your abilities?

How did your vocabulary fare on the reading sections (especially the SAT's sentence completion questions)? Were you significantly better or worse at one of the subjects? Keep these thoughts in mind.

Weeks 1-5: Acquaintance with and Mastery of the Questions

Now the real work of improving your ability to take the SAT and/or ACT begins. The first of the two major phases of your preparation, which we've previously alluded to, is to build your skill in correctly answering the tests' questions. This is best achieved by taking practice tests (official ones whenever possible) carefully and slowly.

We discussed this strategy in Chapter 4, the first part our PERFECT Approach. Ensuring you know – and internalize for later use – the route of reasoning from each question to its answer is the cornerstone of your preparation at all stages. During beginning preparation, it should be your focus. For example, if you encounter any surprising passage question answers or a novel grammatical or mathematical concept, pause and spend the time to learn what you need to in order to master questions of the sort. Perhaps employ our strategy to Think Like a Test-Maker (see Chapter 5).

Because you don't need to strain your mental stamina just yet, don't take whole tests at once during this phase. Break it up and take chunks of one or two subsections each sitting, so you're fresh to dive deeply into the material. The questions we recommended you pose in order to learn from your diagnostic testing come into play now: Spend more time working on your weaker subjects. If you had favored one test between the SAT and ACT by a decided margin, prepare for that test exclusively. If you don't know which you prefer, prepare with both tests for the first two to three weeks of your preparation, eventually settling on one to focus on for the remainder of this preparation cycle.

These first several weeks of preparation are also your time to learn the supplemental knowledge necessary for answering some test questions. We don't think vocabulary lists are universally advisable, but if you feel that vocabulary is holding you back on the sentence completion questions on the SAT, spending ten or fifteen minutes a day reviewing high-hit-rate word lists, as we discuss in Chapter 6, is time efficiently spent. You may also need to dedicate sessions to learning new math topics online or from textbooks or other SAT/ACT guides. If the English questions on either test are stumping you, the deficit is almost certainly in your grammar knowledge (see our detailed coverage in Chapter 7). Once you know your concepts, mindful practice and application are all that limit you from mastery of the questions.

Weeks 6-9: Training for Time

Untimed mastery of all question types that appear on the SAT or ACT is integral to scoring your best. Alas, both tests are in fact officially timed. Speed should be the final skill you develop in your preparation.

Speed is not particularly teachable. We cannot meaningfully impart to you through description how fast you should go and how you go that fast without compromising your mastery of question-answering.

Speed is, however, *learnable* – by practice. Take timed subsections. Work up some sense of haste and benign anxiety as you take each subsection; challenge yourself to go as speedily as you can, while still coolly applying the techniques and knowledge you've crystallized. Much of the difficulty associated with testing under tightly timed conditions derives from an inability to cope well with the stress. Your speed training should attempt to introduce some stress so you can work on handling that element, too.

The perfect pace is individual. Given similar preparation backgrounds, some students are nonetheless able to go more quickly than are others before focus falters. Such students may naturally have more time to dedicate to reviewing their answer choices after they've finished a section. Certainly, though, all students can accelerate and improve their pacing by progressively increasing speed whenever they feel they can do so without starting to miss more questions as a result.

We have provided a number of strategies throughout our previous SAT and ACT coverage that assist in taking the tests efficiently. We believe that Chapters 6's strategies on how to take the reading sections are especially conducive to finishing within time. Chapter 5 – *Acing the Math Section* – too, has some tips that aspire to help you work fast (see, for instance, "Stamping out silly mistakes" at the end of that chapter).

Note that "training for time" should not be interpreted as mutually exclusive of continuing to develop your mastery of simply answering the questions. To that end, even though during this phase you will be observing the allotted time limits, when time is up but you haven't confidently answered every question, proceed with the same strategy we advised in the last preparation phase: Meticulously spend the time you need to in order to fully attempt each question and, later, to understand exactly why you missed any questions you did.

Week 10: Finishing Strong but Relaxed

If you've got focus and a smart plan, you don't have to spend many grueling months to reach a great score on the SAT or ACT. As we've laid out in this plan, a few months of effective preparation yields an excellent chance of skyrocketing your score.

The same cannot be said of the final week before your official administration. It's all too common to hope to push all the work to the days before the test, when the pressure's on so late in the game. But this sort of procrastination is just a mechanism to handle uncertainty about how to prepare or a lack of motivation. We hope our words in this book prevent both, so that you do the work to improve while time is on your side.

Your days of preparation should not be focused on learning new information – don't be the student cramming formulas and vocabulary lists on the car ride to the test center. Last-second knowledge acquisition efforts almost certainly won't stick, and they will cloud your mind with extra stress, making it tough to remember what you had earlier taken the time to learn. The first weeks of your preparation should be when you internalize the concepts that were weak points for you.

The final week is foremost an opportunity for mental preparation. Employ our previous recommendation to visualize your testing room experience: Imagine as vividly as you can the process of taking the real SAT or ACT, seeing yourself calmly handling the questions and intelligently tackling any tough questions. Reinvigorate your motivation to do well and your confidence that you can. Briefly review the vocabulary terms, grammatical concepts, and mathematics that you focused on in your early preparation.

Continue some speed practice so you feel sharp. Review the tests you've already taken for questions that originally stumped you, in order to sharpen your analytic sense of how to answer the hardest questions they can throw at you. Sleep plentifully in the several days before the test. Enter the testing room with assurance that you are so capable that the test is a challenge on which you are prepared to achieve outstanding success.

Room for Flexibility

The time guidelines provided above aren't rigid. If you see an individual need to differ from them, don't hesitate to do what works for you. For instance, if you know that, throughout most of school, you've been excellent at figuring out the correct answers on tests but always critically pressed for time, consider spending a little longer on time training. (Certainly, though, never forgo the more important phase of mastering the questions.)

We structured these time recommendations on the assumption that you would begin preparing about ten weeks out from your first official administration of the test. Most students who have taken the time to read through this book will probably start to prepare earlier. This is generally a good thing: All else equal, the more time you allow yourself to prepare, the more potential to progress. With that said, mindful of the diminishing returns of exhaustively long preparation periods and that you have lives outside of a test booklet, we do believe that a short preparation schedule, as we've outlined here, is sufficient to satisfactorily approach your optimal performance on the SAT or ACT. The key is to always have a purpose in your preparation: Outline in advance of your preparation what you will be specifically working to improve and when.

If you find yourself with fewer than ten weeks before the official test and you haven't begun to prepare, it's time to reevaluate whether you need to take the test at that time. Unless you will otherwise miss a college or scholarship application deadline, postpone the test to a later month so you can comfortably prepare.

Mock Test Dates

No matter how much and well you prepare, there's something unique about the official administration of the test: It's for real this time. Confidence in your question-answering skills, speed practice, and visualization preparation are all potent tools for tempering test-day nerves, but we offer one final tactic to make the stressful test day a bit more familiar and, therefore, an opportunity to showcase the unfettered magnitude of your abilities: mock test dates.

During your preparation, set up at least one date (preferably a Saturday or Sunday) on which you will pretend that you are taking the real SAT or ACT. Wake up at the time you plan to for the official test and allow yourself the same time conditions for each section and breaks. Take the whole test. Psych yourself up ahead of time, telling yourself that this practice session counts. Embrace the nervousness as a way to enhance your focus.

In the days after this experience, retrospect critically on how it went. What did you do well on? What weaknesses presented themselves and how should these be addressed in the remaining time in your preparation schedule? How can you learn from this test simulation so the real test feels as comfortable as possible?

When to Take the Test

Some particularly motivated students are eager to take the SAT or ACT early in their high school careers, thinking that this will give them a foundational score on which they can later build. Others, driven by their fear or dislike of the tests, put the chore off as long as possible, cramming it into their schedule during the first semester of senior year.

Generally, waiting until senior year to first take the SAT or ACT is a mistake. You will already be busy enough trying to keep your grades in a healthy range for college applications while fighting the demotivating force that is senioritis – as well as filling out those college applications and writing the associated essays – that standardized testing is not a stressor that you should pile on. Additionally, there's little time to prepare for a retake should you wish to improve your score.

At the time same, however, there's little reason to take the test much earlier than that. Freshman and sophomore test-takers will be at the disadvantage of having had less time to develop their vocabularies, general reading skills, and mathematical tools. They can still do very well if they are advanced in their education for those grades and their preparation is smart, but they would do at least as well – and likely better – if they were to hold off for a year or two.

We recommend first taking the test sometime in your junior year. Some students prefer to spend the summer on SAT or ACT preparation, when they aren't balancing their time with schoolwork. For such students, taking the test early in junior year works very well. As long as you take the test officially at least once in junior year and begin your concentrated preparation about ten or more weeks out, you are under excellent circumstances to perform exceptionally well on the test.

Retaking

Much has been said of the perennial debate of whether to retake the SAT or ACT after achieving a score lower than desired: "Retake only if your score is really bad." "Retake only if you are applying to really selective schools." "Always retake, as long as you have time." "Never retake, because it's a waste of time."

We apply the following rule in advising whether to retake: If the amount of work you intend to exert in preparing to retake will earn a sufficiently significant score increase and you will not regret having not spent it on other things, retake the test. In other words, if you are willing to work hard and meaningfully to improve your score, do so, unless you feel the time could be better spent.

Be realistic about how much you can improve your score. If you didn't prepare much for the first test (or not in the efficient ways we have espoused), there is great potential for improvement, and it's probably worth your time to prepare again and retake. But if you have already spent months preparing in effective ways and improved your score by a large margin but just want to eke out those last few questions, understand that small score differences are usually negligible; spend the time on your schoolwork, your applications, or some non-academic endeavor.

If you do decide to retake, reevaluate whether you are pursuing the appropriate test for you: Maybe you're better suited for the ACT than the SAT, or vice-versa, so give that one a go this time. Also take care to cater your preparation schedule to the areas you most hope to improve. Now that you have experience under your belt, you know whether you need to emphasize time training, question mastery, or knowledge acquisition. Divvy up your time resources accordingly, so you make the most out of this new opportunity.

APPENDIX
RESOURCES FOR STANDING OUT

We have included, as supplements to this book, a few resources below that should help you stand taller. Please visit our website at k12.osmosis.org for additional resources.

General

- k12.osmosis.org

Math

- www.khanacademy.org

- www.erikthered.com/tutor

Vocabulary

- www.professorword.com

Reading

- www.newsela.com

English

- www.noredink.com

- public.wsu.edu/~brians/errors

Science

- www.successwithscience.org

AP/SAT II

- k12.osmosis.org

College Admissions and Discussion

- www.collegeconfidential.com

52661935R00136

Made in the USA
Lexington, KY
06 June 2016